COLLABORATIVE MANUFACTURING

Using Real-Time Information to Support the Supply Chain

COLLABORATIVE
MANUFACTURING
Using Real-Time Information
to Support the Supply Chain

Michael McClellan

S^t_L

ST. LUCIE PRESS

A CRC Press Company

Boca Raton London New York Washington, D.C.

Library of Congress Cataloging-in-Publication Data

McClellan, Michael, 1940-
    Collaborative manufacturing : using real-time information to support the supply chain /
Michael McClellan
        p. cm.
    Includes bibliographical references and index.
    ISBN 1-57444-341-0
    1. Production management. 2. Business logistics. 3. Real-time data processing. I. Title.
II. Series.
TS155 .M3455 2002
658.7'2—dc21

2002068208

Visit the CRC Press Web site at www.crcpress.com

© 2003 by CRC Press LLC
St. Lucie Press is an imprint of CRC Press LLC

No claim to original U.S. Government works
International Standard Book Number 1-57444-341-0
Library of Congress Card Number 2002068208
Printed in the United States of America 2 3 4 5 6 7 8 9 0
Printed on acid-free paper

Dedication

To my wife Pamela

Preface

Collaborative manufacturing can be a totally different way of doing business. There are many facets to this idea, but the most significant is the change of business buy and sell roles, from adversarial relationships to cooperative and then collaborative arrangements, based on identified elements of mutual interest and trust. The concept of collaboration means that participants contribute something for the betterment of the whole. In doing so, the relationship changes from traditional business rules to those based on mutual trust; these are enhanced by performance and contribution. One example is the sharing of new product development information with a vendor. The first commitment a vendor must provide is one of absolute confidentiality: information will not be shared beyond those required to contribute. The supplier agrees to product development confidentiality while the host agrees to not share product innovation or production ideas provided by the supplier. The results are better ideas, lower cost (perhaps shared), and committed production benefiting both supplier and host. It's a win/win arrangement that is likely to provide a better product and improved business success for both parties. For many years, this relationship has been evident in certain industries and some companies, including automotive and electronics manufacturers, and contrasts sharply with the tough adversarial beat-down-the-price and beat-up-the-vendor relationship that exists in many supply chains.

One of the best starting points of collaboration is to provide each supplier partner with accurate information regarding product demand. Are your major suppliers in the dark as to your expected purchases or can they plan operations based on a shared forecast? With better information, a stronger commitment of delivery and performance to the agreed schedule are possible. How many times has your company used an estimated forecast to generate a master production schedule only to find that the forecast was substantially inaccurate, with quantities either under- or over-estimated? Either instance causes considerable upheaval, now or later, in eventually responding to the real demand requirement, either by driving up inventory costs or by missing sales opportunities because the product was not available. One of the primary objectives of collaborative manufacturing is to synchronize the production processes of the value chain network to reduce or eliminate this dysfunctional process, thereby lowering costs and more consistently meeting market demand requirements. Although conceptually simple, the idea of synchronized inventory/production requires true collaboration. One goal is to eliminate or improve management of events that result in just-in-case inventory, the historic method of responding to events that might affect delivery performance. With even a minimal degree of success, the savings are enormous.

To apply collaboration in manufacturing companies, begin by removing obstacles that stand in the way of cooperation for a small group (two to four) of supply chain partners within the supply chain network. The process begins with steps that identify and set out the objectives of the arrangement. The second phase establishes the requirements, responsibilities, and methods of each partner in meeting the determined objectives. The third phase is the ensuring of compliance or the confirmation of facts based on absolute truth. This is the most vulnerable point of the process, where trust alone can bridge the gap between partners.

Trust is gained through confirmed compliance using on-line, real-time information. In the case of product design, on-line information is basic to the process of tracking and recording each event and contribution throughout a product's entire life cycle. In the production environment, trust is ensured through generation and presentation of real-time information from the plant-floor production process that confirms agreed-on planned events and product compliance processes. Assumptions, paper transmittals, or promises will not suffice, as any misinformation will detract from the fundamental element of trust, the foundation of the collaboration agreement. Actual information gained through process visibility is the *only* data source that confirms truth. There is no substitute.

Another important area of collaboration is accomplished through the use of information technology systems and the Internet to simultaneously include partner collaboration in product design and to collect and manage product definition information from design to product disposal. Generally referred to as collaborative product commerce or product life-cycle management, this form is characterized by the idea of broad, perhaps global, inclusion of participants in product design.

Companies have been exchanging manufacturing and product data with customers and suppliers for many years. This has taken the form of direct contact with the plant floor or production updates provided on some planned basis. Collaborative manufacturing, at its minimum, takes this simple passing of information one or two dimensions higher, to an actual confirmation of successfully meeting the committed performance requirements.

This book examines the application of collaborative manufacturing processes through at least four categories, ranging from collaboration in product life-cycle management to collaborative tools used in manufacturing management. It addresses collaboration as it might be applied to business processes within companies on a department-to-department basis and externally to designated supply chain partners on both the demand and the supply side of the supply chain network. It includes some reasons you should change your practices, and provides details on how to achieve change.

The business assumptions are that you are looking to improve your ability to convert incoming inventory to a greater value-added product, and you want to include partners within the supply chain network to get the maximum impact and result.

Two messages will be presented:

- Collaboration is a good thing. Linking partners within the supply chain network can accumulate numerous advantages through collaboration as a formal business alliance or simply through the sharing of business process information. Collaboration can be as simple as linking internal interdepartmental business processes or as complex as synchronizing an eight-tier supply chain.
- Real-time, on-line information from production processes is crucial to improving success across the supply chain network. Without real-time information, the most solid information is based only on assumptions. Mutual trust is hard to build on assumptions. Only true, current, and accurate information will suffice. There is no substitute for real-time production data.

Collaboration may or may not be a paradigm shift, but the momentum exists and is likely to continue to grow because leading companies, such as Daimler-Chrysler, Dell Computer, and Cisco Systems, have seen its success and the opportunities are nearly endless.

The book's chapters and appendices are summarized below, followed by a table that lists the relative value of each chapter for readers by area of responsibility, department, and industry.

- Chapter 1 is an introduction to the general idea of collaboration as used in manufacturing companies. It describes how working together with shared objectives in a nonadversarial environment can have positive impact. A general explanation of enterprise resource planning systems, supply chain management, and real-time information from production and logistics processes shows their role in the extended enterprise and their fit in a collaborative environment.
- Chapter 2 defines four collaboration strategies: product life-cycle management; collaborative planning, forecasting, and replenishment (CPFR®); synchronized inventory management; and manufacturing enterprise collaboration. The chapter contains a list of considerations applicable to collaboration and a discussion regarding the value of truth as a crucial element in nonadversarial business relationships.
- Chapter 3 provides details on CPFR, the version of collaboration that has been developed to serve the manufacturer to retailer environment. Through the efforts of the Voluntary Interindustry Commerce Standards Association, an organization of major retailers and consumer goods producers, standards have been developed to guide companies in their efforts to more effectively serve the retailing industry.

- Chapter 4 describes the bullwhip effect of demand distortion within supply chains and provides some answers to alleviate the consequences. This chapter addresses the idea of synchronized inventories and the issues of inventory management in the era of mass customization or lot sizes of one. The early government-sponsored collaborative manufacturing study (Demand Activated Manufacturing Architecture) in the textile industry is outlined along with a presentation of its process for multitier collaboration.
- Chapter 5 provides an outline of why and where to apply collaborative strategies across the extended enterprise including internal and external supply-chain network partners. The idea is to better support your existing business processes with people-centric applications of technology and to tie disparate silos of information into more effective business-process support mechanisms using real-time information.
- Chapter 6 provides in-depth information on how to use collaboration tools to improve product design processes. It also explains product life-cycle management and what can be done collaboratively to reduce new product introduction time and to track a product throughout its lifetime. A primary objective is to keep every part of the supply chain network current and aware of product issues, including engineering change orders and critical supply items.
- Chapter 7 offers an overview of the role of enterprise resource planning systems and their evolution from the early finance-oriented, material-requirements planning systems to the modern business tool of today. A brief description of the major functional areas, including customer relationship management and supply chain management roles, is provided.
- Chapter 8 discusses the significant role of the supply chain and supply chain management. It shows how the supply chain has evolved to become a solid competing entity of its own with supply chains competing against each other based on a collective competitive advantage.
- Chapter 9 details the idea of real-time, on-line information that exists across entities within the supply chain network or extended enterprise. A full list of information sources and some ideas regarding accessibility are shown. The general theme is that collaboration is built on trust and only current actual information from production and logistics processes can provide confirmation of the events that are anticipated by collaboration partners.
- Chapter 10 outlines industries that are candidates for collaborative efforts. There is an extensive discussion on standards development efforts by various industry associations, each seemingly aimed at the long-term goal of business-process information exchange.
- Chapter 11 looks at some earlier manufacturing management ideas and how the continuous evolution of management practices has led to the current age of information and collaboration. Early collabora-

tion comes with much history from the Toyota manufacturing processes that have been transferred and copied internationally as lean manufacturing.

- Chapter 12 provides the academic view of collaboration and other cooperative forms of business relationships. Alliances, joint ventures, and collaboration are all about working together for the greater value of the cooperation effort. The roles of culture and honesty are discussed as part of winning relationships and alliances.
- Chapter 13 provides an overview of how collaboration is being applied in the automotive industry and what is driving the industry toward closer relationships with suppliers and their customers to reduce the billions of dollars in supply chain inventory.
- Chapter 14 shows how collaboration is impacting regulated industries, including medical device and pharmaceutical manufacturing. Business drivers include mass customization and improved inventory management in a collaborative environment.
- Chapter 15 examines how collaborative processes are being used in the electronics industry where so much of the manufacturing is done by third-party suppliers and product life cycles can be measured in weeks. This global industry works with up-to-the-minute information from far-flung production facilities and engineering change orders that can obsolete millions of dollars in inventory in hours.
- Chapter 16 deals with collaborative manufacturing in the continuous segments of process industries such as pulp and paper, refining, mining and metals, and chemicals.
- Chapter 17 is a summary of collaboration ideas and their uses in the general area of manufacturing. Some suggestions for getting your collaborative initiative under way are provided.
- Appendix A contains a discussion of the hierarchy of supply-chain software system applications.
- Appendix B provides an example of a fully integrated enterprise resource planning system. Functions of the PeopleSoft 8 system (PeopleSoft Inc.) are described.

Relative Value of Chapters by Area of Responsibility, Department, and Industry

	Chapter															
---	1	2	3	4	5	6	7	8	9	10	11	12	13	14	15	16
CEO	X	X	X	X	X	X	M	M	M	M	M	M	M	M	M	X
CFO	X	X	X	X	X	X	X	M	M	M	M	M	M	M	M	X
CIO	X	X	X	X	X	X	X	X	X	X	M	M	M	M	M	X
VP manufacturing	X	X	X	X	X	X	M	M	X	M	M	M	M	M	M	X
VP engineering	X	X	X	X	X	X	M	M	M	M	M	M	M	M	M	X
VP supply chain	X	X	X	X	X	X	X	X	X	M	M	M	M	M	M	X
VP sales	X	X	X	X	X	X	M	M	M	M	M	M	M	M	M	X
Procurement	X	X	X	X	X	X	X	X	X	X	M	M	M	M	M	X

Relative Value of Chapters by Area of Responsibility, Department, and Industry *(Continued)*

	Chapter															
	1	2	3	4	5	6	7	8	9	10	11	12	13	14	15	16
Information technology	X	X	X	X	X	X	X	X	X	X	M	M	M	M	M	X
Manufacturing engineering	X	X	X	X	X	X	M	M	X	M	X	M	M	M	M	X
Product development	X	X	M	M	M	X	M	M	M	M	M	M	M	M	M	X
Retail	X	X	X	M	M	M	M	M	M	M	M	M	M	M	M	X
Industrial manufacturer	X	X	X	X	X	X	X	X	X	M	X	M	M	M	M	X
Consumer goods	X	X	X	X	X	X	X	X	X	M	M	M	M	M	M	X
Electronics	X	X	X	X	X	X	X	X	X	M	M	M	M	M	M	X
Process industry	X	X	M	M	X	X	M	M	M	M	M	M	M	M	M	X
Automotive industry	X	X	X	X	X	X	X	X	X	M	X	M	M	M	M	X
Regulated industry	X	X	X	X	X	X	X	X	X	M	M	M	M	M	M	X

Reader value key: X = significant value; M = moderate value.

Acknowledgments

I required assistance and input from many people in writing this book, and I extend great gratitude to all who participated. A special thank you goes to Jon Tschaikovsky for his unending support and most of the information in the chapter on life science industries. Another special thank you goes to Robert Jansen for his early comments regarding the subject of collaboration and much of the information in the chapters on the automotive industry and manufacturing enterprise collaboration. Major information contributors include the Original Equipment Suppliers Association, Automotive Industry Action Group, Agile Software, PeopleSoft Inc., Rockwell Automation/Propack Data, ARC Advisory Group, the Voluntary Interindustry Commerce Standards Association's CPFR committee, Lean Learning Center, Performance Measurement Group, MSI magazine, and MESA International.

I am also grateful to all the people who have put up with my questions and information search, and to those who gave feedback on the text and general theme of the book. Other major contributors include John Carlson of Riverside Graphics and Marjorie Hoye, Ph.D., who does a great job of editing my text so that it is grammatically correct and much easier to read.

Michael McClellan

About the author

Michael McClellan has over 30 years of experience serving and managing manufacturing enterprises. He has held a number of positions in general management, marketing, and engineering, including president and CEO for companies supplying capital equipment and material management systems to nearly every type of manufacturer. In 1984, McClellan and a group of associates founded Integrated Production Systems, a company that pioneered the use of computer systems to manage and track production events on the plant floor. These systems are generally referred to as manufacturing execution systems and have found extensive use in varying forms in production facilities. His book, *Applying Manufacturing Execution Systems*, defines manufacturing execution systems and explains the reasoning and history behind them. He is a frequent speaker at company meetings and manufacturing conferences, has presented a number of papers on plant information systems, and holds one patent.

For a long time, McClellan has participated in and supported systems that improve manufacturing effectiveness. In his view, applying collaborative manufacturing concepts is of utmost importance in shaping and responding to supply chain effectiveness opportunities. He strongly believes that such application must be based on the accurate and current information that exists or is generated within the production infrastructure by partners across the supply chain.

McClellan currently lives in Washington state and is president of Collaboration Synergies, Inc., which provides consulting services in the areas of plant-floor information systems, manufacturing execution systems, and collaborative manufacturing system development and implementation. His interests span all types of manufacturing environments and locations.

Collaborative manufacturing is relatively new as a management strategy and there is strong enthusiasm for its broad implementation across the extended enterprise. The leading-edge information in this book will soon be eclipsed as the technology progresses. If you will provide your name and e-mail address, McClellan will endeavor to maintain contact with regular updates regarding collaboration application information. Use the following website to contact the author and/or to register for updates: www.collaborationsynergies.com. Your comments, including experiences, ideas, challenges, and contributions are appreciated and of great interest. You can also access a short executive overview of this book from the website.

Contents

Abbreviations

AIAG	Automotive Industry Action Group
DC	direct customer
POS	point of sale
APS	advanced planning system
APICS	Educational Society for Resource Management
BOM	bill of material
BR	batch record
CAD	computer-aided design
CAE	computer-aided engineering
CAM	computer-aided manufacturing
CIM	computer-integrated manufacturing
CPFR	Collaborative Planning, Forecasting, and Replenishment
CRM	customer relationship management
DAMA	Demand Activated Manufacturing Architecture Project
DCS	digital conversion system
ECC	engineering change control
EDI	electronic data interchange
EIP	enterprise information portal
ERP	enterprise resource planning
FDA	U.S. Food and Drug Administration
GMP	good manufacturing practice
GUI	graphical user interface
HMI	human–machine interface
IT	information technology
JIT	just-in-time
JMI	jointly managed inventory
LIMS	laboratory information management system
MCO	medical client offering
MES	manufacturing execution system
MRO	maintenance and repair order
MRP	material requirements planning
MRPII	manufacturing resource planning
NEMI	National Electronics Manufacturing Initiative
OEM	original equipment maker
OESA	Original Equipment Suppliers Association

PDA	personal digital assistant
PDM	product data management
PDX	Product Data Exchange
PLC	programmable logic controller
PLM	product life-cycle management
PM	production management
PMG	Performance Measurement Group
RFQ	request for quote
ROI	return on investment
SCADA	supervisory control and data acquisition
SCC	Supply Chain Council
SCM	supply chain management
SCOR	Supply Chain Operations Reference
SPC	statistical process control
SQC	statistical quality control
VICS	Voluntary Interindustry Commerce Standards Association
VMI	vendor-managed inventory
WIP	work in progress
WMS	warehouse management system

chapter one

Introduction

This is the *collaborative era*: trust is in and adversarial contingencies are out; real facts and shared information are the foundation for business decisions and business relationships; estimates or assumptions are regarded as guesses; working together with shared and confirmed information is the norm, not the exception; and supply chains compete against supply chains, which is a major change beyond company against company.

The current hot issue in manufacturing is collaborative manufacturing. Is this a hyped overstatement of the simple idea of companies sharing product data information? Is the objective only to share product schedules or can a group of suppliers led by the big gorilla customer truly create improved value (and reduced cost) by working closer together? Will this new world require computer science knowledge, an industrial engineering or manufacturing engineering education, or what? Who will drive these projects — the company president, marketing executive, supply chain management, or manufacturing managers? Is return on investment still part of the justification or are there bigger-picture issues that make collaborative manufacturing simply necessary to do business? The answer to each of these questions depends on your company and how you want it to operate.

There is no quick and easy definition for collaborative manufacturing because it includes a number of categories. However, collaborative manufacturing concepts generally focus on greatly expanding information sharing throughout your internal company-wide operations and external supply chain partner sphere, generally referred to as the extended enterprise. Stating the general objectives will probably give you a warm and cozy feeling, but like so many of life's obvious directions, the devil is in the details.

Like the decision to implement your new enterprise resource planning (ERP) system, collaborative manufacturing is a significant business strategy commitment. (Unlike ERP, it need not be expensive.) The basic premise is that competitive ability and the broad sense of customer service can be greatly improved when specific business process information is shared with extended enterprise partners most effectively. Collaborative manufacturing is a grouping of ideas and processes designed to greatly enhance the effectiveness of the extended enterprise. One analogy is to think of a large philharmonic orchestra. If each orchestra member worked from his or her individually selected sheet of music the result would be cacophony. Each member working from the identical sheet of music and led by a good conductor can produce real harmony. Collaborative manufacturing is the process of fine tuning for each member and each process of the extended enterprise to obtain greatest harmony and as a group, the greatest competitive position.

Is this a real paradigm shift? I think not. In the recent past, nearly every major company has pared its list of vendors from thousands to hundreds based on the idea of working closer with fewer suppliers more sharply focused on mutual objectives and mutual interests. This movement was enhanced by electronic equipment manufacturers, such as Cisco Systems Inc. and others, who work extensively with contract manufacturers around the world. To mitigate the risks of *not* having the manufacturing facility within walking distance or within the direct purview of management, new rules had to be developed and deployed.

There are three major legs to this idea, illustrated in Figure 1.1. The overriding leg is the ERP system where overall management of corporate planning begins. Included are the processes of corporate inventory management and forecasts, financial objectives, manufacturing requirements, and the general focal point of information technology.

A fully integrated ERP system is the core management tool of most major companies today (Figure 1.2). This tool is the primary method to keep everyone within the company on the same sheet of music by presenting business information in a consistent and formal way using one integrated database and information presentation as defined by managers at the highest level. Modern corporations function much like the human body with the ERP system as the brain that provides sensory sensation recognition and response. Functions are continuously occurring in response to the cadence set by the brain whether that be a rapid heart beat rate or tactile response

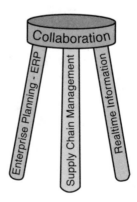

Figure 1.1 Three legs of collaboration. (Reprinted with permission from CRC Press.)

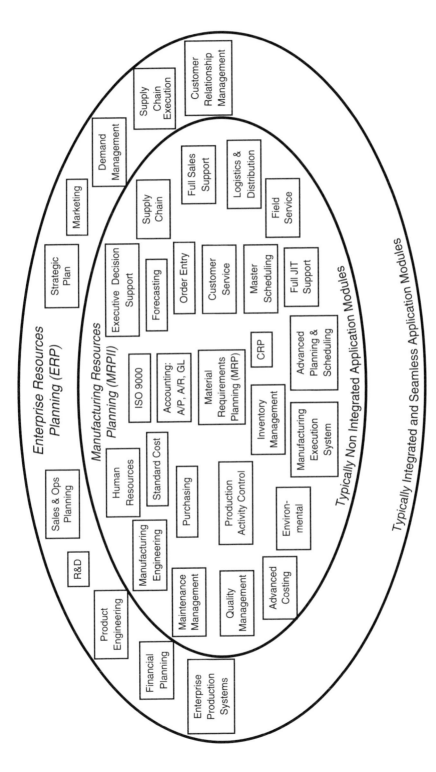

Figure 1.2 Fully integrated ERP system. (Reprinted with permission from CRC Press.)

Suppliers   **Manufacturer**   **Customers**

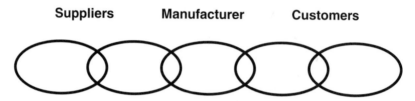

Figure 1.3 Supply chain. (Reprinted with permission of CRC Press.)

to a hot stove. In the business sense, the ERP sets the company-wide pace. The ERP system drives the business plan, monitors concurrence to objectives, and is sensitive to significant events. One function example is the currency exchange component found in most ERP systems that converts worldwide international receipts to a common presentation of dollars or some other currency. Another common example is the aggregation of inventory data with details presented at appropriate points of use. Another example is the roll-up of financial data from widespread sources into a single consolidated, reliable financial report. Having been deployed by most major companies around the world, these systems are broadly accepted as the central business management tool. Chapter Seven provides a full description of planning systems and how they have evolved during the past 30 years.

Many companies do not yet have a fully integrated resource planning system, although these systems are generally well accepted. Other similar but less functional systems are used in company management, and there are still a few companies that use manual tools to understand and direct their business. These too provide many cost-effective collaboration opportunities.

The one seemingly universal condition of any manufacturing business is the concept of the supply chain (Figure 1.3), an interlinking system of suppliers, manufacturers, and customers. The second major leg of collaborative manufacturing is the supply chain in its broadest sense and in all its permutations, upstream and downstream to and including the end customer.

The following definitions are used by Ayers (2001):

> **Supply chain**: Life-cycle processes comprising physical, information, financial, and knowledge flows whose purpose is to satisfy end-user requirements with products and services from multiple linked suppliers.
> **Supply chain management**: Design, maintenance, and operation of supply chain processes for satisfaction of end-user needs.

Poirier and Bauer (2000) provide other definitions:

> **Supply chain**: Core business processes that create and deliver a product or service, from concept through development and manufacturing or conversion, into a market for consumption.

Supply chain management: Refers to the methods, systems, and leadership that continuously improve an organization's integrated processes for product and service design, sales forecasting, purchasing, inventory management, manufacturing or production, order management, logistics, distribution, and customer satisfaction.

Supply chain management emerged as a business tool in the late 1980s and has since grown to a significant management position in the enterprise because of excellent cost-reduction results and improved customer service. In some companies supply chain management is focused on logistics and warehousing but in this book we are taking the broadest view to include all components in the supply chain from product concept to disposal and recycling. Collaborative manufacturing relies on and centers on ever-closer relationships between members of the supply chain and how they can collectively improve business functions. Chapter Eight elaborates on supply chain concepts and where this technology is leading.

The third major leg is the specific information necessary to keep all parts of the supply chain properly oiled with clean, timely, and correct data. There are many sources of information necessary to build closer relationships but centermost is the necessity for real-time/on-line plant floor and logistics information. The full array of the production-management-system infrastructure must be available to give openness and real-time/on-line shared information (see Figure 1.4). There are a number of obvious reasons to support this idea.

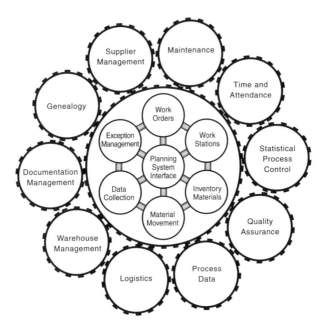

Figure 1.4 Manufacturing execution system.

An enormous amount of data is required to run a business and, once the data exist, using the data elsewhere is relatively easy. A short list of data sources would include access to production planning, inventory management information, quality assurance measurements, schedule revisions, material location, engineering change-order management, production variances, statistical process control, and engineering change orders. In most cases, the sources exist and are already being used within production management systems up and down the supply chain.

With everyone in the supply chain working with consistent, current, and synchronized information, contingencies can be more effectively managed. Supply-chain to supply-chain competition is here and will grow in the future. Each partner can benefit through collaboration and the full effect is synergistic.

Real-time information from the many production facilities within the supply chain is largely underutilized. As the idea of collaboration within the supply chain gains adoption, the need for truly accurate, reliable information will be the key. With customer service as a primary competitive element of the supply chain, it is not enough to rely on estimates or contingency planning. Only actual information from on-line sources will suffice.

Wight (1984) suggests that a fundamental opportunity in business is trust and that the prevailing adversarial relationships are counterproductive. This was an important idea behind building rational and logical computer planning systems (manufacturing requirements planning, MRP); they could be trusted.

In Chapter 18 of *Management Tasks, Responsibilities, Practices*, Drucker (1973) develops the idea of making work productive. Drucker explains that the process of production requires built-in controls such as its direction, quality, quantity, and standards. In Chapter 19, he discusses the worker and the process of work, including Theory X and Theory Y as developed by McGregor (1960). The basic idea is that theory X managers see their employees (and by implication supplier companies) as lazy and adversarial and that they need both carrot and stick to be coerced to perform. On the other hand, Theory Y managers see people (and suppliers) as having a psychological as well as financial need for success in work achievement and responsibility, and will do the right job if they have the correct tools (information).

The idea of management control built on positive fulfillment and nonadversarial leadership is particularly evident in many of today's technology companies. Bringing this philosophy to the plant floor and the production management infrastructure up and down the supply chain is a new approach. It is not suggested that this new world dawned and everyone changed their spots from being adversaries to partners overnight. I do suggest that using available information technology as a proactive management tool can be a nonadversarial approach to support the idea that people will perform most effectively if they are part of the team and have accurate and current information to work with.

Eliminate the walls of coercion, inaccuracy, and distrust. Build trust and collaborate to the betterment of all. Easy? Not on your life. But when leading companies such as Cisco Systems, Intel, Volvo, Procter & Gamble, Pharmacia, or Chrysler can make this work with resulting reduced cost and improved customer fulfillment, can the rest of the world sit back and not take note? Making this approach an effective management tool will not be easy but there are those who believe collaboration will have an even greater positive impact on business management processes than resource planning systems.

For the sake of consistency, the term "supply chain network" or "extended enterprise" is used to describe what some call the supply chain, the supply chain constellation, the value chain, and the value chain network. The supply chain network is made up of each department within each company that is linked at any point within the supply chain, either on the supplier side of the business or the customer side, and extends from the original producer of any part or service to the final user and eventual product disposal. As we will see, collaboration can range from an interdepartmental activity that is simply sharing business process information more effectively to collaboration activities that span any number of companies around the world. It may or may not be a paradigm shift but collaboration is definitely an important part of how business will be done in the future.

References

Ayers, J.B., *Handbook of Supply Chain Management*, St. Lucie Press, Boca Raton, FL, 2001.

Drucker, P.F., *Management: Tasks, Responsibilities, Practices*, Harper & Row, New York, 1973.

Langenwalter, G.A., *Enterprise Resources Planning and Beyond*, CRC Press, Boca Raton, FL, 2000.

McGregor, D., *The Human Side of Enterprise*, McGraw-Hill, New York, 1960.

Poirier, C.C., Bauer, M.J., *E-Supply Chain*, Berrett-Koehler, San Francisco, CA, 2000.

Wight, Oliver, *MRPII: Unlocking America's Productivity Potential*, Oliver Wight Publications, Williston, VT, 1984.

chapter two

Collaboration strategies

There are at least five forms of collaborative strategies currently being applied to support manufacturing companies. Collaborative manufacturing is not new but is getting greater attention as a corporate strategic initiative because the supporting information technology is firmly in place and examples of collaborative success are extensive in product design management, supply chain production management, and product distribution. Informal collaborative alliances have been around a long time as some companies have intentionally built closer relationships with their suppliers and customers as a normal part of supply chain management. Collaborative manufacturing is simply an extension of that process with some new possibilities that have come available only recently due to technological advances and evolving market forces.

- Information technology allows information to be shared in near real time. Regardless of whether the tool is the fax, the Internet, or integrated computer technology, the ability to transfer data between interested parties removes any reason to not be informed.
- The increasing emphasis on mass customization requires manufacturers to have production systems built to support production agility that responds to small lot sizes and individualized customer requirements.
- The possibility of synchronized inventories across the supply chain network is an idea with great economic potential. The tools are here and some companies are making significant progress.
- Product design done through collaborative efforts of supply chain partners has been very cost effective.

John Kay of Daimler Chrysler (2000) points to three major challenges confronting the automotive industry (illustrated in Figure 2.1) and suggests how they will be met:

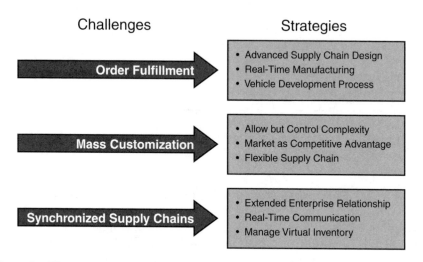

Figure 2.1 Three major challenges confronting automotive industry.

- **Order fulfillment** — Delivering cars and trucks that have been built to meet an individual customer's requirements in days rather than weeks is the new automotive industry obsession. Kay states that today's goal is to deliver an individualized car in single-digit days instead of the year 2000 practice of up to 35 days. To meet this objective, collaborative strategies will have to be in place.

  Advanced supply chain design — Supply chain relationships must be thought out and realigned to satisfy new customer expectations.

  Real-time manufacturing — A streamlined real-time manufacturing process must be built from the ground up.

  Vehicle development process — The ability to share product design and innovation information across the extended enterprise, in- cluding providing information to contributing nodes wherever in the world they may be located must be realized.

- **Mass customization** — Mass customization allows customers to have the vehicle built to their requirements. At Mercedes, the number of permutations of an S-Class vehicle can reach into the millions, and building a car with any combination within days is what the market will demand. Meeting this individualized product market will re- quire different strategies than are currently in place.

  Allow but control complexity — Work toward the idea of individual customization but do so with some control over the process and combination possibilities.

  Market uniqueness as a competitive advantage — Providing each customer with the ability to build his or her own vehicle could be a factor in the market.

  Manage a flexible supply chain — The most significant issue is how to manage the supply chain to deliver the unique vehicle in the targeted time span. This will be possible only through synchronized inventory management across the enterprise or an enormous inventory buildup. The forecast must near 100% accuracy, as the orders will have been confirmed with each component identified. Variances will only occur due to customer cancellations or changes and other unanticipated events.

- **Synchronized supply chains** — The supply chain will respond to an avenue of information and knowledge sharing from the car manufacturer to the lowest tier, with the decision-making process an event rather than a reaction. This will require the following strategies:

  Extended enterprise relationships — The relationship will be based on trust and delivery commitments for every company across the supply chain network.

  Real-time communication — Only real-time information to and from supply chain partners will provide the receipt and confirmation of order information as well as track each item through its production and delivery process.

  Manage virtual inventory — Inventory management will be accomplished through on-line real-time information systems. *If it becomes necessary to physically see or count the inventory, deliveries will have already been missed.*

This vision is far reaching but within the grasp of current technologies and management thinking. The obvious heart of these strategies is very close collaborative manufacturing, centering on real-time information.

An article by Hewlett-Packard (2000) shows the evolution of enterprise collaboration; it extends to a "customer-centric collaboration" made up of value collaboration networks that virtually integrate members of their community into flexible value chains as needed, allowing quick responses to market dynamics and customer requirements. Their road map to this objective identifies three phases of development, shown in Figure 2.2.

Collaboration ideas are not far-out ideas coming to us sometime in the future. They are part of today's business activities. In a recent article in *Information Week* (Konicki 2001), John Burdett of Lockheed Martin Aeronautics makes the following comments regarding the company's successful effort to win a recent Defense Department contract for jet fighter aircraft: "It is unlikely Lockheed would have won the contract without the modern collaboration system. This is a new era in how we contract for business and how we execute on contracts. The collaboration system gives the company visibility into the inventories and production schedules of suppliers. The system automatically alerts the appropriate manager if a supplier is having problems meeting inventory deadlines."

According to Lisa Koenig, director of re-engineering at IBM's Personal Systems Group (Balijko, 1999), one business unit of IBM has seen the following results of implementing a collaborative system:

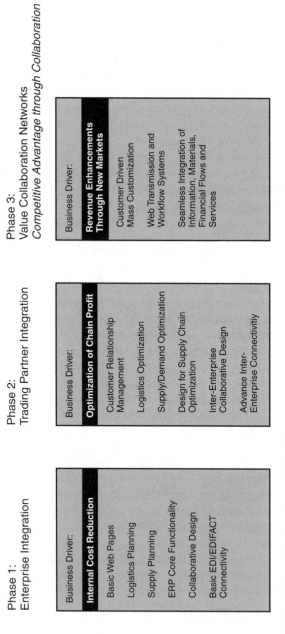

Figure 2.2 Evolution of enterprise collaboration.

Order scheduling time reduced by 66%
Channel inventory trimmed by 80%
Supply-commit cycle time shaved by 50%

Collaboration between companies is not a new idea. In its simplest sense, collaboration is not much more than simply working closely together toward mutual objectives. Can collaborative manufacturing be so simple as to be nothing more than sharing information? In some instances the answer is yes.

> *Collaborative manufacturing can be defined as sharing information between business processes across internal or external partners in the supply chain network.*

or

> *Collaborative manufacturing is to automate, link, complement, or support business processes across departmental, plant, enterprise, or supply chain boundaries.*

Historical evidence of companies working in close alliance is easy to find. Examples include locating supplier plants near the customer, such as a container plant next to a brewery or a supplier facility near an automotive assembly plant. Another example is the highly successful idea of vendor-managed inventories known as collaborative planning, forecasting, and replenishment. In the bottling plant example, the relationship is based on historical business approaches of supply chain management through improved logistics. It is obviously less expensive to ship products a few feet between plants than to ship the same product 100 miles over the highway. Collaboration partnering in today's terms is generally thought of as something beyond traditional supply chain management that uses information technology as the enabling tool. Information technology is not a factor in the bottling example unless it includes the ability of the downstream customer (the bottling plant) to examine and affect the work-order progress, current cycle time, or current inventory issues of the container manufacturer by accessing and using real-time information. Supply chain management initiatives are still an important part of the management process but the aim of this book is to address new and potentially greater opportunities available through the use of modern information technology to view production facility events as they are occurring and to optimize the variables to fit a synchronized result.

There are no fewer than four categories to describe collaborative manufacturing. They are described briefly here as part of the definition of collaboration. Each category will have an explanatory chapter providing much greater detail.

Product life cycle management — The practice of sharing and collaborating on product design using supply chain partners has emerged as a significant management tool, especially in industries using outside contract manufacturing facilities and those with multiple design engineering input locations. Included in this category is real-time information sharing on product tracking and product genealogy throughout the life of the product. These data could include the following: complete product design history from initial concept to product disposal, quality assurance data, and use and repair information throughout the useful life of the product to disposal or recycle.

Synchronized inventories and production — The intent in these applications is to synchronize inventories across supply chain partners. This means removing the inventory buffers that most companies put in place to protect their ability to provide products to customers when unanticipated adverse events impact the production plan. Another major factor is basing production plans on a demand forecast that is shared between supply chain partners as much as is practical and useful. Within this view is the growing requirement of mass customization to meet individual customer desires. Inventory management is a crucial element in accomplishing individualized unit production without a major adverse cost impact, and the key to inventory management is to produce to *actual demand*, not anticipated or forecast demand.

Distribution order fulfillment — The most successful implementation of collaboration to date appears to be Collaborative Planning, Forecasting, and Replenishment (CPFR®), a model developed by the Voluntary Interindustry Commerce Standards Association. The CPFR standard guidelines have been implemented by a number of companies building on earlier models of vendor-managed inventory (VMI), an idea that has been very successfully implemented in retailing industries. Their success and the guidelines that have been published are very important but are only a part of the process envisioned in this book as the CPFR model stops with order affirmation. The inclusion of the CPFR model plus collaborative relationships across the extended manufacturing enterprise, the use of real-time process information, and the concept of a virtual inventory provide a broader view of the opportunities of collaboration in manufacturing.

Manufacturing enterprise collaboration — Sometimes it simply makes good sense to share information. This too is collaboration. As our information systems applications have matured, we have developed large silos of information that have provided more information and in most cases better resulting data. Unfortunately, we have constructed walls around and between business processes. These walls exist between departments within companies and between supply-chain network partners in spite of the best intentions. Another opportunity for manufacturing enterprise collaboration is to link companies and facilities that have come together through acquisition or merger. Although there might be a quick connection at the planning system level, the real-time information from the plant floor may be necessary to support business processes.

In manufacturing enterprise collaboration systems the idea is to simply share information because it better supports the common everyday business processes that people work with as a matter of course. Historical efforts to tie systems together through tight integration have been very expensive, unreliable, time consuming to develop, and difficult to change once in place. Collaborative manufacturing methods use these systems as network nodes that are linked to retrieve or exchange information that can be interpreted and passed to interested parties and/or other systems.

One example is to link quality assurance data from within the manufacturing execution system (MES) with a supply chain event management system to monitor yield information and broadcast results to internal or external recipients. An additional step might be to provide that information to the planning and scheduling system for an automatic response to the actual yield quantity and to revise the schedule accordingly. To extend this further, we might inform downstream partners of the quality assurance data, the resulting yield, the revised schedule, and current shipment information as developed in the logistics management system. One more step might be to advise the supply-chain event management system of the new priority-enhanced schedule by using a logic requiring notification by the MES if the revised schedule for the order does not begin on the date specified.

This category of collaboration may be as simple as information transfer through e-mail to designated receivers, browser access, or as sophisticated as on-line, computer-information sharing with internal and or external users.

Collaborative competitive advantage and other cooperative strategies — This application of collaboration includes those instances where the participants join for the purpose of gaining a distinct competitive edge over other companies or supply chain networks. There are many ways to gain a competitive advantage through closer collaboration with one or more supply chain partners. In most cases, the advantage may be cost oriented, but other possibilities can apply, including faster product to market and geographical advantages, among others.

There are other forms of cooperative relationships, including partnering, consortiums, joint ventures, alliances, networks, and collaboration among competitors. Some relationship forms will include manufacturing collaboration and product information sharing but these cooperative arrangements are usually formed for reasons other than manufacturing information sharing and are mentioned here for reference purposes only.

At least two categories of collaboration are aimed specifically at supply-chain inventory management. A fundamental part of the ideas behind both synchronized inventories and CPFR collaboration is an intense focus on manufacturing products to an *actual demand* as opposed to a *forecast demand.* Although any production environment other than a build-to-order method will have some degree of an estimate, the idea is to eliminate as much of the guesswork as possible and to use time buffers, not inventory buffers, to address any discrepancy. This is best accomplished through a scheduling system that integrates each node of the supply chain into a single schedule and provides actual demand information to each participant. This approach requires complete visibility and accuracy of production events and processes, and is a part of the trust equation that is so important to successful collaboration.

To develop an effective collaborative manufacturing strategy, it is necessary to view the supply chain network in a holistic sense. The islands of information throughout the plant or plants of each supply chain partner should operate interdependently, similar to a finely tuned orchestra. Again, the orchestra analogy is the appropriate holistic sense. Think of the conductor as the customer and the first violinist as the supply chain host. We key off of the first violinist with each member using finely honed skills (the real-time contribution) to provide the harmonious result. All participants have their sheet of music (the demand forecast), understand their position in the orchestra (the supply chain), and produce in harmony (real-time synchronized result).

Dyer (2000) provides an excellent overview of collaboration within the automotive industry, particularly Chrysler and Toyota, and describes the management of their relationships through the past decade. Dyer explains the thinking behind proactive supply chain management via collaboration and measures the effectiveness of Chrysler and Toyota against Ford and General Motors. The book is highly recommended, as it provides excellent insight regarding collaboration and lends strong reinforcement to what may seem obvious in hindsight: Suppliers managed as supply chain partners in a strategic sense are much more effective than suppliers managed through coercion and intimidation.

Dyer uses the term "collaborative advantage" to describe the competitive advantage jointly created and shared by teams of firms within a value chain. He goes on to define the term "extended enterprise" as a value chain in which the key players have created a set of collaboration processes that allow them to achieve virtual integration and to work together as a virtual team. The term "extended enterprise" is used frequently in this text because it so well describes the relationship that is possible through mutually beneficial collaborative relationships.

Many instances of forced collaboration have met with only limited success and have simply aggravated the adversarial relationship. One example, long a part of supply chain management, is just-in-time inventory management. Instead of reducing inventory, this frequently accomplishes nothing more than moving the inventory back one step to the supplier. The enticement is generally "take it or leave it"; if you don't do it, your competitor will. This is a "good-for-me" perspective that rarely translates any benefit to the suppliers or the end customer. Collaboration must be mutually beneficial in a "good-for-us" sense for all parties involved, or success will not meet expectations.

Supply chain management is the effort of continuously improving chain-network-partner performance. Collaborative manufacturing goes one step further to include supply chain partners in the virtual corporation as if they were part of the company. As a collaborative partner at any location in the supply chain network, the focus must be on the end customer. The commitment to and the support of meeting customer needs as a supply-chain network entity provides for the collaborative advantage of the network. This applies regardless of whether the supply chain network is a group of non-related companies, plants of a multidivision corporation, or departments within a company.

Strategic deployment of collaborative manufacturing formally addresses at least two issues within the supply chain:

- A modern company can have a global supply chain of suppliers, factories, logistics, distribution centers, and customers. This many entities with their myriad functions will encounter normal dynamics that cause incidental performance failure. Integrating links must exist within the supply chain so performance failures can be recognized early and proactively, thereby mitigating their impact.
- The second strategic view is the use of core competencies within the extended enterprise to gain a competitive advantage. This can begin with product development or product life-cycle-management technologies and continue through the production and distribution processes of each member of the extended enterprise network. The collaborative advantage benefits the entire supply chain network and rises to the level of supply chains in competition with other supply chains.

Collaboration can be a very effective and successful business strategy but it is not easy or simple and will require some new thinking, openness, and trust. Using new names to identify old processes is not enough. The most significant ingredient is trust between the partners but there are additional considerations.

- Trust is the fundamental building block of collaboration. Each partner must be able to share information without fear of being taken advantage of. This includes such sensitive information as product design, cost information, and occasional performance deficiencies.
- Only accurate, timely, available, and real-time information gives everyone the ability to react in the interest of the supply chain network.
- The purposes and objectives for collaboration should be consistent and mutually aligned among all partners across the supply chain.

- There should be high visibility and accuracy of all data sources. Assumptions are unreliable and therefore unacceptable. Only accurate information allows trust.
- The old cliché still applies: A chain is only as strong as its weakest link. Reliability is a key factor in collaborative network performance and there is no substitute.
- To obtain reliability there must be a consistent allocation and commitment of resources.
- The ability to make delivery promises must be based on sound data and resource allocation.
- All partners must buy into the ideas, methods, and objectives.
- There must be a simple, well-defined data transfer methodology.
- There must be consistent and shared performance benchmarking standards that are measured and shared on a regular basis.
- Companies in a supply chain can hardly work at opposing ends. They must work together as an aligned team; they must collaborate.
- Chain partners must reduce or eliminate the adversarial tone between themselves. Supply chain partners must be seen as departments of the extended enterprise with the common objective of enhanced supply chain performance.
- Utilizing effective information technologies toward the focused objective is a must. The enterprise resource planning system or an equivalent is in place in most companies. The collective information management of the extended enterprise must be used.

Trust is seen as the fundamental element in collaborative relationships. In his book, Dyer elaborates on trust as follows: *Trust is one party's confidence that the other party in the exchange relationship will fulfill its promises and commitments and will not exploit its vulnerabilities.*

Dyer goes on to describe how trust is important as it affects the following areas:

- Trust leads to superior knowledge sharing.
- Trust facilitates investments in dedicated assets.
- Trust lowers transaction costs.

The first two items are reasonably intuitive but the transaction cost element deserves more explanation. Transaction costs involve all of the costs associated with conducting business between firms. They can be divided into four areas:

- Search costs — the costs of gathering information to identify and evaluate potential trading partners.
- Contracting costs — the costs associated with negotiating and writing the contract.

- Monitoring costs — the costs associated with monitoring the agreement to ensure that the parties fulfill the obligations of the transaction.
- Enforcement costs — costs associated with resolving nonperformance.

Trust can provide a substantial cost saving when viewed in the context of an extended supply chain.

In the manufacturing environment trust comes from measuring and confirming events as they occur and making this information available to partners. Whether this is called visibility or corroboration, having access to production information as manufacturing is occurring is a necessary exposure. Trust is then built on confirmation of events through information technologies.

Tactical applications of collaboration are unfolding rapidly. Applications can be simple or complex, between two departments or any number of companies or across the broader extended enterprise. Some initiatives are easily recognized and allow quick implementation. Other initiatives are long-range projects implemented through a team or teams of professionals over a period of years. Early projects aimed at obvious opportunities can be quickly brought on line with a very fast return on the investment. A starter list of tactical application ideas using collaboration tools for improvement follows:

- Initiate new product development efforts using a broader range of input and review from extended enterprise partners.
- Improve a product design for manufacturability using the full range of competencies within the supply chain network.
- Synchronize the inventory across the supply chain beginning with first-tier suppliers.
- Provide schedule information to support producing to actual demand, not to an anticipated or assumed demand.
- Improve logistics cost across the supply chain network.
- Reduce the time to market for new product introduction.
- Reduce the manufacturing cycle time for designated partners.
- Develop a formula to measure overall supply chain cost and view tactical managerial initiative opportunities using that cost as the baseline.
- Initiate a benchmarking performance review of the supply chain network.
- Obtain maximum data input from all partners.
- Examine how collaboration might be used to more closely align production with distribution channels.

Except in the simplest form, collaboration needs to have some foundation of formality. In later chapters, specific steps to develop and implement collaborative strategies are discussed, but the following guidelines are good thought starters.

Alignment: Collaborative manufacturing requires companies to have mutually aligned interests. Collaboration is not about coercion. It is about sharing information and objectives in a way that the total is greater than the sum of the parts. Alignment helps to ensure that the people understand the objectives and view the process alike. One aid to alignment is benchmarking a few key performance indicators. Whatever examples are used will form the basis for operation as people tend to focus on those things being measured. Include the partners' interests in alignment to gain a win/win situation and maintain a "what-is-good-for-us" perspective.

Dedication: Dedication to the ideas and objectives is a fundamental requirement of collaboration at any level. Whether the exchange is between departments or between companies, the commitment must be mutual and complete. Asset dedication, such as plant location or capacity set aside, is a part of the dedication. Collaboration cannot be business as usual.

Visibility: The primary thrust behind collaboration is to raise the visibility of current and near-future conditions within all partners of the supply chain. For all the partners across the supply chain, this includes visibility of production data, logistics information, quality assurance and yield data, product development and enhancement, engineering change-order issues, customer reorder or order changes, work-in-process status, genealogy information, granular inventory information, and so on. Decisions and commitment based on visible information develop trust and good business relations. The other side of visibility is the bad news component. Surfacing an unanticipated event of nonperformance early may allow timely downstream responses to minimize the effect on supply chain performance.

Adaptability: The supply chain network must respond to the combined requirements of the customer. Involvement in identifying and meeting those requirements necessitates a capability to adapt to new products, new ideas, and other cultures quickly and completely.

Accessibility: Access to the data flowing within the collaborative system is a must. Some form of information systems integration between partners in the supply chain is absolutely crucial to ensure that information is visible and consistent. The system must be able to support the objectives of the collaboration agreement.

Glass supply chain: The supply chain partners should seek to provide a full and open exposure to all partners. The ability to review and confirm events provides control over the process, something that is lacking with passive business cultures.

Engagement: Collaboration is not a one-time thing or a business practice that you put in place and walk away from. Full engagement on a long-term basis is required to address marketplace and performance changes and to continue building an ever more successful alliance. Collaboration is a process, not an event.

Production information: All manufacturing plants have some infrastructure to manage and measure their production. This may be a fully integrated MES, a stand-alone warehouse management system, a quality assurance system, a production scheduling system, a distributed process control system, a data collection system, a genealogy system, a supply-chain execution system, or any other combination of systems and methods. In some cases, the existing system or systems can accept or provide real-time production information. In other cases, it will be necessary to determine how to obtain or provide the required information and design the connection as necessary. Having systems integrated to the extent that data can be exchanged, reviewed, and discussed is fundamental to collaborative manufacturing.

On-line: On-line real-time information is the source of data that is accurate, reliable, and available. Some sources of production data may not be available electronically but that is the first option. Gathering data manually and entering it into the information system is not error free. Waiting for paper-borne information is not reliable or fast enough. Systems other than plant floor sources, such as the enterprise resource planning systems or the advanced planning system (APS), may not be capable of real-time or on-line availability.

Network: The supply chain is made up of a network of interrelated companies and interrelated functions. The relationship may be only for a single product for a single node of the supply chain, but the responsibility as a link in the chain represents the commitment to the network. Collaboration is about all nodes being in step with each other through accurate information and access to other supply-chain network partners. Whether the network consists of nodes within a company or across the extended enterprise, the inclusion of parties with access to on-line information is a key to success. Collaboration is about the network and what is good for "us" as an entity.

Security: There has been a lot of comment made about sharing information and visibility across the supply chain network but this is not about indiscriminate information access. Security is just as important here as in any other system.

Scalability: Initial collaborative arrangements are likely to grow. As early systems are being considered, design into your process the ability to increase traffic and the number of participants.

Culture: Collaboration is about bringing people closer together. Culture is a part of every group of people and must be a consideration in the process of collaboration development.

Leadership: There is an old axiom that business is not a democracy and that is no less true today. Collaboration may be closer to democracy but it is still business and it requires strong leadership, not just good cheerleading. It is a business strategy that must be led effectively by the supply chain host and accomplished with qualified supply chain partners that share in the benefits. This is a two-way win/win process, but leadership for collaboration initiatives clearly rests with the production entity whose product is identified to the distribution and marketing process. This entity usually has better insight on customer issues, the greatest product exposure, the greatest business risk/opportunity, and the greatest leverage of all partners within the supply chain.

People: Collaboration is a people-centric concept. Bringing people closer together with the proper supporting tools to bridge business-process gaps is the essence of collaborative strategies. Business processes provide the framework and information technology is the enabler, but the applications must be people-centric.

Implementations of collaborative strategies have just begun, and enabling technologies will continue to be developed to provide easier ways to connect across the supply chain network. The following chapters provide in-depth information on each type of collaboration along with application examples and ideas on how to define objectives and guide system implementation.

References

Andersson, P., Automated Collaborative Execution and the Real-Time Supply Chain, An Ericsson Case Study, paper presented at Educational Society for Resource Management (APICS) Conference, San Antonio, TX, 2001.

Balijko, J.L., Supply chain management: involve partners to enhance processes, *Electronic Buyer News*, May 17, 1999, p. 60.

Campbell, A., and M. Gould, *The Collaborative Enterprise*, Perseus Books, Cambridge, MA, 1999.

Dyer, J.H., *Collaborative Advantage: Winning through Extended Enterprise Networks*, Oxford University Press, New York, 2000.

Hewlett-Packard, Evolution to an E-services enabled collaborative Internet economy, in *Manufacturing Leadership through the Extended Enterprise*, Technology Publishing Ltd., London, 2000, p. 18.

Kay, J. The virtual automotive market — who's driving today's competition?, in *Manufacturing Leadership through the Extended Enterprise*, Technology Publishing Ltd., London, 2000, p. 105.

Konicki, S., Collaboration Is Cornerstone of $19B Defense Contract, *Information Week*, Nov. 12, , 2001.

chapter three

Collaborative planning, forecasting, and replenishment

This chapter provides an in-depth explanation of collaboration specifically aimed at retail industries and the manufacturers serving this business segment. The history of traditional interaction and inventory decisions is explained to provide a basis for newer methods of vendor-managed inventories (VMI) and jointly managed inventories (JMI) that have evolved into a true collaborative approach. The focus is on processes and methods regarding inventory management between the manufacturer and the retail store, and methods for determining demand in the value chain. Although the methods presented here are most applicable to the processes outside the manufacturer, they are excellent bases of ideas and experiences to jump-start the thinking processes to apply collaboration deeper in the supply chain network.

The term "collaborative planning, forecasting, and replenishment" (CPFR) is a registered trademark of the Voluntary Interindustry Commerce Standards Association (VICS). VICS is made up of a number of large-scale, consumer goods manufacturers and retailing corporations that set out to improve manufacturing scheduling and responsiveness to demand fluctuations. A study by participants indicated that the problem resulted from cascading forecasts. One example in the study was disposable diaper manufacturing; the product intuitively should have had a steady demand requirement that followed the birth rate but didn't. With as many as four intermediaries in the chain from manufacturer to the retail outlet, forecasting was following the Forrester effect with precision. These companies set out to do something about the problem and as part of that process established operation guidelines to reduce these fluctuations and improve cost and inventory management. Much of the information presented in this chapter is taken from one of their documents published in 1998, "Collaborative Planning, Forecasting, and Replenishment Voluntary Guidelines."

The guidelines are based on the observation that significant business improvement opportunities are possible through more effective practices in the following areas:

- Revenue opportunities — Reducing lost sales due to a mismatch in demand and supply in front of the customer will create revenue opportunities.
- Inventory reductions — Collaboration can have a major impact on the management of the value chain uncertainty and process efficiencies, the drivers for building and holding inventory.
- Improved return on investment (ROI) — The ROI from CPFR for most companies can be substantial.
- Improved technology ROI — Technology investments for internal integration can be leveraged through extending these enabling technologies to trading partners.

According to a 1996 study, retail product stock-outs occur at an average rate of 8.2%. In other words, for every 100 customers going to a store to buy a specific product, eight will not find the item they wish to purchase because it is not in stock. These out-of-stock occurrences represent 6.5% of all retail sales.

For the retailer, 3.4% of the 6.5% figure is offset by alternative sales; the remaining 3.1% of sales are lost. (This does not take into account other intended purchases at the time of the visit that may also have been lost.) These percentages translate financially into the loss of significant margin opportunities and a possible increase in marketing expenses.

Customer dissatisfaction also affects the manufacturer. Of the 6.5% in lost sales described above, only 1.5% is recouped by alternative purchases from the same manufacturer. The remaining 5% becomes an opportunity for competitors. In addition, just as customers may lose patience with a retailer and go elsewhere, retailers may decide to allocate shelf space to another supplier.

The traditional answer to addressing customer service problems has been to increase inventories. If inventory is in the pipeline, including the stores, then consumers will never have to deal with products being out of stock. Unfortunately, inventory is expensive in terms of capital consumption and expense. Participants have also found that inventory management initiatives frequently involve as much shifting of inventory burden as direct inventory reductions. The result is that the impact on the value chain still leaves considerable room for improvement.

To understand how collaboration can affect inventories it is worthwhile to examine some of the issues that drive inventory decisions. The most significant driver in nearly all inventory decisions is management of uncertain demand. The more unpredictable the demand, the more inventory is required to manage the risk of lost sales. In addition, the farther away from the consumer an inventory buffer is in the value chain process, the more demand variability that inventory buffer will have to address. This is referred to as the Forrester effect. The Forrester effect is created by the lack of coordination of downstream demand information with supply processes back through the value chain. Each demand and supply pairing is managed independently. The cost of inventory generated by this lack of coordination ultimately is buried in the product cost to the consumer.

Another potential source of inventory distortion is the uncertainty of supply processes. Supply variability drives inventory at both the beginning and the end of value chain nodes. There can be several reasons for its occurrence. One of the most common reasons at the input stage of a supply chain node is a supplier failing to deliver what is ordered. At the output stage of a supply node, inventory depends on the flexibility of the node process, expressed as process cycle time, to react to demands on it. It is fairly common for output inventories to be equal to the node process cycle times. (Finished goods inventories for manufacturers are frequently equal to production lead times.) It is also common for process cycle times to have hidden time buffers to compensate for process inconsistencies. These time buffers are ultimately equal to output inventory buffers. Collaboration allows value chain participants to coordinate the planning for supply processes to reduce the multiple sources of supply variability and subsequent inventory.

Inventory has a way of hiding inefficiencies in processes and generates some of its own. The supply process variability mentioned above is an area where significant inefficiencies are usually found. These include costly activities like expediting transportation or production, resulting in added costs for that activity and also in the disruption in the flow of other products. Inventory also drives what is frequently unnecessary storage costs and increases the handling of products. Inventory inhibits flexibility. Within the store, for example, inventory affects shelf productivity and impacts assortment opportunities.

A basic assumption behind CPFR is that technology investments for improving internal integration can be leveraged if companies extend the technologies to their trading partners. These technologies include the investments in enterprise systems and supply chain planning systems. These systems represent a sizable investment, and extending the technology to trading partners can be relatively low.

For most companies, the return on investment generated by CPFR will be substantial. Investments in the technology necessary for CPFR are relatively small compared to technologies that it leverages such as ERP systems. The other area of potentially significant investment is the change management required to move to a corporate culture that supports collaboration. Financial improvement comes through revenue growth due to improved customer service, balance sheet improvement from reduced inventories, and expense reduction from improved supply-process efficiency and productivity improvement.

To develop an idea of where progress can be made, begin with an examination of the current process. Currently there are three forecasting and replenishment processes being used by the retail value chain (see Figure 3.1). The most widely used approach is the aggregate approach. The other two are VMI and JMI.

	Aggregate Forecasting	Vendor Managed Inventory	Jointly Managed Inventory
Joint Business Planning	Limited joint business plan development	Limited joint-business plan development	Heavy emphasis on joint-business planning and coordinated execution planning
Assemble Data	Syndicated data and historical sales	POS, warehouse withdrawal data, syndicated data	POS data by product, store, and week; syndicated data
Sales Forecasting	Sales forecast done at a high level of detail: category, week or month, market or region	Sales forecast generated by: product, customer DC, by week. Store-level VMI is by product, store, week	Sales forecast generated at the store level by product by week. Identifies micro-marketing and micro-merchandising opportunities
Order Forecasting	Primarily focused on manufacturing support to its own distribution centers. Frequently not done by retailers	Focused on retailer DC driven by inventory and transportation cost targets; store-level VMI focused on store inventory; still focused on supply coming from supplier DC	Time-phased replenishment of stores, retail DCs, and supplier DCs
Order Generation	Generated by retailer expecting 100% fulfillment from supplier	Generated by supplier based on the pull from store replenishment or consumer demand for store-level VMI	Could be generated by either party based on store-level sales that are time-phased to supply capabilities
Order Fulfillment	Supplier provides what is available at its DC	Supplier fills orders from its DCs, giving priority to VMI customers	Supplier fills orders from its DCs or manufacturing, depending on the extent of integrated planning

Figure 3.1 Three forecasting and replenishment processes used in retail value chain. (Courtesy of VICS.)

The prevailing aspects of the existing planning and forecasting practices follow:

- Most companies generate multiple, independent demand forecasts for different purposes.
- Most forecasting is done at a high level of detail that focuses on a product category or family, a market or region, and a period of weeks or months.
- Forecast accuracy is not measured frequently.
- Operational forecasts usually focus on interaction between two nodes on the value chain. These forecasts are not time phased across the value chain.
- Manufacturing usually pushes inventory to its distribution centers based on manufacturing economics and not on forecasted consumer demand.

Aggregate forecasting and replenishment are the traditional methods of interaction between business trading partners. The manufacturer and retailer views of this process along with some of their deficiencies will be reviewed. The manufacturing approach generally follows these steps:

Assemble data: The core data used for forecasting include historical shipments, syndicated data, and sales forecasts. Typically, the data are aggregated to the product family or brand level by week or month, and by market regions. Data inaccuracy is compensated for or buried through an aggregate process.

Forecast sales: The available data input and plans from marketing that focus on influencing demand are used to generate an aggregated consumer demand forecast. The best practice is to use this forecast to drive integrated planning across the corporation. Frequently this does not happen, as the desire for meeting short-term targets often preempts the best forecasting algorithms.

Forecast orders: The aggregated consumer forecast drives a coordinated effort to create a supply plan that supports the designated level of sales. In today's environment the demand and supply are matched by planning the customer-order flow and finished-goods inventory flow into distribution centers. Planning systems with conventional distribution requirements are sometimes used to facilitate a customer pull-through process.

Order generation: As the execution phase begins, a retailer places a purchase order. One primary driver of the ordering process is replenishment activity. The key to this is warehousing withdrawals by stores. Other input involves the basic ordering parameters that factor inventory targets and transportation costs into ordering quantities. The third primary driver is promotional activity.

Order fulfillment: Once retail orders are received, manufacturers look to the available inventory and determine whether the order will be filled completely. If an allocation needs to take place, the manufacturer notifies the retailer. This contact marks the first collaboration within the process. Frequently the first notification of a shortage occurs when the retail receiver opens the back of the truck. In either case, given the short order cycles, the retailer and the manufacturer have little recourse for remedying the shortage. If the retailer has been carrying enough inventory, the consumer may not be disappointed. If not, sales are lost. Either outcome is costly.

The retailer goes through the following series of steps, which is similar but different from the manufacturer:

Assemble data: Historical sales, syndicated data, and input from suppliers on promotional plans and changing product offerings are the key data sources. Other input involving store openings or closing and retail promotional activities are the primary drivers.

Forecast sales: The assembled data lead to a category or merchandising plan determined by major market areas. The level of detail varies but is generally high. Independent sales forecasts may be generated by procurement, logistics and store operations to support operating plans. As with the manufacturing approach, the financial plan may prevail over the consumer sales forecast when it comes to operational planning.

Forecast orders: The forecasting of material flow is concentrated around distribution inventory and processing. Many retailers do not forecast for regular replenishment business. However, they do attempt to predict orders for seasonal and promotional activity because of the operational impact on the business. Most businesses expect 100% responsiveness from their manufacturers in meeting orders within short time frames.

Order generation: Orders often are placed independently by replenishment, promotional, and seasonal buyers. Each has targeted inventory and sales plans to support. While lead times may vary for different processes, the level of coordination with manufacturers is on an exception-driven basis — coordination takes place only when problems come up.

Order receiving: Demand and supply come together for the retailer at the receiving dock. At this point, there is little time to react to shortages.

The VMI approach was developed to avoid some of the process problems identified above. A key technology component that has made VMI possible is the ability of supply chain applications to manage inventories at retailer locations. Demand and supply now come together at the retail receiving location. This is frequently the distribution center, yet store-level VMI is also common. VMI practices and technology provide a broader view of the inventory holding locations and pipeline activities; this gives the manufacturers better information for planning inventory deployment across the pipeline. It also allows the manufacturer to be more customer-specific in their planning and to plan at a much lower level.

The key process activities in VMI reside primarily with the vendor or manufacturer. They involve the same process steps described earlier.

Assemble data: The primary data driver for VMI programs that focus on distribution centers is warehouse withdrawal from retailer distribution centers. Some companies complement this with point-of-sale data so that store-level activity and inventory have greater visibility. Store-level VMI uses point-of-sale data as its primary driver.

Forecast sales: The primary forecasting effort of most VMI programs is warehouse withdrawals from the retail distribution center. Store-level VMI is consumer focused. Retail customer-specific sales need to be reconciled with the overall market sales in the complementary aggregate forecasting process.

Forecast orders: Order forecasting is controlled by the manufacturer and generally works to agreed-on retail inventory target and transportation cost objectives. This allows the manufacturer to plan inventory for specific customers.

Order generation: The manufacturer controls the generation of purchase orders. These are driven by the store replenishment pull on the distribution center or actual consumer demand for store-level VMI. Since the manufacturer controls the process, the customer usually receives priority service when shortages occur.

Order fulfillment: The manufacturer fills product primarily out of inventory.

VMI has advantages but there are also some limitations:

- The overall level of collaboration is limited.
- The level of detail for planning is still generally high.
- The focus on warehouse withdrawals for distribution-center VMI is not as effective as for the store-level or consumer-level focus.
- Most companies fail to leverage customer-specific data effectively for planning manufacturing operations. Instead, they continue to make to stock.
- In some cases, reserving finished goods inventory in the manufacturer's distribution centers actually causes shortages to other customers.

The JMI approach focuses on collaboratively planning and executing the business at a much lower level of detail. This allows an increased focus on the consumer and on exploiting opportunities frequently hidden in the aggregated data. Jointly managed inventory uses teams of people working only with key accounts. Frequently, team members are located geographically close to each other, which allows frequent face-to-face meetings. This fosters open communication between functional counterparts, which in turn furthers process customization. The improved understanding of each other's operations and the increased interaction that results helps foster trust between the trading partners.

The five functional steps described earlier are also part of the jointly managed inventory process. Normally, these are guided by the previously completed joint business planning. JMI, however, involves a much more intense joint planning effort and coordination of execution before the process steps begin. The level of customization of the process steps is driven by the capabilities of each trading partner, with a focus that is much more consumer-centric.

Although there has been substantial progress in the ability to improve customer service and inventory management there are still opportunities for improvement. CPFR principles have been developed from the best practices of both VMI and JMI. The trading partner framework and operating processes focus on consumers and are oriented toward the value chain process.

1. Trading partners manage the development of a single shared forecast of consumer demand that drives planning across the value chain.
2. Trading partners jointly commit to the shared forecast through risk sharing in the removal of supply process constraints.

One key finding in this development process is that no single business process fits all trading partners or all situations between trading partners. Trading partners have different competencies based on their strategies and investments. They also have different sources of information and different views of the marketplace.

Retailers see and interact with the end consumer in person and infer consumer behavior using point-of-sales information. They also see a range of manufacturers, and their product offerings and plans for marketing those products. Manufacturers see a range of retailers and their merchandising plans. They can also monitor consumer activity, with some delays, through syndicated data. Given these different views, the trading partners can improve their demand planning capabilities through an iterative exchange of data and business intelligence without breaching confidences. The end result is a single shared forecast of consumer demand at the point of sale. This single, shared demand plan can then become the foundation for all internal planning activities related to that product for the retailer and the manufacturer. This gives us value chain integration.

Embedded in the concept of a *single shared forecast* is the orientation of forecasting toward a level of detail that supports the identification of consumer opportunities. While information sharing and demand planning at some level of aggregation are practical, the ability to work together to discover and exploit these opportunities requires an interactive flow of information within a framework of collaboration.

The value of having a single demand plan, if nothing else changes, is to better coordinate value chain process activities. This coordination would yield significant, but not dramatic benefits. Dramatic benefits come from using the demand plan to affect the constraints inhibiting supply process performance. An example of a significant constraint would be manufacturing flexibility.

Manufacturing capacity is not used because retailers' normally short order-cycle times are inconsistent with longer manufacturing-cycle times. By extending the retailers' order cycle and thus making it consistent with the manufacturing cycle, production could move to a "make-to-order" process for some products. This removes the need to hold a significant number of finished goods inventories in the value chain and improves customer service. Another example of constraints that could be addressed involves dynamic inter-enterprise scheduling to optimize asset utilization across manufacturing, transportation, and distribution centers. Optimization across the value chain depends on collaboration to ensure a consistent and focused view of the interests of all parties in the value chain.

Collaboration is not something that is a naturally occurring phenomenon even though the advantages seem to serve everyone. The guidelines (illustrated in Figure 3.2) provide a process model that identifies the steps necessary to gain alignment among the value chain partners.

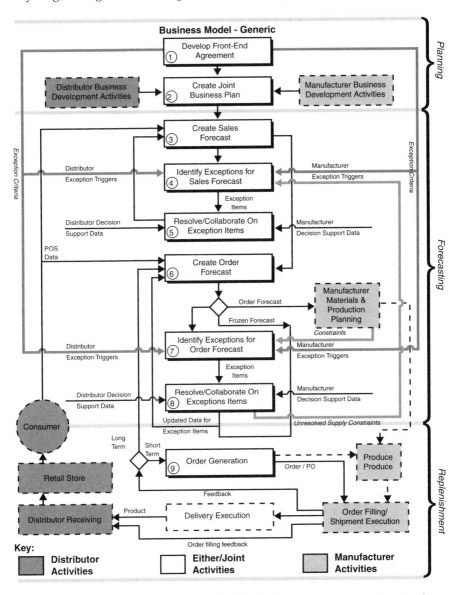

Figure 3.2 Guidelines to a process model identifying steps necessary to gain alignment among value chain partners. (Courtesy of VICS.)

Step 1. Develop a front-end agreement

Purpose — This step is where the retailer/distributor and manufacturer establish the guidelines and rules for the collaborative relationship. The front-end agreement addresses each party's expectations and the actions and resources necessary for success. To accomplish this, the retailer/distributor and manufacturer co-develop a general business agreement that includes the overall understanding and objective of the collaboration, confidentiality agreements, and the empowerment of resources (both actions and commitment) to be employed throughout the CPFR process.

Output — The output of this step is a published CPFR front-end agreement that gives both partners a co-authored blueprint for beginning the relationship or redefining it in accordance with the CPFR standard. The document clearly identifies the process in practical terms. It also identifies the roles of each trading partner and how the performance of each will be measured. In addition, it spells out the readiness of each organization and the opportunities available to maximize the benefits from their relationship. The agreement also documents the commitment to pursuing a higher level of performance and willingness to exchange knowledge and share the risk.

Step 2. Create a joint business plan

Purpose — In this step, the manufacturer and retailer exchange information about their corporate strategies and business plans in order to collaborate on developing a joint business plan. The partners first create a partnership strategy and then define category roles, objectives, and tactics. The item management profiles (e.g., order minimums and multiples, lead times, and order intervals) for items to be collaborated on are established.

Output — The result from this step is a mutually agreed-on joint business plan that clearly identifies the roles, strategies, and tactics for the items in the agreement. The joint business plan is the cornerstone of the forecasting process. Having such a plan at the front end should greatly reduce exceptions and the need for overly excessive collaboration.

Step 3. Create sales forecast

Purpose — In this step, retailer point-of-sale data, casual information, and information on planned events are used to create a sales forecast that supports the joint business plan.

Output — A sales forecast is initially generated by one party, communicated to the other party, and then used as a baseline for the creation of an order forecast.

Step 4. Identify exceptions for the sales forecast

Purpose — This step identifies the items that fall outside the sales forecast constraints set jointly by the manufacturer and distributor.

Output — The output from this step is a list of exception items. This information is necessary in Step 5.

Step 5. Resolve/collaborate on exception items

Purpose — This step involves resolving sales forecast exceptions by querying shared data, e-mail, telephone conversations, meetings, and so on and submitting any resulting changes to the sales forecast.

Output — Collaborative negotiations between the retailer/distributor and the manufacturer resolve item exceptions. An adjusted forecast is then submitted. The increased real-time collaboration fosters effective, joint decision making and increases confidence in the eventual committed order.

Step 6. Create order forecast

Purpose — In this step, point-of-sales data, casual information, and inventory strategies are combined to generate a specific order forecast that supports the shared sales forecast and the joint business plan. Actual volume numbers are time phased and reflect inventory objectives by product and receiving locations. The short-term portion of the order is used for order generation, while the long-term portion is used for planning.

Output — The result of Step 6 is a time-phased, netted-order forecast. The order forecast allows manufacturers to allocate production capacity against demand, while minimizing safety stock. It also gives retailers increased confidence that orders will be delivered.

Step 7. Identify exceptions to the order forecast

Purpose — This step determines what items fall outside the order forecast constraints set jointly by the manufacturer and distributor.

Output — The result is a list of exception items that have been identified based on the predetermined criteria established in the front-end agreement.

Step 8. Resolve/collaborate on exception items

Purpose — This step involves the process of investigating order forecast exceptions through querying of shared data, e-mail, telephone conversations, meetings, and so on and submitting any resulting changes to the order forecast.

Output — The results of this step are the output of the negotiation and resolution of item exceptions, which are then submitted as an adjusted forecast. The increased real-time collaboration facilitates effective joint decision-making and fosters confidence in the order that is eventually committed.

Step 9. Order generation

Purpose — This step marks the transformation of the order forecast into a committed order. Order generation can be handled by either the manufacturer or distributor, depending on competencies, systems, and resources. Regardless of who completes the task, the created order is expected to consume the forecast.

Team Members, Roles and Responsibilities			
Role	Responsibilities	Typical Position Buyer	Typical Position Seller
Sales Collaboration	The sales collaboration team is responsible for establishing sales forecasts, promotion plans, collecting and reporting sales results. The team is also responsible for recommending and implementing changes to the replenishment system.	Category, Manager Buyer, Replenishment Analyst	Sales Representative (Account Relationship Owner)
Replenishment	The replenishment team determines the order forecast, and collects actual order and inventory information.	Inventory Analyst Buyer	Customer Service Manager, Forecast Analyst, Order Management Analyst
Collaboration Technology	The collaboration technology team sets up the collaboration environment, monitors technology effectiveness, and evaluates technical rollout requirements.	IT Coordinator, Project Manager, Systems Manager	IT Coordinator, Project Manager, Systems Manager

Figure 3.3 Roles and responsibilities of team members. (Courtesy of VICS.)

Output — The result is a committed order generated directly from the frozen period of the order forecast. An order acknowledgement is sent as a result of the order.

The VICS's CPFR committee (1999) later developed the following road map to guide and assist companies as they began CPFR initiatives:

Step 1. Evaluate your current state — CPFR begins long before piloting with an assessment of the company's needs, values, strategies, culture, partner relationships and track record of implementing best practices. This step looks for areas where change is needed to implement CPFR successfully. Only after this step is done will your company be prepared to articulate a meaningful vision for CPFR. In addition, the senior leadership of your company must not only understand the concept of CPRF, but must also openly offer their support.

Step 2. Define scope and objectives — After the vision is created, the next step is building the team and setting initial objectives (see Figure 3.3). Step 2 requires:

- Gaining commitment from trading partners.
- Assigning team members and establishing their roles.
- Selecting products and locations that will be included in the process.
- Deciding which parts of the nine-step process to test.
- Establishing key performance metrics to measure the initiative's success.

Step 3. Prepare for collaboration — In Step 3, the project team studies the details of the CPFR business process and identifies the technology and additional resources required to support it. Sales and replenishment team members develop ground rules for managing exceptions and changes. Collaboration technology team members install and configure the information systems (purchased, developed, or simple spreadsheets and e-mails) used to support collaboration between partner pilot teams. At the end of this step, collaboration is ready to begin.

Step 4. Execute: performing the pilot — In Step 4, the sales and replenishment collaboration teams begin to exchange forecasts with each other, modifying them to respond to changing conditions. The collaboration technology team gains experience managing the environment, and prepares for rollout to a large number of locations and projects after the pilot is complete.

Step 5. Assess performance and identify next steps — In Step 5, the team and its management reviews progress, reports results to their respective organizations, and makes preparations for broader CPFR rollout. The suggested next steps include:

- Expanding to other CPFR processes.
- Adding more products to the initial lineup.
- Increasing the level of detail by going from warehouse information to store-level information.
- Automating the process. The vision of CPFR is that of managing forecasts by exception, which can best be achieved through an automated process — especially when the number of products and trading partners is high.
- Adding trading partners.
- Integrating the results. For the supplier, this means using the collaborative forecast in the production planning, capacity planning, and materials requirements planning processes as well as financial planning. For the buyer or retailer, this means integrating the collaborative forecasts into buying, merchandising, replenishment, and financial planning processes.

The underlying principles of the process are what generate the dramatic potential benefits of collaboration. Building a trading partner framework, creating a single forecast of consumer demand, and synchronizing manufacturer- and retailer-order cycles all focus on creating an inter-enterprise, value chain environment that reduces waste and cost. Collaboration supports marketing, promotion, management, manufacturing, transportation, and planning activities. The information shared as part of this process enhances the accuracy of the forecast and order fulfillment. The extension of the collaboration into the value chain environment is the fundamental change that creates new opportunities.

A large portion of the information in this chapter has been taken from the "Collaborative Planning, Forecasting, and Replenishment Guidelines" (VICS, 1998) and "The Roadmap to CPFR: The Case Studies" (VICS, 1999). For more information, see the VICS website, www.vics.org, and the CPFR

Committee website at www.cpfr.org. The CPFR Committee has done an outstanding job of guiding development and implementation of collaboration and are now engaged in the Global Commerce Initiative to expand the application of CPFR and define n-tier CPFR as a multitiered collaborative solution across the supply chain. Their pioneering work at the distribution to retail level has gone a long way in developing collaboration as a viable business strategy. Their assistance in providing information for this book is very much appreciated.

References

Bowman, S., McKinney, J., and Morgenstern, R., Collaborative Planning, Forecasting, & Replenishment (CPFR), white paper with case study, Computer Science Corp., El Segundo, CA, 2000.

Lewis, C., Roth, L., and White, A., Global Commerce Initiative Interim Report Update 4, CPFR Committee, Voluntary Interindustry Commerce Standards Association, Lawrenceville, NJ, 2001.

VICS Merchandising Issues Committee, CPFR Committee, Collaborative Planning, Forecasting, and Replenishment Voluntary Guidelines, Voluntary Interindustry Commerce Standards Association, Lawrenceville, NJ, 1998.

VICS Merchandising Issues Committee, , Roadmap to CPFR: The Case Studies, Voluntary Interindustry Commerce Standards Association, CPFR® Committee, Lawrenceville, NJ, 1999.

White, A., n-Tier CPFR, white paper, Logility, Inc., Atlanta, GA.

chapter four

Synchronized production and inventories

Collaboration in this instance has the specific purpose of synchronizing inventories across supply chain network partners. The objective is to substantially reduce or eliminate excess inventory by producing to actual current demand and by synchronizing with supply-chain network partners on the demand and supply side, one common schedule with visibility for each participant.

Cost reduction opportunities are enormous. In the pharmaceutical industry supply chain, beginning with the retail drugstore outlet to the distributor to the manufacturer to their suppliers and their suppliers, the inventory can be as high as 100 days of supply. In the electronics industry where the supply chain has at least as many layers, it is said that the inventory can exceed 1 year's supply, a particularly significant issue in an industry where products can become obsolete overnight. The reasons for the existence of this inventory are many. Some reasons are valid and some are questionable. A full examination within the context of the broad view of the value chain will bring a new perspective with potentially impressive cost reduction opportunities.

In *Industrial Dynamics* (1961), Jay W. Forrester recaps his study of the process of information feedback characteristics within companies and within supply chains. His study led to the conclusion that an increased demand level at the final customer level causes an amplified demand wave when it reaches the manufacturer level. This is known as the Forrester effect or demand amplification. Forrester identified the following as the main causes:

- There was no demand visibility along the network. Responding to current information or demand changes was not possible.
- Information distortion was constant with participants affecting the process with their own interpretation of events and data.
- Intentional adjustments made by one party had compounding effects at other nodes of the supply chain.

One of the major factors effecting inventory overbuild is the distortion of demand information as identified by Forrester. One of these distortions is called the bullwhip effect; it describes the demand amplification primarily due to misinformation as requirements move up the supply chain. Demand distortion is generally used to describe an over-reaction to actual demand but it could equally describe an under-response. The under-reaction would have adverse effects in that customer service could suffer and sales likely would be lost. Over-responding or amplifying the demand information results in peaks and valleys in manufacturing causing problems of cost and inventory buildup.

Lee, Padmanabhan, and Whang (1997) describe the bullwhip phenomenon in terms of causes and possible actions to mitigate its effects. The four major causes follow:

Demand forecast updating — Every company prepares forecasts to guide their organization on subjects such as production quantities, inventory levels, material requirements, and financial requirements. Because people are using available information when making or adjusting forecasts, they tend to react to obvious demand information. When a customer places an order with a supplier, the individual receiving the order is likely to see that as an indication of future demand. Forecasts are based on historical and the latest current information with individuals likely to over-react to positive trends by increasing their orders to upstream suppliers to ensure their ability to deliver. In a supply chain of any size, the cascading effect of the distorted demand can be very significant.

Order batching — Ordering cycles can distort demand by accumulating quantities into infrequently placed orders. An example is a company that sells one of an item each day but places orders every 2 months because of internal reasons. The supplier sees something quite different from the actual demand of one per day.

Price fluctuation — Special pricing, such as promotions or seasonality, can cause customers to overbuy to meet future needs resulting in inventory that exceeds current demand.

Rationing and shortage gaming — A shortage, real or imagined, can be seen as a threat to future supply causing buyers to overbuy today to ensure inventory availability tomorrow.

Suggested responses to the bullwhip include:

Avoid multiple demand forecasts — Base forecast information on a single schedule available to members across the value chain.

Break order batches — Collaborate with value chain partners to devise rules for order batching that provide smoothing of demand.

Stabilize prices — Review internal pricing programs to avoid forward buying.

Eliminate gaming in shortage situations — During shortages it might be an improvement to allocate products based on historical sales records. Sharing actual inventory and production information can also alleviate customer concerns.

Lee, Padmanabhan, and Whang (1997) contend that the bullwhip effect is the result of rational decision making by members of the supply chain. By understanding the underlying issues, companies can reduce the effects through more effective information systems and more collaborative relationships with supply chain partners.

Another aspect of the Forrester effect exists within companies as plants, departments, and individuals accumulate inventory that was produced to counteract adverse events within production processes. Usually referred to as buffer inventories, they can exist anywhere in the supply chain production process. Some production systems have automatic built-in buffers in areas such as lot sizing or scheduling algorithms. Other systems can be affected by individuals at decision points by *under-* or *over-reacting* to real demand as in this example. An order is received for 100 widgets from a customer expected to order 50 per month. Believing this to be the new business level, the annual forecast is revised upward. A check of on-hand inventory finds 30 in stock. The manufacturing economic order quantity has been set at 200, so production is scheduled for 200 units. Yield has been trending downward on the last three production runs to 90%. To offset the yield problem, production planning sets the quantity at 215. Purchasing uses the initial order quantity to order sets of purchased material for 200 widgets and then revises the order upward when production planning revises the quantity to 215. This is not a problem for suppliers except for the two vendors that made separate shipments, one for the original order and another for the addition. As the production order makes its way through the plant the yield is up, reaching 95%, but one of the separated vendor shipments is lost, leaving 15 unfinished pieces currently stored on the floor at the final assembly station waiting for the remaining components to be found and assembled. As a result of many decisions, we now have an inventory that is not synchronized with demand.

Collaboration is used to address the fundamental causes of what are obviously dysfunctional system processes by first giving visibility to the processes and events on a holistic basis. It is not enough to view just a department or a plant, but each decision point of the entire value chain must be included in the examination of existing methods. The solution will include most of the following steps:

Synchronization of demand and supply: This requires the participants to see the actual demand requirements with the value chain host providing leadership on demand identification for all value chain participants and processes. Decision points must be highly visible with absolutely correct real-time information and a single schedule.

On-line information transfer: Communications channels must provide timely and accurate transmittal of compliance, as well as condition change information, such as quantity revisions or exceptions to planned events. Modern information technology, including Internet access, e-mail, and automatic integrated system updates, are required.

Time buffers: Time buffers should be the tool used to respond to unanticipated events, not inventory buffers.

An excellent example of synchronized production has been accomplished by Ericsson Radio Systems, a manufacturer of cellular base stations for telephone companies. Over a 2-year period, they envisioned, developed, and implemented a system linking five plants that includes multiple level suppliers across the supply chain. Today all customer requirements are open to the supply chain partners. All resources are available for review and on-line commitment allowing an account manager to provide a delivery confirmation response within 10 seconds, down from 24 hours. An order received by Ericsson is transmitted immediately to the supply chain partners providing a true pull environment. A graphic schedule is used to transmit the demand requirement to each partner. The systems include linked ERP, supply chain event monitoring, and real-time information transmittal and availability down to the machine level and warehouse management system.

Synchronized inventory is a vast opportunity for business improvement. The auto industry wants to reduce the pipeline from 30 days to 5. The electronics industry with 1 year of inventory supply is ripe for improvement, made even more necessary by rapid product obsolescence. Reducing the 100-day pharmaceutical industry inventory would reduce costs, substantially affect warehouse and transportation costs, and could likely reduce the time from manufacture to customer use. There is probably no industry that could not benefit from synchronized production and those companies that improve their processes will have a tremendous advantage over their competition.

Collaboration between partners seems to be intuitively correct. People working together can usually accomplish more than people working against each other treating the other party as the adversary. If this is true for people, it should apply to companies as well — but sometimes things are not as we might want to see them. Manufacturing collaboration does in fact have a great number of success stories to tell. The progress in product life-cycle management as companies use collaboration to reduce time to market and improve manufacturability seems widespread. The application of collaboration in retail industries has gotten excellent reviews and the CPFR committee can cite a number of successful case histories. Analyst organizations are also very strong in their assessment of collaboration, its impact on companies that have applied collaboration, and the expected investment in applying collaborative methods.

But there are some issues to consider. In a study by Mentzer, Foggin, and Golicic (2000), interviews were conducted with supply chain executives of 20 major companies to learn what experience has taught those who have applied collaboration ideas in their organizations. The study sought to gain insight on questions such as, What exactly is collaboration and what enables it to take place? What are the obstacles and is achieving supply chain collaboration worth it?

The study found that there were certain enablers required to achieve success.

- Common interest and benefit sharing — It is necessary for the collaborating parties to have a common interest and a win/win result from their efforts. The relationship must be based on a "what's-in-it-for-*us*" perspective.
- Openness — Collaboration requires being open with information that may be considered proprietary. This does not mean full exposure of all company information, but it does require sharing information that allows each partner to see itself as part of the team, not as an adversary.
- Recognize who and what are important — Not all partners and activities are equal. Choose those that provide the greatest benefits.
- Cooperation and mutual help — Collaboration is about teams that work together to achieve a common goal. Coercion and punishment are not effective methods to improve team relationships.
- Clear expectations — All parties need to know what is expected of them and others in the partnership.
- Leadership — Without someone to lead and guide the collaboration effort, nothing significant will get accomplished.
- Trust — Trust must be evident throughout the organization at every management and functional level.
- Technology — Technology is not the panacea, but it is essential to enabling a collaborative relationship across the supply chain.

Items found to be impediments to collaboration in the study follow:

- Doing things the old way — Resistance to change continues to be a part of human nature even when there is a benefit.
- Limited view of the supply chain — It takes leadership to help individuals see the broader picture of the supply chain partnership or the extended enterprise.
- Time investment — Collaboration takes time and work. To get people to make the commitment they must truly understand the objectives and the benefits.
- Inadequate communication — When communication between partners is inadequate, the potential for problems increases exponentially.
- Inconsistency — Behavioral attitudes and operational executions must be consistent at all levels within the relationship.
- Betrayal — Lying, misleading, misrepresenting, or anything else that is not a positive element of trust is the ultimate barrier to success.

- Other impediments include conventional accounting practices that focus too much on historical views of business cost allocations and annual supplier/customer negotiations that can be adversarial.

Some of the issues that were published in this study are repeated over and over in the available literature. A research project called Demand Activated Manufacturing Architecture Project (DAMA) was recently completed after a seven-year study effort. It was funded by the Department of Energy through the American Textile Partnership (AMTEX) to develop collaboration technology in the textile industry. This study examined the full supply chain beginning with the fiber to the fabric provider to the garment manufacturer to the retailer to the consumer. The final report (Chapman et al., 2001) listed the following issues as barriers to collaboration:

- Lack of trust is a major deterrent to collaboration. When companies do not trust each other, collaboration attempts fail. As a prerequisite, collaboration requires sharing more proprietary information than is currently shared. Only limited information is shared when there is lack of trust. Lack of trust was seen as a critical issue between companies, but also as an obstacle where lack of trust exists between divisions of the same company.
- Lack of trust in the ability of technology to provide adequate data.
- The inability of companies to identify what information should actually be shared.
- Failure of the collaboration champions to clearly demonstrate the benefits expected from collaboration to upper management.
- An inherent risk-adverse attitude within the company.
- Internal software to support collaboration is not in place within the companies wishing to participate.
- Companies are not currently organized to support collaboration, that is, resources are inadequate.

After trust, the next major hurdle against collaboration appears to be culture. Hofstede (1991) defines culture as "the collective programming of the mind which distinguishes the members of one group or category of people from another." Culture, for the most part, appears to be learned and shared through social interaction in our work and where we live. The important part is that culture can have a direct effect on cooperation.

Collaboration, by design, brings people from different organizations together to work on common objectives. Each of the organizations in a collaborative partnership will have developed a culture that is distinctive and unlikely to be easily modified. In some companies, the culture allows people to arrive late but work well past the end of the normal workday. Some companies have a quiet soft-spoken demeanor, where others may be loud and very forceful. Some may lean toward a very conservative position while others may be eager to push the boundaries.

Culture can be a barrier to cooperation and team building, so it is important to recognize early on that attention must be paid to cultural issues and how this aspect of collaboration is to be managed. This should be a consideration in choosing collaboration partners and in staffing assignments. Organizational culture is not necessarily the Achilles heel of collaboration but it can be a serious issue if not adequately recognized for its possible impact.

On the other side of the culture discussion are instances where cultural diversity can be an advantage that allows the partnership to use the competencies and knowledge of each partner's culture to foster improvement and benefit the overall partnership. This thought extends to the idea that the collaboration partnership is likely to form its own culture. Continuous learning and cultural evolution are hallmarks of a successful relationship as organizations coming from different cultures work together toward widening relationship objectives.

Culture was found to be an issue in the DAMA study (Chapman et al., 2001). In 1997, the focus was changed from a technology-driven approach to a business process approach that addressed the following business requirements:

- Knowledge of the industry culture and business practices
- Development of maps of industry models of information flow
- Construction of collaborative frameworks for business practices
- Deployment of information systems to support the collaboration

After developing, simulating, and implementing a collaborative model that was built around business requirements, the study reported these key findings:

1. A necessary ingredient for collaboration is an accepting culture. This may require modifying corporate value structures and activities to support collaborative relationships.
2. The primary target for a company must be the consumer or end user of the product, no matter where the company is in the supply chain.
3. There is an evolutionary path that companies follow as they move toward a true collaborative environment that takes them from a focus on internal processes and systems to a global view of the supply chain.

The DAMA report suggested three distinct phases to develop a collaborative supply chain.

Phase One, Preparation — This phase encompasses cultural change and development of methods and processes. The report cited that a significant amount of preparation is required, particularly if a company is not ready for change. Included in this phase is the need to identify and address cultural barriers to be overcome. Once the cultural issues are being resolved, the next step is to ensure that each partner's internal processes are in order to support collaboration.

Phase Two, Pilot — The best way to reduce risk is to first do a small-scale pilot. The piloting phase is manpower intensive as the team works to identify operational processes that fit each partner.

Phase Three, Scaling — The scaling phase is where the scope of the pilot is increased to include more products, more collaborative functions, and/or more participants.

The ten-step preparation program outlined in the DAMA study is essentially a gearing-up process to determine if supply-chain inventory synchronization has a place in your environment. The full outline of a collaboration process follows this preparation and pilot phase outline. This program follows the three-phase process indicated above.

1. Select trading partners.
   a. Identify all partners in a supply chain.
   b. Identify the products that will serve as the basis for collaboration.
   c. Obtain executive-level commitment to participate.
   d. Secure a signed front-end agreement from all partners, which includes but is not limited to:
      i. Statement of intellectual property
      ii. Data security
      iii. Confidentiality
2. Select collaboration opportunities.
   a. Investigating possible opportunities for collaboration may involve a very formal analysis of the supply chain or a very informal analysis that results from a discussion between trading partners.
   b. Selected trading partners choose opportunities to leverage through collaboration.
      i. Improve sales forecast.
      ii. Improve order forecasts.
      iii. Reduce lead times.
      iv. Reduce inventory levels.
      v. Increase visibility of information throughout the supply chain by bill-of-material explosion from the end product through the supply chain.
3. Identify information to be shared.
   a. Determine what information will be required to support collaboration for each product focus.
   b. Determine the information-sharing format.
      i. Electronic data interchange (EDI) transactions or other software system linkage
      ii. Excel spreadsheets
      iii. Memos

4. Select the method for collaboration.
   a. Identify the methods that will facilitate the collaboration.
      i. E-mail, faxes, mail
      ii. Conference calls, video conferences
      iii. Face-to-face meetings
      iv. On-line collaborative software linkage
   b. Identify the resources, including the computing resources (network connection, software installations, PC requirements, etc.) required to support each method selected.
   c. Determine the time required to support each method that will be used and the frequency of collaboration.
5. Specify roles, responsibilities, and team members.
   a. Specify the team leader for each company.
   b. For each company, determine the business role and function that can supply the appropriate information and support for successful collaboration.
   c. Determine and outline the responsibilities for each of the identified roles.
   d. Identify the individuals who are responsible for the corresponding roles.
   e. Specify the estimated time commitments for each individual in his or her role.
6. Define measurements of success.
   a. Identify quantifiable measurements that will be used to determine if the collaboration was successful.
   b. Ensure that the collected information will support the defined measurements, including benchmark data.
   c. Determine who will be responsible for collecting and analyzing data.
   d. Use metrics as an improvement to the collaborative process, rather than letting metrics drive the process.
7. Document the process for collaboration.
   a. Study business practices required and develop business process activities and information flows to accomplish the collaboration opportunities.
   b. Develop a new business process model to define this activity. The process model will identify specific work practice changes.
      i. Identify areas in the business that will require change to support collaboration.
      ii. Determine if the current business practices will allow the change required.
      iii. Identify alternate practices that the business will support for collaboration.
      iv. Business process examples:
         A. EDI forecast transactions will be integrated into the planning software and made available to all supply chain members at the same time.

      B. Purchase order commitments for the pilot will be submitted through EDI transactions that are derived through the collaborative process.

8. Develop a time line for collaboration.
    a. Specify collaboration start and completion dates.
    b. Identify and schedule training sessions to be conducted.
    c. Schedule meetings.
    d. Specify milestones.
    e. Include the frequency of collaboration.

9. Agree on a reporting process.
    a. Specify a reporting template.
    b. Determine contents to be included.
       i.   Company names
       ii. Pilot objectives
       iii. Methods and technology used
       iv. Measurements for success
       v. Resources involved
       vi. Business practices and processes implemented
       vii.Summary of pilot effectiveness
       viii.Benefits realized
       ix. Trading partner relationship changes
       x. Recommended changes
    c. Determine who the report recipients will be.
    d. Determine a timeline for reporting.

10. Implement the collaborative process.
    a. Implement methods and technologies.
    b. Collect data.
    c. Analyze data.
    d. Review processes.
    e. Review business processes.
    f. Implement change as required.

The first nine steps are included in the preparation phase and help define the steps necessary to implement a successful pilot. Step 10 is included in the piloting and scaling phase.

Once the decision to collaborate has been reached, the DAMA model outlines the following activities:

- **Develop business planning agreements**. It is necessary that each trading partner begin by developing a business planning agreement. Each company must assess its own strategy and goals to ensure that these are incorporated into the partnership agreement. The goal is to arrive at a win/win situation for all players. This requires sharing some risk and rewards, in addition to sharing common goals.
- **Populate the supply chain utility**. In this activity the trading partners populate a supply chain utility that is envisioned to be a collaborative

software system that should support product definition; supply chain planning; supply chain visibility; and select, secure data sharing. The initial population would require each trading partner to provide initial information in the following areas:

- Manufacturing information, including lead times, process times, and transport times
- Capacity that has been allocated to the partnership
- Manufacturing information, including bills-of-material, product specifications, and boundary constraints
- Exception criteria
- Assistance in establishing a common vocabulary

- **Define the products**. Collaboratively defining products in a supply chain requires increased supply chain visibility of all partners to the product lines in each sector (fiber, fabric, apparel, and retail). The process begins with market research about customer demand. The partnership collaborates to develop products to meet demand. Once the product is developed, a product definition is provided to each member in the chain.
- **Collaborate on exceptions for product definition**. If a particular product attribute is not available, an exception is generated. Resolution and/or collaboration of the exception may involve phone calls, e-mail, or on-line interaction. Resolution may require adding a product or manufacturing capability by changing the product mix or outsourcing to a third-party supplier who is not a member of the collaborative partnership.
- **Forecast and plan capacity commitments**. One or several partners in the supply chain may develop the forecast. Once the forecast is developed, it is made visible to all members through the supply chain utility. Each forecast must be reflective of the portion of the order that will be filled by the next member in the supply chain. The initial loading of the supply chain utility will ensure that the correct proportions for an order are maintained. Based on the forecast received, each manufacturing member of the partnership should then provide a capacity commitment to the forecast for the specific product line.
- **Collaborate on forecast or capacity to meet forecast exceptions**. A forecast may exceed original capacity commitments or fall short of the commitments. When this exception occurs, the affected partners must collaborate and either find additional capacity from an increase in demand, or share associated risk of a reduction in forecasts. The partnership agreement should provide guidelines for handling these exceptions.
- **Schedule production and product delivery**. The supply chain utility will balance a final order commitment against initial capacity commitments. Using that information, in addition to manufacturing capability data, the utility will generate work orders for each manufacturer in

the supply chain. Each manufacturer then processes these work orders individually.

- **Collaborate on product ship date-exceptions**. Resolving and/or collaborating on product ship-date exceptions leads directly into the expedite production and delivery step. A late ship date on fiber could impact all members along the supply chain. But the textile manufacturer might have yarn in inventory that was not previously entered into the supply chain utility. The supply chain utility processes the updated data for exceptions.

- **Expedite production and delivery**. Manufacturers' ship dates generated from the process of collaboratively scheduling production will be compared to delivery status provided by each manufacturer on a regular basis. If ship dates and delivery status for product are not meeting the agreed-on product ship dates, an exception will occur. Most exceptions will be made available to the trading partner who is initially impacted by the exception, usually the next downstream partner.

- **Execute delivery**. The carrier handles the execution of delivery and provides delivery status information. The supply chain utility determines if the target ship dates are being met.

The objective of the DAMA project was to determine how and what to do in the textile-industry supply chain to reduce the inventory pipeline. The study began long before supply chain management software and the Internet became part of our vocabulary. There was some effort to commercialize the ideas and system software as the study reached certain milestones, but there was little interest from systems providers to exploit the technology at the time.

The following quote by Michael Hammer, former professor of computer science at Massachusetts Institute of Technology, now president of Hammer and Company, is offered as an end to the discussion on the subject of culture. It is taken from the final report on the DAMA project (Chapman et al., 2001) and is in response to a question regarding trust and companies working together: "Companies often look at themselves as sort of a self-contained medieval enterprise, a city state if you like. Everybody else around them is their enemy. In fact, many companies operate as though their customers were their number one enemy, their suppliers their number two enemies, and other departments inside their company are their number three enemies."

The processes that have been outlined in the DAMA model are oriented to consumer goods sold through retail systems. In other industries, such as electronics or industrial equipment, where the consumer is not so easily defined, demand generation uses different sources of input. Although the DAMA outline is an excellent starting point, each initiative should be examined to include other industry-specific steps that might modify the process.

References

Chapman, L.D., R. Lathon, M. Petersen, and Lovejoy, J.L., DAMA Final Report, Sandia National Laboratories and Textile Clothing Technology Corp.; distributed by Textile Clothing Technology Center, Cary, NC, September 2001.

Child, J. and D. Faulkner, *Strategies of Co-operation*, Oxford University Press, Oxford, 1998.

Forrester, J.W., *Industrial Dynamics*, Pegasus Communications, 1961.

Hofstede, G., *Cultures and Organizations: Software of the Mind*, McGraw-Hill, New York, 1991.

Kanter, R.M., Collaborative advantage: the art of alliances, *Harvard Business Review*, July-August, 1994, .

Lee H.L., Padmanabhan, V., and Whang S., The bullwhip effect in supply chains, *Sloan Management Review*, 38, 93, 1997.

Mentzer, J.T., Foggin, J.H., and Golicic, S.L., Collaboration (Keys to Successful Supply Chain Collaboration), *Supply Chain Management Review*, 4, 52, 2000.

Taylor, D. and Brunt, D., *Manufacturing Operations and Supply Chain Management*, Thomson Learning, London, 2001.

Umble, M. and Srikanth, M.L., *Synchronous Manufacturing: Principles for World Class Excellence*, South-Western, Cincinnati, OH, 1990.

Womack, J.P. and Jones, D.T., *Lean Thinking*, Simon and Schuster, New York, 1996.

chapter five

Manufacturing enterprise collaboration

As earlier forms of collaboration were developed, specific purposes addressed particular business processes and corresponding road maps to implementation. In manufacturing enterprise collaboration, there is a broader but less specific objective: link information from disparate business-system applications to better support business processes. Visibility is a key word. Synchronizing information is a key process. The perspective is holistic information empowerment to better support manufacturing-related business processes within a plant, within a company, or across the extended enterprise.

There are a number of similar ideas being advocated by industry analysts. Some focus on closer ties and coordination with suppliers. Others point at internal opportunities to provide information visibility to departments or plants within an enterprise. In each case, the message is very similar — improve your business by linking data from the many business process sources. This is a strategic view that sees information as a resource that is largely underused due to lack of visibility.

Manufacturing enterprise collaboration is based on two ideas:

1. Computer system applications have been developed around specific business processes, such as accounts payable, quality assurance, production scheduling, or warehouse systems. This has provided silos of information that should be linked to fill gaps that exist within or between business management processes. Significant gaps can exist through company or facility acquisitions, leaving companies with sometimes hundreds of very useful system applications that are isolated from each other, unable to provide any transfer of information. There are also changes that take place in organizations and processes that can create information gaps or change the information required to best perform a business function. Linking these disparate sources to improve operational information visibility can enhance business operation (see Figure 5.1).

Evolution to Collaboration

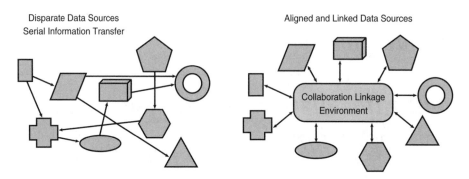

Disparate Data Sources
Serial Information Transfer

Aligned and Linked Data Sources

Figure 5.1 Evolution to collaboration.

2. The linking mechanisms between business processes are usually peo-
    ple using their ability to bridge gaps by providing judgment and
    experience to complex business issues. There is a significant oppor-
    tunity to improve company performance by better supporting these
    people-linked business processes. The support mechanism can be
    very simple, such as an e-mail to confirm an event has taken place,
    or rather complex, such as integrated systems sharing inventory or
    schedule information across the supply chain.

Companies have been implementing systems that address specific business issues for many years. These applications have tended to be somewhat
inward looking providing a service that is focused on a particular business
area. That has left an assortment of acronym soup systems that probably
serve their original constituency reasonably well, but service outside of that
constituency can be very obscure or abruptly nonexistent. An obvious example, illustrated in Figure 5.2, is to consider the functionality of a typical
manufacturing execution system and a simple customer relationship management (CRM) system. There are many possible links, but it is a rare system
that has any connection.

One more example of narrow use is a quality-assurance point solution
that was implemented to meet the requirements of the quality assurance
department. The application may have included all the bells and whistles that
fit the needs of the department but the information typically was (and usually
still is) very difficult for others to see or use. Another example is the advanced
planning and scheduling system that is not receiving information feedback
from the plant floor that identifies available resources or production yields.

These systems typically provide excellent information depth for the
original users but little or no visibility or access for others. The departments
of a manufacturing plant floor might include scheduling, order tracking,
quality assurance, process control, resource planning, genealogy, and maintenance, each with its own software system specifically chosen or designed

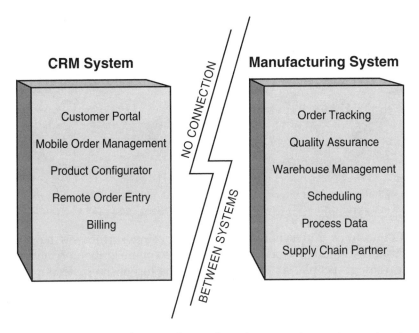

Figure 5.2 Functionality of a typical manufacturing execution system and a simple customer relationship management system.

to meet the needs of that department. Planning systems range from modern fully functional corporate-wide systems to nonintegrated, manufacturing-resource-planning modules. The result is a collage of applications across the plant, across the company, and across the enterprise, each doing its own specific job very well but meeting the requirements of the wider entity very poorly. Successful companies are made up of an interdependent linked set of business processes. Building the various software system components into improved business process support is the impetus behind manufacturing enterprise collaboration.

Industries will always be consolidating and many companies will continue to grow and change through acquisition, providing opportunities and requirements to link business processes more closely. As companies or plants have been acquired, the difficulty of systems integration has proven to be a substantial obstacle to information sharing. A very weak process information system can result when combining acquisitions with the globalization of firms, the expansion of their supply chains, and worldwide markets.

The need to inform and be informed with real-time business process information is heightened with miles of separation, multiple facilities, and global supply chains. Manufacturing enterprise collaboration is the tool to help ensure business process support (see Figure 5.3).

Manufacturing enterprise collaboration will automate, link, complement, or support business processes across departmental, plant, enterprise, or supply chain boundaries.

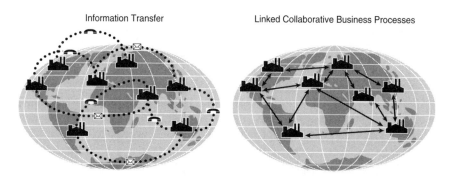

Figure 5.3 Illustration of information transfer (left) and linked collaborative businesses processes (right).

Connections and synergism between business processes have been accomplished through expensive software system integration or, more effectively, through people. As we get close to the top of the systems pyramid with ever higher-level business processes, the need to apply the judgment skills of people with integrated information from across the extended enterprise is ever more obvious. Instead of better-informed people, we see business processes in one area not linked to processes in another, forming larger silos of information. The business process gaps are connected through swivel-chair or sneaker-net technology, or in many cases, the link is simply not made.

The following typical examples give more insight to what manufacturing enterprise collaboration can do.

- Provide real-time, production-run yield information to the planning and scheduling system so that schedule regeneration can be based on actual production system results.
- Provide warehouse inventory information to the CRM system for view by a salesperson. Give the salesperson the ability to commit inventory to a customer order.
- Provide corporate production planning with real-time, enterprise, individual plant-capacity information to facilitate where-to-build decisions.
- Provide production planning with the latest demand information from the customer on a daily basis to optimize the production schedule and reduce build-to-forecast inventories.
- Give customers the on-line ability to track the logistical progress of their order.
- Share product design information with internal or external supply chain partners on-line.
- Provide design engineering with a vendor's tool capacity information.
- A broader example is linking quality assurance data from within the manufacturing execution system with a supply chain event management system to monitor yield information and broadcast results to

recipients internally and/or externally. An additional step might be to provide that information to the planning and scheduling system for an automatic response to the actual yield quantity, and to revise the schedule accordingly. This can be extended further to inform downstream partners of the quality assurance data, the resulting yield, the revised schedule, and current shipment information as developed in the logistics management system. One more step might be to advise the supply-chain, event-management system of the new priority-enhanced schedule using system logic that requires notification by the production management system if the revised schedule for the order does not begin on the date specified.

Informal collaboration has been a part of business since the first customer was found and when the first employee was hired. In today's view, collaboration is a strategic business tool that sees information as an underused corporate resource that could be better deployed. Following are a few ideas to begin a strategic use of collaboration and to set some objectives.

- View information and collaboration in the broadest sense across departmental, company, and extended enterprise boundaries.
- Examine business process gaps where decisions are based on poor or nonexistent information, assumptions, or information that is not current.
- View information as a corporate resource, not as departmental property. There is extensive information generated and accumulated each day that could enhance business processes if it were visible.
- Examine collaborative opportunities from the view of each group of users and information sources.
  - Internal users across the enterprise
  - External suppliers and partners
  - External customers
- Collaboration is not an all-or-nothing process. There should be incremental progress based on defining places of need and acceptance by the users.
- There is no single best answer. Collaboration is about filling gaps in existing business processes by providing linkage between applications. Your applications and your business processes will define the path.
- Collaboration is not about technology. Technology requirements, if too great, will deter partners from willingly supporting projects.
- Collaboration should not force a dramatic change from existing business methods and practices. Collaboration should be the enabler that brings incremental improvement.
- Aim to use tools that can be revised without information technology (IT) management resources wherever possible.

- Revisit specifications for all control systems and IT applications to ensure adaptability to collaborative use by providing information visibility. Internet access should be a standard requirement.
- Linking the various points and communicating in real time can provide an organization with a single mind acting on real-time information.
- Consider the broadest span of business processes from the plant floor systems to the customer and the most upstream supplier.
- Certain collaborative situations are meant to be temporary and some relationships that seem so solid now may change. For these reasons, coupling and decoupling should be part of collaboration considerations.

Mikurak (2001) further argues the case for collaboration as a *people-centric* process. He suggests two requirements for collaborative processes. First, technology must deliver the right information to the right people in the right context at the right time to make a decision. Second, the information must be in the right form for people to use it effectively. People-centric systems

- Break down data and process barriers and allow relevant information to flow to whoever needs it.
- Provide capabilities for users to adjust processes that need to be changed without requiring IT support.
- Provide a process-centric environment that spans tasks, applications, and departments.
- Support both behind-the-screen processes and collaborative processes that involve people.
- Provide workflows that can be granular or high level, depending on the user's experience and knowledge about a process or issue.
- Co-exist and leverage the existing infrastructure of applications, systems, and communications.

Formal collaboration mechanisms are being applied in some industries at the product design level and some areas of the supply chain. But there has been little or no formal process that addresses the internal requirements between the front office and production functions. While there may be some integration between applications within a particular business function, there is little integration across them. Business processes are typically lined up in these categories (see Figure 5.4). An examination of the sublevels of each category will find smaller silos of information that have not been integrated into the other systems in their category or even less, those outside of their category (Figure 5.5).

Enterprise collaboration requires integration of production information across these silos to better support people-centric business processes. Figure 5.6 illustrates an example of what this plan might look like.

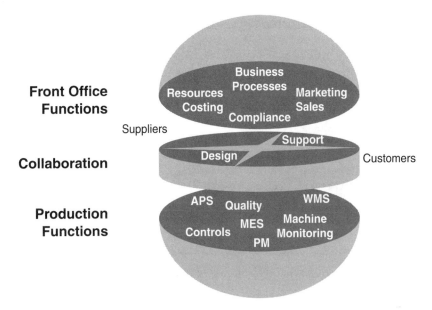

Figure 5.4 Formal collaboration mechanisms as applied in some industries by business process categories. (Courtesy of ARC Advisory Group.)

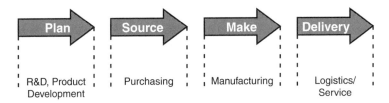

Figure 5.5 Sublevels of business process categories.

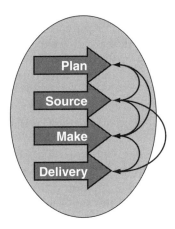

Figure 5.6 Integration of production information to support people-centric business processes.

The Enterprise   Business Partners

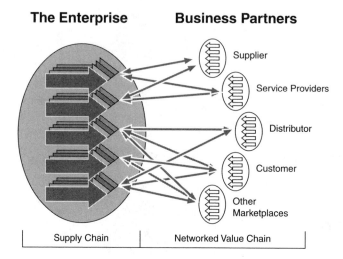

Supplier

Service Providers

Distributor

Customer

Other
Marketplaces

| Supply Chain | Networked Value Chain |

Figure 5.7 Illustration of synergy achieved via linkages between the enterprise and business partners.

Once synergy has been achieved across these silos (Figure 5.7), a whole new world of collaborative possibilities with the supply chain opens up, including optimizing market-facing business processes between the internal supply chain and external supply chain network.

Manufacturing enterprise collaboration has many of the same inherent inhibitors as might be seen in external supply chain partners. The two primary issues are culture and trust and their impact can be just as profound within an enterprise as might be seen between competitors. Culture can extend to interdepartmental relationships that should be constructive but quite often are anything but. Trust and commitment are also as important but sometimes more elusive within organizations. Does your production organization work precisely to the marketing forecast or is there a fudge factor? Have manufacturing and/or purchasing had an opportunity to collaborate on new product design or are they expected to do as they have been told? Can a salesperson or a customer determine the current status of an order or is information provided only on a need-to-know basis — and when provided, is it trustworthy?

Similar to other forms of collaboration, the first step in enterprise collaboration initiatives is a general assessment of the current condition.

> **Step 1.** Review the current condition. Begin by establishing the review boundaries along with the breadth of the review and the perspective. The view of the chief information officer will be different from the supply chain manager of the same corporate unit. Is the view to be a corporate-wide perspective, from the IT view, from the managerial perspective, plant manager, supply chain manager, or manufacturing support? What is the breadth and depth of the analysis?

Step 2. Examine the current environment to see if there are collaborative processes in use today that follow any of those outlined in this book? What is the level of informal collaboration and could a different approach with real-time information provide better support? If there are systems in place, what are the scope and the impact? What was the origin of these systems? What problems arose as they were getting to full operation?

Step 3. Examine the culture of the company regarding information systems. Is information seen as a proactive strategic tool either internally or externally? Do people interact with the information systems only as a data entry point or is there a flow of information both ways? Is information locally owned or is it available for broader business use? How are systems accessed? Is technology in place for technology reasons or is it truly based on business process support? Are we data disadvantaged where the information is too stale to be of value? Does the culture inhibit modern business systems or embrace them as tools? What is the culture response to ideas other than IT, such as sharing customer information with suppliers or product development with suppliers — or market demand information? Can we be open enough to expose vulnerabilities? Are suppliers and/or customers adversaries or partners? If trust is lacking, can this situation be changed? Does the outside world see us as trustworthy? Two issues are basic to manufacturing collaboration. One is openness and vulnerability and the other is factual information. Do those correspond with our culture?

Step 4. Develop a preliminary supply-chain map using a few threads based on either products or market sectors. Map the internal supply chain. Identify how demand is determined and where that information is used. Define all sources of internal supply within the company. Define and map external sources. Examine and lay out the supply chain indicating relationships, sales history, physical proximity, financial issues, and likely future. Categorize high-volume vendors as collaborative prospects, keeping in mind that not all vendors are equal. Outline the information transfer methods — computer, mail, personal, and so on. Indicate information systems capabilities at the planning and plant floor levels and the willingness to use electronic methods to send and receive information. Look at issues such as material management, scheduling, capacity planning, order tracking, and engineering change-order tracking.

Step 5. Examine current business processes to determine the time deficit of information sources. Are you in a time deficit where the available information is always old? If so, how old? Are promises made with data that are not current? Trust is a critical point of collaboration, internally as well as externally, and late information may not be reliable enough to maintain trust. It is not safe to make predictions based on yesterday's data. Real-time information from the point of activity will provide a better basis for judgment and decision-making.

Step 6. Identify decision points. Where and how are business processes affected by individual decisions? Pick two processes and map the decision points as an example of how this can affect the operation. Identify how the decision process works and what the inputs are, and determine whether they can be affected by collaboration. Examine some exceptions and the method of reaction at the decision points.

Step 7. Collaboration, regardless of its form, requires a commitment, and requires a company vision statement to identify that commitment. Effective initiatives must have backing and support from the highest level and a champion to drive and implement them.

ARC Advisory Group (2001), a provider of analysis guidance for collaborative manufacturing, has identified the following seven requirements that manufacturers should be considering:

1. Synchronize business processes with manufacturing processes. A key step is to surface more information for sharing with other audiences and make production systems more responsive and flexible.
2. Optimize the supply-side value chain. Tools and methods are available to manufacturers that provide actual demand information in real time throughout the production network and a competitive edge.
3. Automate business processes across departmental and business boundaries. First movers can expect to realize significant competitive advantage by capitalizing on the agility and responsiveness of adaptive business process control.
4. Generate value by empowering people and measuring results. Web-based tools such as portals can provide information from a variety of systems throughout the enterprise.
5. Implement collaborative design and engineering. This includes the management and collaboration of specification and product development information, as well as the design and collaboration on manufacturing processes across multiple specialized nodal manufacturers.
6. Link operations with customers. In this new environment, close collaboration among nodal manufacturers raises cooperation to a new level. It is now possible and necessary to transmit real-time information in two directions among the nodes. Production information on quality, materials availability, and production status must flow to customers while information on orders, inventory levels, specifications, and change orders flows to the supply chain.
7. Enable collaborative maintenance and manufacturing support. As delivery promises must be met, it will be necessary to avoid equipment failures and downtime through effective plant asset management systems.

Figure 5.8 illustrates the application(s) used in people-centric collaboration efforts. The software systems industry has developed many products

People-Centric Collaboration

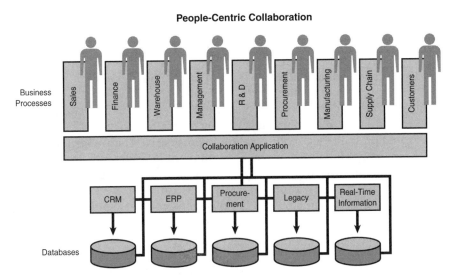

Figure 5.8 People-centric collaboration. (Courtesy of Montgomery Research, Inc.)

that are applied in various places in the enterprise and supply chain hierarchy; a listing and description of most product categories appear in Appendix A. Manufacturing enterprise collaboration does not have a specific collaboration software product that addresses the needs outlined in this chapter, but there are two applications that seem particularly appropriate for use in these activities. Plant portal solutions and the closely related category of enterprise manufacturing-intelligence applications are gaining acceptance as tools that can be used to aggregate, analyze, and present information generated by disparate plant-level systems and process control solutions.

Portals are websites that allow a specific group of users to access, view, and interact with specific data items and software applications. The idea is to gather and integrate data and applications needed by a user into a virtual single repository. Although they are relatively new to most businesses, portal development has gone through three stages, beginning as simple websites that allowed employees to view company news or employee benefits. The next generation brought in information from outside the company to include such things as stock quotes, maps, and other extraneous information. The next generation provided access to structured information for analysis and began to build extensions to a broader environment. Newer systems are being developed that fit the requirements of the user organizations and provide access to a full range of data sources, including existing applications such as the enterprise resource planning systems. Newer portal applications are referred to as enterprise information portals (EIPs) and should meet the following characteristics:

Single point of access — The portal can provide a single point of access for all corporate data. The enterprise information portal should be designed to collect information from a wide variety of heterogeneous data sources into a single repository. Users can search the repository, or the portal can be configured to alert users when new, pertinent information is added.

Knowledge management — By providing a single point of access, an enterprise information portal establishes the infrastructure necessary for knowledge capture and sharing. A key to sharing data is users' ability to publish documents to the portal, and to subscribe to information that they require or are interested in. The publish-and-subscribe model allows workers in different departments, locations, or companies to easily share business-critical knowledge.

Corporate customization — Companies can customize the portal to provide access to a range of applications and data sources. Roles can be defined by the system administrator and applied to categories of users, such as marketing, sales, engineering, manufacturing, accounting/finance, human resources, customer support, or senior managers. Corporate customization also includes defining security policies and procedures, and defining how data will be categorized in the portal.

End user personalization — Corporate users can personalize their portal interface by selecting from the catalog of data sources and applications that they have access to according to the parameters of their assigned roles. The personalization process allows users to quickly locate information that they require and to filter out extraneous information. This increases productivity by reducing the amount of time wasted locating and consolidating information situated in a variety of heterogeneous sources.

The extended enterprise — An enterprise information portal addresses the challenge of streamlining supply chains by providing business partners with secure, controlled access to corporate data and application. These business partners include suppliers, distributors, original equipment makers/value-added resellers, and customers. The enterprise information portal allows companies to increase competitiveness by accelerating the flow of corporate information.

Another software tool called a manufacturing intelligence system, illustrated in Figure 5.9, is being applied in many industries. This off-the-shelf package is designed to collect data from many plant-focused devices and systems and to bring appropriate information into context for presentation and analysis.

The application processes include:

Extract real-time process and production information from all plant-focused systems, leaving each source unchanged.

Aggregate the information that provides context to data from dissimilar sources and correlate it as if it came from the same system.

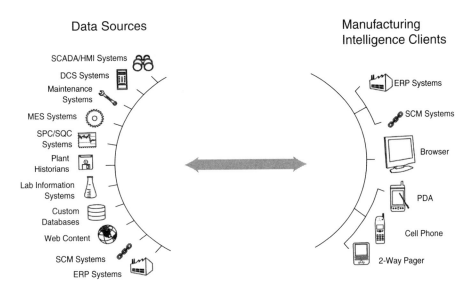

Figure 5.9 Manufacturing intelligence system. (Courtesy of Lighthammer Software.)

Transform the information into actionable manufacturing intelligence through customizable analytics.

Personalize the information for each user.

Deliver the information to browsers, wireless devices, and enterprise business applications.

The tie between these systems and collaboration efforts is straightforward and direct. Both are about sharing information across a broader range of people for the purpose of making better decisions.

After even a simple review of the existing condition in your manufacturing enterprise, it is very likely a number of opportunities will be obvious. Collaboration opportunities in this category are much like choosing little improvement tasks around your house. If you cannot find them, you are not looking very hard.

References

Cookson, C., Linking supply chains to support collaborative manufacturing, in *Achieving Supply Chain Excellence Through Technology*, Vol. 3, Montgomery Research, San Francisco, 2001, p. 56.

Davis, D., Synchronous advantage, *Alchemy*, January 2002, p. 25.

Gorbach, G., ARC Advisory Group, Collaborative Manufacturing Management Strategies, white paper, ARC Advisory Group, Boston, 2001.

Greenbaum, J., PeopleSoft and Enterprise Collaboration: A People Centric Approach to Collaborative Business, white paper, Enterprise Applications Consulting, Daly City, CA, 2001.

LaLonde, B., Connectivity, collaboration, and customization: new benchmarks for the future, in *Achieving Supply Chain Excellence Through Technology*, Vol. 3, Montgomery Research, San Francisco, 2001, p. 168.

MESA International, white paper, MESA International, Santa Ana, CA, 2001.

Mikurak, M.G., Putting people back into collaborative commerce, in *Achieving Supply Chain Excellence Through Technology*, Vol. 3, Montgomery Research, San Francisco, 2001, p. 241.

Quinn, F.J., Collaboration: More than just technology, in *Achieving Supply Chain Excellence Through Technology*, Vol. 3, Montgomery Research, San Francisco, 2001, p. 222.

Building Enterprise-Class E-Business Portals, white paper, 2000.

chapter six

Product life-cycle management

Product life-cycle management describes software information systems used to manage the information and events associated with a product from concept through design through manufacturing through distribution; it also includes user feedback processes. The capabilities of an effective system enable interaction among departments within a company or an extended enterprise of supply chain partners.

This category of collaboration currently goes by many names, including product life-cycle management, product chain management, collaborative product commerce, collaborative product development, or collaborative product data management. Sidney Hill, Jr., executive director of *MSI Magazine* (2002), describes this area of collaboration as a class of software and services that use Internet technology to permit individuals to collaboratively develop, build, and manage products throughout the product life cycle.

The market is currently very upbeat with major suppliers rapidly growing their product offerings. Current enthusiasm is obvious in this comment by Kevin O'Marah of AMR Research: "The idea of using collaborative technologies to support product development across extended groups of experts is irresistible. It's too good an idea not to do."

Modern applications of product life-cycle management are built around a closed-loop process that begins with customer requirements information management and concludes with collection and management of customer feedback information to start the process over again. These systems have evolved from early computer-aided design (CAD) and computer-aided engineering (CAE) to product data management systems that support and connect global network nodes with proactive system tools built around creating, storing, and managing product and process information across the extended enterprise. The use of the Internet provides a global reach that can include real-time interactive sessions with participants anywhere.

Collaboration is based on the idea of interactive co-development and management. Participants in co-development may be within a company sharing information among product development, manufacturing, marketing and purchasing. Extend that to a multiplant company and then to a multicompany enterprise. In many businesses, the participants include suppliers and their suppliers, and it is not unusual to include customers and their customers at some points in the process. Some companies have hundreds of people involved on product project teams that can last for years.

In discrete item manufacturing there are two phases of product collaboration. The process begins with product definition starting at the earliest concept of the product. This includes every step in the design and every detail of the product ranging from the bill of material listing of components and their suppliers, to recipes, routings, tooling requirements, assembly methods, and process parameters. All documentation and software that are connected to or used in the manufacture or product use are part of the product definition.

The actual production of design information is usually accomplished through collecting and blending information from various engineering and design sources. The design competencies can be brought together in a virtual conference room to review documents, make changes, and keep current through immediate access to previous session information. This collaboration can include such diverse groups as customers, suppliers, marketing, manufacturing, and professional designers able to work concurrently and collaboratively on design issues. Information can be imported from various CAD sources and presented in three-dimensional form providing easier knowledge sharing and a common view. A particularly important part of the process is the ability for manufacturing process and tooling design as well as other departments to participate in the early phase of product development. Initial design and engineering account for an estimated 60% to 80% of product cost (Figure 6.1). Collaborative design tools allow participation at an early development stage with a wider range of participants at the time when input relative to cost can be more effective. This early input can have a significant effect on reducing changes later in the development cycle.

The second major category of product life-cycle management is the management and processing of the product design information through the production and delivery processes across the supply chain network to cus-

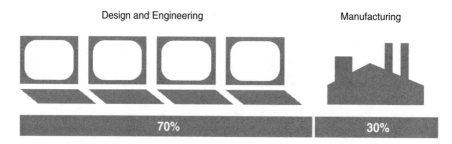

Figure 6.1 Product cost defining areas.

Product Lifecycle Management

Figure 6.2 Product life-cycle management.

tomer delivery and product disposal. This includes managing issues across the supply chain, such as product change, engineering change orders, product and product information obsolescence, data integration and entry into and from the enterprise resource planning (ERP) system, product service and improvement, sourcing management and tracking, and material and information flow. Functionality can include collection and distribution of product process data generated during production, including who, what, and when for each step in the production process, logistics, delivery, maintenance history, and customer use. In some industries, functionality can include details such the name of an operator at a supplier's plant, laboratory test results for a specific lot, complete genealogy data for each item in the bill of material, and it could extend to maintenance information as provided by the end user or a third-party service provider. Figure 6.2 provides an outline of the many collaborative instances and the continuous process that can occur throughout the life of the product.

A recent study by the Original Equipment Suppliers Association (2001), an association of suppliers to the automotive industry, was done to build an internal business case for collaborative product development. The study focused primarily on the efforts within the industry to collaboratively design and manage product information. The study group listed the following current-state conditions that were felt to be opportunities for improvement.

1. Document access and retrieval can be cumbersome. Because information is handled by e-mail, fax, and mail, there are frequent routing errors, lost information, extended approval cycles, and resubmission

due to incorrect or missing information. There can also be considerable time delays and various revisions in the systems at the same time.

2. Considerable documentation and data are generated during the life of a development program. The data tend to reside with the author/owner and are distributed when needed. In many companies, common documents are available; however, substantial effort may be required to access documents because there is no central repository of information.

3. Customer satisfaction is often compromised by timing delays resulting from the need to interpret multiple formats of information, and the lack of a common distribution approval process. Processes cannot be easily automated as information and capabilities are contained in separate systems with no interface capabilities.

4. Communication and program data errors are common due to multiple data sources containing inaccurate or out-of-date information. Multiple versions of documents may also exist within the design systems but there is no mechanism to guarantee that team members are accessing the latest information.

5. Data and documents are generated by many sources. The document owner must be contacted each time to ensure that the document in question is correct. This is not always possible and errors occur when old or inaccurate documents are used. Team membership over the life of a program may change and documentation may be lost in the transition of new team members.

6. Maintaining accurate records of product version status among all supply chain members working on a specific project can be complicated, error prone, and the cause of continuous frustration. In addition, the viewing of CAD drawing data is generally limited to individuals with CAD access; paper copies are required for anyone else needing to review the data. This lack of access often results in duplication of activities, a lack of organizational learning, continuous improvement, root cause analysis and the inability to balance resources.

7. The inability of product development teams to access pertinent information for decision making in real time results in delays and nonoptimal decisions. In addition, most suppliers do not have standard revision control over design information or the ability to review past information.

8. Program data and information are not centralized, resulting in ineffective use of product development resources spent in searching multiple repositories for such information and associated timing delays. In addition, lack of centralized data across multiple products limits opportunities for commonality of parts, tooling, equipment, and technology.

9. In many cases, archiving of hardcopy documents is done using minimal indexing data. Data are then stored in hardcopy boxes. Usually

only the employee's name, data, and one- or two-word descriptive text of the contents of the box are available. Current lack of document control methods can create legal exposure.

10. Companies usually store data on shared, local-area-network hard drives. Data are often duplicated across locations. Confusion and conflict occur as a result of not knowing which version of a specific document is the latest or the correct one.

The study went on to outline the following direct benefits of using a collaborative product development system.

1. Collaborative design allows participants of an interactive design session to discuss design concepts and direction. Several concepts may be developed and discussed in a single interactive session using an on-line system. Design teams may interact via a Web browser and review several variations of a design done interactively using input from both the customer and in-house design teams. This interaction allows a free exchange of ideas and concepts. The ability to collaborate with colleagues in different locations around the world results in the best ideas being exchanged simultaneously, reducing re-engineering efforts and the best product offerings at the lowest costs throughout the program.

2. Faster product development cycle times (fewer design turns) and greater efficiency also result from automated workflow, 24/7 capability, and effective sharing and visibility of common information.

3. Many suppliers believe that the potential exists for significant reductions in product development time using collaborative tools and processes.

4. Workflow functionality can ensure that necessary follow-up actions take place, thereby avoiding potential delays and allowing engineers to meet key milestones.

5. Real-time review and approval of data and program-related information allow customers, suppliers, and internal users to improve efficiency and quality through earlier design involvement and participation.

6. Travel times to discuss feasibility and review designs can be substantially reduced. Teams will be able to mark up and annotate designs and provide manufacturing feasibility in a real-time capacity.

7. Using workflow to manage access and approval of designs in a central repository would reduce cycle time in the development process and facilitate informed decision making.

8. A collaborative development system will allow process/procedure tracking and an audit trail useful in ISO 9000 certification. This same audit trail can be used in a "lessons-learned" review for process improvement.

9. New employee effectiveness can be enhanced as a result of the pre-defined workflow process and documentation availability through a central repository and virtual workspace.
10. Standardized processes for completing development tasks can be communicated more effectively within organizations.

The situation is similar in many companies and industries and the task of managing product data becomes more difficult as the geography and number of interactive partners increases. Some companies make such extensive use of collaborative product applications that they have developed formal contractual relationships with supply chain partners. Cisco Systems Inc. uses a process among major supply chain partners that spells out responsibilities, procedures, delivery dates, statements of work, and dispute resolution methods. There is also a three-level management structure made up of the project managers and development teams, a relationship management committee, and a joint executive sponsor from each company.

Flextronics Corporation is a global electronics manufacturing services provider that serves major electronics original equipment manufacturers. As an integral part of the supply chain of a wide range of companies, it became necessary to develop an evaluation process where both the companies and the customer examine the relationship and how it will be managed. These formal agreements among collaboration partners are common, but most instances of collaboration are less formal relationships built on historical ties or company competencies.

Agile Software is a provider of product life-cycle management systems with extensive capability to collect and manage product information and provide a direct interface with manufacturing facilities and supply chain partners. Their system is divided into the following six modules: Product Definition, Change Collaboration, Supplier Management, Design Integration, Manufacturing Integration and Partner Synchronizing.

Product Definition enables a company to create, maintain, reuse, and share core product information and make the information instantly available on-line to any member of its extended supply chain partners. This will provide partners with immediate access to the latest information and enable them to:
- Locate preliminary and released information about any part, document, or engineering change.
- Create, view, and redline a bill of material.
- Identify where multiple parts or documents are used.
- View which items would be affected by a change.
- Send changes, parts information, or documents to a reviewer.
- View released and pending changes.
- Generate reports based on product definition.

Change Collaboration automates the product change process, enabling users to create and approve changes on-line. Supply chain partners can collaborate in real time throughout the product change process, providing shorter change-cycle times and reducing time and cost in the manufacturing process, and thus enabling them to:

- Create, route, modify, and approve change requests through a Web browser.
- Notify reviewers when a change is ready to be reviewed.
- Keep supply chain partners involved in the process.
- Manage and control the change with a workflow system.

Supplier Management allows manufacturers to collaborate with their supply chain network to make decisions regarding quality, cost, and availability of components, both during new product introduction and over the product life cycle. They can:

- Define commodity components and their manufacturers for each bill-of-material item.
- Control and communicate changes to the approved manufacturers list.
- View data sheets and files associated with a manufactured part or the manufacturer.
- View the released and pending changes to a part's approved manufacturer list.
- Identify duplicate part numbers and consolidation opportunities.

Design Integration enables companies to quickly and efficiently share engineering data with manufacturing by seamlessly connecting and transforming data from multiple CAD sources. Companies can:

- Aggregate and transfer data from disparate CAD tools.
- Improve the new product introduction process.
- Improve the product change process.
- Enable the ramp-up of manufacturing resources.
- Simplify the aggregation of raw product information.
- Make critical product chain information available for immediate use to other systems.

Manufacturing Integration publishes product chain information from the system to a wide variety of enterprise business application and users both internally and across the extended enterprise. Businesses can:

- Synchronize manufacturing with up-to-date detailed product information.
- Increase information availability and accuracy across the supply chain network.
- Integrate the data with enterprise business systems.

Partner Synchronizing is a tool that publishes critical product information to the supply-chain network partners using Product Data eXchange (PDX). This allows customer, supplier, and design partner to participate in the review and approval process by providing product data to a wider variety of business applications and users. Partners can:

- Publish critical information to supply chain partners without regard for system compatibility.
- Send and receive PDX documents in real time.
- Eliminate manufacturing delays caused by incomplete or old product information.
- Make better decisions using the most current information that everyone can work from simultaneously.

The business value of these systems is broader than the obvious idea of a community of stakeholders sharing information. Following are just a few of the extensive business benefits that come in a number of forms.

- Businesses can develop and introduce new products faster. With the full product design always up-to-date and available for collaboration from entities anyplace within the supply chain, it is easier to make revisions to products under development or to authorize changes to existing products. With the consolidated information it is easier to convert engineering information to manufacturing information.
- There is special value during new product introduction and manufacturing ramp-up by maintaining a current database of problems, workarounds, and changes with easy visibility. This allows quick information exchange between the manufacturing process and the design team with interactive responses from anywhere in the extended enterprise.
- Product shortages and replacement options can be met with a quicker response due to predetermined part compatibility and source information.
- Engineering change orders can be more effectively issued and tracked across the supply chain.
- Part genealogy and production information can be aligned with production lots or serialized product-item numbers.

Product life-cycle collaboration is not just for discrete product manufacturing companies, although that is where the earliest implementations and the most growth have occurred. Process industries, including specialty chemical, pharmaceutical, consumer packaged goods, and food and beverage producers, also use this technology to distribute and maintain product information across global plant locations and third-party manufacturers. A consumer goods manufacturer with 16 manufacturing sites requires visibility of information and on-line collaboration between product development, the various manufacturing facilities, and the many supply chain partners. Daily production issue resolution is the same here as in most businesses but is compounded by variations in raw material and by subsequent adjustments in recipes and processes. It is also not unusual to update and reconfigure products to stay current with the market, consumer tastes, or competition. This involves collaboration across the enterprise to react collectively and quickly.

Process industry applications begin at early laboratory phases and continue through introduction into manufacturing, with that cycle being repeated numerous times for innovations and changes during a product's life. For process companies today, that is a mostly sequential series of steps that pass a product from department to department. At each step, product data are passed on in an unstructured, ad-hoc way to the next department, resulting in delays and costly errors. Industry-wide standards for product definition, such as CAD, are not available as they are in discrete industries, such as electronics and automotive. This results in longer time-to-market and time-to-manufacture periods, causing companies to lose valuable time in the early stages of new product innovations when margins are the highest. A related problem is that new product portfolios are not organized for a collaborative environment nor are they consistently judged against objective criteria making go/no-go decisions more complicated and subjective. Unstructured product definitions, lack of a collaborative environment, and inadequate information required to fully prosecute manufacturing options result in products that are committed to a specific manufacturing location early in the process, leaving little room for flexibility.

The value propositions in both discrete and process industries are very similar and are based on achieving real business benefits that increase the profitability through increased revenue, decreased risk, lowered costs and better utilization of assets. The following system application information was provided by Sequencia Corporation, an early supplier of product life-cycle systems in the process industries:

Increased revenue — Accelerate the delivery of product innovations to market and increase product innovation throughput (50% improvement from the current range of 12 to 24 months). Companies gain market advantage over their competition by getting product innovations to market more rapidly. In addition, they increase innovation throughput without increasing investment costs.
   • Complete product visibility and collaboration capability from design through retirement
   • Automated research and development tools
Decreased risk — Increase the success rate of the innovation portfolio (100% improvement from the current success rate of 10% to 40%). Customers can ensure that market innovations are taken from concept to product flawlessly. Flawed projects are identified quickly so that they can be corrected or eliminated proactively.
   • Comprehensive portfolio management
   • Broader view to design for customer need
   • Internationally recognized standard product definitions
Lowered costs — Increase the profitability of products by minimizing product cost structures. Increase the profitability of new products by ensuring that products are introduced with the most competitive product–cost structure.

- Integrated design for manufacturability
- Optimized least-cost recipe configuration
- Strategic material substitution and consolidation capabilities

Better utilization of assets — Avoid capital expense by more flexible utilization of available assets (current capacity utilization is frequently as low as 50%). Customers can achieve a greater return on assets by fully utilizing all of the available capacity and capability in the value chain, both internally and externally. Capitalize on more market opportunities by adding the flexibility to enter new markets without the risk of adding additional manufacturing assets.

The system is made up of several integrated modules that can be used independently or individually.

- **Standards for communicating process-industry product definitions** — Similar to CAD in the high-tech world, the system is the enabler for providing a common language (S88 via XML) for developers of products to communicate among themselves and with supplier and manufacturing facilities, either within or outside the product company.
- **Complete specification requirements** — Defines all aspects of the product, including formulation and packaging, presented both graphically and digitally. The system supports specialized requirements, such as nutrition and labeling for food and beverage and multiple packaging configurations for CPG.
- **Rationalization of manufacturing capability** — Model any target manufacturing facility either company-owned or via contract by allowing the users to define hundreds of attributes and capabilities. Using the detailed information in the system, product requirements can be compared to plant capabilities, including qualified contract manufacturers, to select plant assets as an ongoing process or, in the case of an acquisition, map new products to existing plants and old products to new plant.
- **Intra- and inter-company collaborative workflow** — The processes involved in collaborative product design and deployment can be configured for each collaborative partner.
- **Portfolio management** — All information collected for a product from all collaborators in a product, including marketing studies, lab results, cost estimates, and so on, are collected under a unified project, making decision analysis for any particular product visible and accessible.
- **Visibility into enterprise applications** — In addition to providing visibility into whom, where, and how a manufacturer can make a product, supply chain and/or ERP information can be accessed and used to make critical decisions.

- **Efficient transfer of product information through the process** — Defines the products and manages the process so that all information collected and required to move a product through various departments within and without the enterprise are available in a common system. Product companies must know from their manufacturing options, both within and without, which can make a product, where they can make a product, and how they make a product.
- **Innovation process management** — Product innovation processes are developed and defined to ensure best practice processes, reduce handoff times and to allow for clear accountability and continuous improvement. Best practices such as stage-gate processes can be defined and enforced through project workflow, routings, and approvals for all elements of the innovation project. Business processes become more transparent providing clear accountability and a fully documented decision trail to allow for continuous improvement through the creation of a full audit trail of discussions and decisions.
- **Design for customer need** — Product innovations are defined with market requirements that are made clearly visible to all authorized collaboration parties. These market requirements, which represent the customer's needs, are an inherent part of the design. The requirements are directly tied to the product characteristics and product specifications required to meet the customer's need. The specifications, in turn, are directly tied to testing procedures required to ensure that customer needs are met at every stage of the design process. This ensures that the customer will rapidly embrace or accept the product innovation when it is introduced.
- **Project collaboration portal** — Personnel across organizational boundaries have full access to projects via the Web. According to security rules, they can quickly see the status of the projects they are assigned to and the actions required. From the workbench, they can view project goals, access project documents and product information, and view project discussions. In addition, personnel will be proactively informed of new project information through alerts and subscriptions that will allow them to proactively manage current projects or new projects that may impact them.
- **Portfolio management** — Projects are clearly defined and characterized in a central project repository allowing projects to be analyzed and prioritized relative to each other to achieve the optimal portfolio mix in terms of value maximization, balance, strategic alignment, and organizational focus. The project portfolio is fully visible to allow projects to be objectively compared, allowing companies to accelerate the projects destined for market success and reduce the time and money consumed on projects that are destined for failure. By focusing on fewer, more strategic projects, companies can increase the success rate of market-winning ideas and focus precious resources on the highest-value projects.

Another supplier has identified the following specific benefits for companies in the food industry:

- A central, global repository minimizes search time, increases formula reuse, and shortens time to market. Product development information maintained includes formulas, specifications, raw materials, test results, and so on.
- Implementation of standard work processes globally to improve product consistency and shorten time to market.
- Actively managed R&D pipeline through real-time visibility into project status, budgets, and resource allocation. Decision making with the latest information and application of portfolio management techniques to the product portfolio.
- Reduction of non–value added activities through standard business processes.
- Reduction of redundant development and testing by leveraging past micro, toxicology, stability, analytical, and compatibility test information.
- Elimination of duplicate effort by reuse of existing projects specifications, raw material, or formulas.
- Capture data in a structured format enabling you to quickly search the global database by properties of raw materials, formulas, specifications, requirements, development projects and programs, and test data.
- Security capabilities that provide secure access to internal and external users within the product development system.
- Integrated modules that enable the secure outsourcing of portions of your product development processes, leveraging technology from global research centers, universities, and technical consulting resources around the world.
- Consistent data through a single, scaleable database and data structure as the foundation for e-commerce initiatives, thus providing a means for customers to give firsthand product performance feedback and product improvement ideas.
- Leverage existing product information to respond faster to new requests; a search of existing formulas and specifications for a starting point to new requests — even search formulas that never made it to production.
- Leverage product and process strengths; differentiated products and improved value-added relationship with customers.
- More accurate and effective estimates of cost.

There are many examples of collaborative applications in today's business press and the experience of BAE Systems (MSI Magazine, 2002) tells the story very well. The global aerospace and defense manufacturer BAE Systems launched its collaborative development efforts by creating a shared data environment (i.e., virtual community) with about 600 participants, including the data exchange infrastructure needed to enable project partners to collaborate through all phases of a product life cycle — from early design through manufacturing and in-service support. Ian Haddleton, integrated systems solutions manager for BAE Systems, says, "With products as complex as a warship, the days of single source are over. Increasingly, our major projects involve a multitude of stakeholders, and in order to deliver our product on time and to cost, it is imperative that we are able to share information easily and openly with one another. To make this happen we did two things. First, we agreed on a set of values with our customer that are now the guidelines and principles for anyone working on the project — i.e., wherever possible information will be shared openly, risks and concerns will be shared early. Second, we established an infrastructure that would support these values, the Shared Data Environment. We now work as a true team, within our own company, with other project partners, and with our customer." Currently, there are about 600 people participating in the on-line community. This number is expected to grow to 1000.

The ability to share information among a large community of designated users simultaneously is fundamental to the intent and definition of collaborative manufacturing. Product life-cycle collaboration is one way to substantially broaden the talent and experience that can be used to address change, development, and product problems all across the various stages of a product life from the earliest concept through manufacture and use, and back to the design process for improvements. Some industry analysts suggest that system implementation growth rates exceed 40% per year.

References

Deck, M., Strom, M., and Schwartz, K., The Emerging Model of Co-Development, white paper, PRTM Consulting, 2001. Available at www.prtm.com.

Ericson, J., Pulling PLM together, *Line56.com*, October 2001.

Formation Systems Inc., product information document for food and beverage industry.

Moore, J. and ARC Advisory Group, Are Process Industries Ready for PLM?, white paper, ARC Advisory Group, Dedham, MA, 2001.

Original Equipment Suppliers Association, CPD Study Team, Collaborative product development business case template, white paper, Original Equipment Suppliers Association, 2001.

Rugullies, E., Total Economic Impact of Collaborative Product Development, white paper, Giga Information Group, 2001. Available at www.gigaweb.com.

Salomon Smith Barney, The Birth of Collaborative Commerce, white paper, New York, 2001.

Sequencia Corporation, Product Overview, Phoenix, AZ.

MSI Magazine, Why Collaborate, *Impact*, March 2002.

Agile Software, San Jose, CA, supplied much of the product data information.

chapter seven

Enterprise resource planning

The evolution of planning systems over the past 40 years has gone through many phases, from an early financial focus to a systems focus that forms the information hub of most modern companies. The primary leg in collaborative manufacturing, the enterprise resource planning (ERP) system, is outlined here to provide those unfamiliar with these systems an overview of their evolution, function, and fit into the information systems structure. If you are familiar with modern ERP planning systems, you may not find much of value in this chapter. If you are not familiar with the terms "material requirements planning" (MRP) and "ERP," this chapter will provide a good outline of what these systems do and how they have evolved. Since companies have a variety of systems from MRP to MRPII to ERP and other systems in between, the term "planning systems" will be used to describe the process, unless the reference is to a specific level of functionality.

Every company has some method of planning its product and some associated tools that determine necessary steps to support production. Whether your company is at the early evolutionary stage of planning systems or you have installed the latest, most modern suite of ERP applications, it is the planning system that forms the starting point for collaborative manufacturing.

These systems have been much maligned in some circles for various reasons, such as a few highly visible installation failures, the substantial implementation cost, and the need for reasonable system-wide uniformity. There may be some validity to these arguments, but there are far more arguments in favor. One of the best supporting arguments is that there is no other tool that can give management an integrated uniform understanding of what is occurring in the total business.

ERP systems are applied in all types of businesses, not only in manufacturing companies. Industries served include:

- Communications services
- Government and public administration

- Financial services companies
- Hospitals and health care
- Museums and associations
- Retail and wholesale pharmaceutical companies
- Utilities
- Transportation services
- Automotive manufacturers
- Wood and paper suppliers
- Furniture manufacturing
- Primary metals producers
- Consumer packaged goods, food and non-food
- Clothing and textiles
- Ship, aerospace, and train construction
- Chemicals
- Electronic/optic and communications equipment

Planning systems have evolved from narrow, single-focus business computer systems to a single giant communications foundation for an entire enterprise that links all functions internally and externally to customers, suppliers, and other business partners (Figure 7.1). Business computer systems did not start at so grand a level, especially as they were applied in manufacturing. Early systems were not very effective as manufacturing management tools.

Original systems were a mixed assortment of applications, including general ledger accounting, accounts payable, payroll, accounts receivable, inventory management, and material requirements planning. Each application was very much a stand-alone package, so it was not unusual to have a payroll system from one vendor and an accounts payable system from another. In some cases, the application packages might be from the same vendor but they were not integrated to the point that data could be shared or passed between them. These systems became connected to manufacturing when MRP, one of the first inventory management tools, was developed.

MRP was not developed to be a manufacturing tool. It was an inventory management idea used to identify when and how much raw material should be ordered to manufacture a specified quantity of a product. The items listed in the bill of material multiplied by the build quantity provide information on what and how many components were required. Purchasing used this information to place orders with suppliers. Manufacturing used the information to confirm what needed to be produced. Other than advising manufacturing what to make, the information was of little or no value to manufacturing management. The information was primarily used to identify inventory investment requirements. Because early computer business use began with accounting, a financial perspective was the basis for nearly every application.

MRP was improved to include time phasing, that is, to include a time factor into inventory management. This was a major step forward that

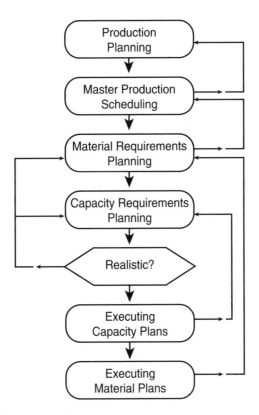

Figure 7.1 Early closed-loop planning system.

allowed the receipt or production of material to coincide with the date of need. By laying out a time line for a specific lot of production, it was possible to view the longest lead-time item. With identified lead times, it was easy to work backward from the longest lead item to the shortest and identify dates when material should arrive at the plant.

These early ideas evolved during the 1970s to include:

Master scheduling became the basis for most company-wide decisions on inventory, purchasing commitments, and manufacturing capacity planning. With information taken from various forecasting sources, decisions were made on what and how many products were to be produced within given time periods. Generally the forecast began with an annual estimate and was then broken down into requirements for quarters or months with adjustments as each period neared. Most systems were based on monthly requirement schedules.

Purchasing was charged with inventory acquisition that would meet the master schedule requirement. Each item in the bill of material had a make or buy decision and an identified lead time. Purchasing was responsible to ensure that the required purchased material was in the plant by the expected time of use but not too early as that would require an earlier-than-needed cash outlay.

Material requirements for items to be built in the plant were computed and delivered to manufacturing as a thick stack of computer printout information that identified all items to be produced for the planning period. It was up to manufacturing management to divine where to start, what sequence to plan, and how to accomplish its task within the specified time frame. Decisions regarding the sequence and processes to be used were based on the assumption that purchased material would arrive just in time for the manufacturing schedule plus a little leeway. At the end of the specified time period, production planning would mark up the earlier schedule printout indicating what was produced, and deliver it to the computer operators to be included as data entry information in the next MRP run, usually planned for on a monthly basis.

Inventory quantity information was adjusted based on material received plus previous period inventory less product shipped. This was a straightforward arithmetic calculation and was a significant management measurement tool. Inaccurate data provided some difficult challenges. Inaccuracies were usually managed through the use of cycle counts — periodic, usually random, physical counts that were compared to the computer-listed amounts and adjusted. There were also periodic full physical inventory counts (usually annually) to confirm accounting records and to adjust them up or down according to the actual count.

Cost accounting information was frequently a part of these systems. Manually entered data from time cards indicating start and end times for each job at a workstation or work segment were used to measure the variance from the published production time standards. These data originally served as an accounting tool used to calculate the inventory value. Eventually the information was used as a variance from standard report to measure manufacturing performance by comparing actual performance to the estimated time standards.

Process industries had a somewhat different evolution but the ideas behind their systems were the same: Satisfy the need to provide accurate financial information used to manage the company and to report financial results. To measure the income of a food processing facility, refinery, or metals producer, the idea followed the same lines: calculate the cost of inbound material plus labor and overhead cost, the value of product shipped, and the value of inventory. The basic concept behind every industry application followed along these lines. The business process improvements provided by early systems were conformity, faster response time, and, hopefully, accuracy. Even if the systems were cumbersome, they were a major step beyond the manual accounting and management methods previously in place.

During the early to mid-1980s, the next step forward was the implementation of a connected set of functions. This new approach was called manufacturing resource planning and was identified by the acronym MRPII to identify something separate from materials requirements planning without losing the acceptance and association with these progressive ideas. Another term used to describe this new accumulation of management tools was "manufacturing planning and control systems." It recognized the movement beyond finance toward a broader user base that included tools to help manufacturing management accomplish its tasks. These systems were growing into an array of functions and some new capability that included:

- A **data library** with computerized data, including product recipes, bills of material, routings, part numbers, time standards, set-up times, and product programs that could be downloaded to programmable logic controllers used to operate and manage processes and equipment.
- **Capacity planning** systems that could measure the amount of work to be performed and compare that to available capacity. This was usually a straightforward calculation based on personnel hours available divided by the personnel hours required to produce the desired amount. If the requirement were greater than the amount available, scheduling overtime or finding outside sources would be necessary.
- **CAD and CAE** systems were developed, applying computer technology to engineering and product data storage. These tools stored computerized design information that could be retrieved and distributed to a limited list of users.
- **Advanced concepts in material requirements** planning included manufacturing lot size, economic order quantities, part period balancing, and group technology and buffering concepts to deal with uncertainties.
- **Logistics planning management** became a part of the manufacturing control system.
- A major impact on all computing systems was the advent of the **personal computer** and the many systems developed for specific applications within manufacturing, such as maintenance management, quality assurance measurement, and extended process control systems.
- **Manufacturing execution systems (MES)** were developed to bridge the gap between the finance-oriented planning system and the real-time world of the plant floor. The manufacturing resource planning system could download a group of work orders planned for a given time period. The MES then managed the work orders through the production process by scheduling and tracking orders based on optimizing current available resources, such as machine, inventory, or tool availability. The system could also combine or split orders, change an order priority in response to current conditions, change

order-fulfillment requirements, or respond to plant floor exceptions, such as quality assurance failure, material shortages, or machine downtime. These systems also served as data collection receptors preparing information to be sent to other users, such as the planning system. A full presentation of MES is provided in Chapter 9 on real-time information sources.

- This period saw a wide variety of applications that were designed for specific functions and users. Examples include quality assurance systems and maintenance management systems that were designed for a limited purpose and number of users. The disparate applications could number 30 or more within a plant with each application having its own sponsor, data sources, and information users. Integration of these applications into cooperating components was nearly impossible due to many technical and political reasons. These systems were then and still are frequently referred to as "silos of information" because of the limited access to other interested parties. Because different system sponsors had their own applications, the same item of data might be collected by no fewer than five different departments, with each department duplicating information collection costs.

The common complaint about these early systems was having a lot of data but not enough information. Imagine a multidivision corporation with many plants and each division or plant having its collage of information systems. In a relatively short period of time, plant systems went from a strong finance leaning to individual operational applications in nearly every department and every level. Planning systems were made up of a chaotic array that was compounded by a variety of applications in operating departments. The problems faced by management to provide or view a disciplined, orderly presentation were significant.

As is usually the case, problems are frequently opportunities in disguise. The idea of the modern ERP system arose from the need for an integrated system that addressed business areas on a consistent company-wide basis with identical data presentations managed in a single database. Systems could be implemented on a modular basis, but the key value point was the common database and data presentation. The system investment and implementation programs were very large, and to be truly effective they had to include broad management structures within the enterprise. This gave rise to many changes within corporate thinking but two are very significant:

- Because of the broad corporate commitment to revise how the company did business, these systems were authorized at the highest corporate-officer level.
- Also because of the broad commitment and very large investment, a department with the responsibility for corporate-wide application of information technology (IT) emerged. This department, under the

direction of the chief information officer, usually reported to the chief operations officer or chief executive officer. This was a very important and positive change in how IT applications would be viewed. Information was starting to become a strategic tool.

Every company uses some process to determine what they will produce. Some rely on pencil and paper, some use simple spreadsheet applications, and others use very sophisticated enterprise resource planning systems. Companies do planning of many kinds and in many areas, but the term was originally used to identify and support steps prior to production. The term "planning system" or "planning level" is still frequently used to describe the complete range of system capability that extends far beyond finance and manufacturing to include customer relations management, human resources management, product data management, supply chain management, and more. If any definition is possible, it might be to say that planning level activities are usually decision support systems that apply to broad business processes at a corporate or business unit level (Figure 7.2).

Current systems are large, complex, very sophisticated, and very effective business management tools. A system can begin with tracking the interest of a potential customer, receiving the incoming order, checking customer credit, entering the order into production scheduling, ordering the necessary material for production, tracking the order through production to the shipping warehouse, and monitoring the logistics process through delivery to the customer. Along the way, the system might issue the invoice, monitor the receipt of payments, maintain cost and accounting information, and revise company financial statements, most of which is done without human involvement.

The modern enterprise resource planning system can integrate all departments and business processes across a company into a single information system that provides combined functionality with a single shared information database. This allows each department to work with software tools designed for their purposes while sharing the same information items. This provides consistent information, a major benefit of integrated systems. One example is the human resource module that provides identical employment applications and benefits information for all employees of a business unit or across the company. Another is the use of the purchasing module to establish and monitor limits that might be placed on vendors or buyers. Gaining consistency across business operations was one of the original benefits of enterprise resource planning systems, as most companies with manufacturing resource planning had many of the same system components, but they were not integrated or broadly based.

These systems are designed to be modular. Modular applications are developed with a list of functions generally suited to specific business processes. In many instances, the components are the same as have been in use for some time. For example, material requirements planning is a part of nearly every manufacturing module and performs the same functions

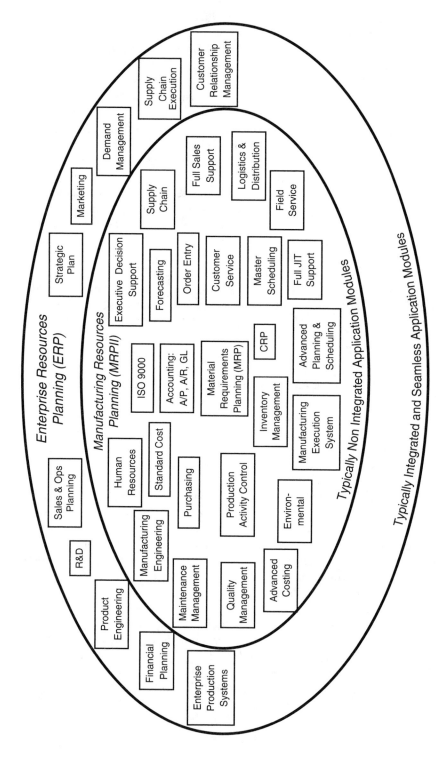

Figure 7.2 Fully integrated ERP System. (Reprinted with permission from CRC Press.)

discussed earlier: calculating the materials required to produce a given quantity of a product. Other components, such as those used in the financial area, are also fundamentally the same as those in use for many years. Because of the modular design, systems are most often implemented on a gradual basis beginning in one area of the business and expanding from there. A company may begin with financial reporting systems and add manufacturing support systems later or not at all. The modular design allows companies to implement as much of the functionality as is necessary at the time. It is also possible to use modules from different suppliers to build what is called a "best-of-breed" composite of integrated system components.

Many vendors offer systems and each differs somewhat from others. Some companies offer a full range of system functionality while others specialize in certain industries or functions. Below is a listing and brief description of typical system capabilities currently provided by PeopleSoft Corporation. A full listing of PeopleSoft modules and respective components is provided in Appendix B.

- **Customer relationship management**, a somewhat recent addition to planning system capabilities, provides an array of customer-facing applications. In days past, companies made things and sold them to someone. That someone may have been a distributor, a retailer, or an end user. Most relationships began and ended with the sale and receipt of payment. Today the customer relationship is thought of as a continuing process that begins at some point and, if supported properly, never ends. This includes identifying unique buyer attributes and supporting ways to satisfy those attributes most effectively. This is the basic thinking behind customer relationship applications. Most systems model the selling process of a company and track events and actions related to specific customers or potential customers. Other functions include sales team management activities, such as call tracking and sales compensation, product promotions, pricing, and financing options. Activities can also include field service management and self-service interactions with the company via the Internet or call centers.
- **Enterprise performance management** provides tools to analyze and measure company performance in nearly any form. This might include data warehousing from sources across the company, financial analysis, customer relationship measurement, and presentation of progress against planned objectives.
- **Enterprise service automation** is an integrated solution for managing services spending and maximizing the value from those services. The system can manage the entire services process from procurement through project and resource management to service delivery.
- **Financial applications** provide the ability to manage the financial aspects of the business, including general ledger, assets, accounts payable and receivable, income statement and balance sheet

information, cash management and forecasting, expense management and control, and financial projects.

- **Human resources management** lets you manage human resource business processes that range from recruitment to retirement. It provides an integrated database of personnel, employee records, compensation, benefits administration, and payroll records. Payroll accounting is individualized to fit the various requirements of countries and states. This module can also be used in career planning, cost allocation, and training programs.

- **Supply chain management** includes functional tools for manufacturing, supply chain management, and distribution activities, including supplier relationship management, inventory, scheduling, engineering, bills and routings, and material procurement. Connection to the plant-floor production management system or systems allows real-time information to be sent and received. In addition, a global view of processes and events across the supply chain is maintained.

The resource planning system is one of the three primary legs supporting collaboration activities as it maintains and drives business processes across the business unit and can have a direct connection to many parts of the extended enterprise. It is the resource planning system that maintains the inventory information, supplier information, customer orders, and production forecast. This is where decisions are made that flow to the operating departments, such as purchasing, production, and the warehouse. Until the resource planning system defines what to make, there is no direction for production scheduling or the quality assurance function, or reason to issue purchase orders. Most collaboration activities fall in the outward flow of that information to the network nodes that react by executing the requests of the resource planning system across the internal and external supply-chain network.

The enterprise resource planning system:

- Collects demand information and determines production quantities and times.
- Maintains the corporate-level inventory information, including what is in stock and what is committed. Local inventory that is carried at a plant or department level may be managed by the MES level as a subset of the total or in a local MES module.
- Determines the quantities to be produced or purchased through the bill-of-material explosion.
- Distributes information to plant-level systems within the internal supply chain and the external supply-chain network and maintains status information through feedback from those entities. The real-time information systems at the execution level monitor production events and provide updated information.

Enterprise resource planning systems are not, by themselves, strategic. They are a resource or storehouse of information and processes that can be used strategically when combined with supply-chain management tools and real-time information sources.

The current leading edge of planning systems applications includes strong support for e-business processes. E-business has evolved from its early stages as a tool to reach the customer via the Internet. Today, e-business includes Web-based activities that surround an effective enterprise. It is defined as the accumulated IT tools used to improve business performance in areas such as the supply chain network and customer service, and to support business processes such as collaborative product development and virtual manufacturing. The planning system enables the planning process through its internal process structure and information database.

This chapter has provided a short overview of the development of planning systems from the earliest stages of material requirements planning, through the manufacturing resource planning stage, to the modern enterprise resource planning system. Although the original functions have changed very little, resource management tools have evolved and grown to serve the broadest global enterprises; they address customer relationships from initial contact to a continuing process of fulfillment, and include the complete range of financial management tools, including accounting, cash management, and banking relations. They also can include a full range of supply chain functions, including inventory, manufacturing management, logistics management, and product data management. Today's planning system supply-chain management tools comprise the hub around which the fulfillment side of the business is managed.

The spectrum of companies utilizing these systems includes large and small companies with some at the leading edge of systems application; others have not gotten past the early material requirements planning stage. Consider also that application of IT is an evolutionary process, not an event. As long as system suppliers can add functionality that satisfies business needs with a proper return on their investment, these systems will continue to expand and to serve a broader constituency.

References

Blain, J. and ASAP World Consultancy, *Using SAP R/3*, QUE, United States, 1999.

Chorafas, D.N., *Integrating ERP, CRM, Supply Chain Management, and Smart Materials*, Auerbach Publications-CRC Press, Boca Raton, FL, 2001.

Langenwalter, G.A., *Enterprise Resources Planning and Beyond*, CRC Press, Boca Raton, FL, 2000.

Norris, G., Hurley, J.R., Hartley, K.M., Dunleavy, J.R., and Balls, J.D., *E-Business and ERP: Transforming the Enterprise*, John Wiley & Sons, New York, 2000.

Oden, H.W., Langenwalter, G.A., and Lucier, R.A., *Handbook of Material & Capacity Requirements Planning*, McGraw-Hill, New York, 1993.

PeopleSoft Corporation product data documents, 2002.

Vollman, T.E., Berry, W.L., and Whybark, D.C., *Manufacturing Planning and Control Systems*, Dow Jones Irwin, Homewood, IL, 1984.

Wight, O.W., *MRPII: Unlocking America's Productivity Potential*, Oliver Wight Limited Publications, Williston, VT, 1984.

chapter eight

Supply chain management

The second major leg of collaborative manufacturing is the supply chain and the continuous effort to improve the process of supply chain management. Supply chain management includes logistics, warehousing, vendor management, information accessibility and sharing, information security, design for manufacturability, scheduling synchronization, production management, and many more. A limited overview of supply chain vis-a-vis collaborative manufacturing is presented here. That view tends to be very broad and even somewhat undefined as we are in the early development stage of collaborative manufacturing. For an in-depth study of supply chain management, Ayers (2001), Langenwalter (2000), Poirier and Bauer (2000), and Schorr (1998) offer excellent information, and there are many more good books on the subject.

My supply chain is better than their supply chain. Is this any way to run a business? Absolutely. Supply chain management works on the idea that all partners within the supply chain can be more effective working as a team with a common objective. Companies must compete on as many fronts as possible and supply chain management is a concept that focuses on at least one step beyond that old standby, cost reduction. With supply chain management, cost reduction is one area of focus along with a number of others, each with a primary emphasis on inventory management. Inventory management includes the inventory of each supplier and their supplier (as affected by our share of their business) on the supply side or upstream side of the company, and the demand or downstream side of each customer and their customer, and so on to product disposal. This is not about low bidders or cheap product cost; it is about how to most effectively satisfy the needs of each member of the supply chain. In this concept of the extended enterprise, having the product where customers want it when they want it can be far more important than price.

Supply chain management goes far beyond logistics and is applied across manufacturing in the sense of the extended enterprise; it includes all suppliers and customers in what can be called the supply chain network. The supply chain network includes suppliers, their suppliers, and their suppliers as far up the chain as practical. No less important, but in some ways easier to see, is the connection to the customer, their customer, and their customer through the full distribution side to product return, recycle, or disposal. There is an element of practicality and industry applicability, but start with a broadened view that extends from the originating point of each component along with each transformation point and each movement of each component, through the full product life to product recycle and disposal. Supply chain management is the practice of continuous improvement of each element within the supply chain network.

Historically, companies have worked on the basis of developing a better product that then provides a period of competitive advantage. Later, when a comparable product is available from other sources, the focus was on reducing cost to be the most competitive. This might occur over a long period of time with a continuous effort to reduce production cost through techniques such as improved quality control, just-in-time (JIT) inventory, larger lot sizes to reduce set-up costs, and so on. That part does not change. Supply chain management includes all of that and casts a broader net to manage cost relative to inventory and its production anywhere in the supply chain network. As was indicated in the introduction, the supply chain describes the interlinked system of all material and services suppliers that affect the process of delivering a product from concept to the consumer and disposal. The profession of supply chain management refers to the process of continuous improvement of the supply chain.

The following supply chain definitions were stated in the introduction. They are repeated here to provide a better context to the subject of supply chain and supply chain management. Poirier and Bauer (2000) provide the following definitions:

> **Supply chain** refers to core business processes that create and deliver a product or service, from concept through development and manufacturing or conversion, into a market for consumption.
>
> **Supply chain management** refers to the methods, systems, and leadership that continuously improve an organization's integrated processes for product and service design, sales forecasting, purchasing, inventory management, manufacturing or production, order management, logistics, distribution, and customer satisfaction.

Note that in the definitions, there is no mention of companies; instead, the word "process" is used. This is intentional to indicate business processes that are within companies, sometimes linked internally between departments within the business enterprise and at other times linked between separate companies. The business processes can be upstream from the supply chain host to include all suppliers and their suppliers that provide a value-added contribution, and downstream through higher-level product manufacturers, distribution channels, or to the consumer. A simple supply chain is illustrated in Figure 8.1.

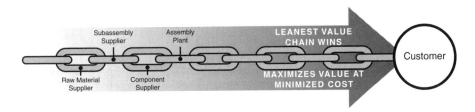

Figure 8.1 Simple supply chain.

Early views of the supply chain referred primarily to distribution and logistics services that are distributed throughout the value-adding manufacturing process as the function of movement and storage occurs between operations and on to the customer. The modern strategic and managerial view of the supply chain includes every step in the product life cycle from concept through consumer delivery to disposal or recycle. Poirier has written extensively and authoritatively on the strategic and tactical implementation of supply chain management. In his books he has identified phases of progress that companies go through as they evolve their supply chain management strengths. Figure 8.2 provides a fundamental view of various business issues that drive the evolution of the process. Where is your company in the process map? Are you still working on logistics or are you focusing on alliances and joint ventures?

In Figure 8.3, which is a revised overlay of Figure 8.2, Poirier has added a new level to the evolution process based on the application of e-commerce as the key enabler to higher achievement possibilities. Some of the data are

	Sourcing and Logistics I	Internal Excellence II	Network Construction III	Industry Leadership IV
Driver	VP-Sourcing (under pressure), et al.	CID supply chain leader	Business unit leaders	Management team
Benefits	Leveraged savings; FTE reduction	Prioritized improvements across network	Best partner performance	Network advantage; profitable revenue
Focus	Inventory project logistics; freight order fulfillment	Process redesign: systems improvement	Forecasting planning: cust. services, interenterprise	Consumer network
Tools	Teaming functional excellence	Benchmarks, best practice, activity-based costing	Metrics; database mining, electronic commerce	Intranet, internet; virtual information systems
Action Area	Midlevel organization	Expanded levels	Total organization	Full enterprise
Guidance	Cost data, success funding	Process mapping	Advanced cost models; differentiating processes	Demand/supply linkage
Reach	Major cost (local) categories	Business unit	Enterprise	Global interface
Model	None	Supply chain – intraenterprise	Interenterprise	Global market
Alliances	Supplier consolidation	Best partner	Partial alliances	Joint ventures
Training	Team	Leadership	Partnering	Holistic processing
	Internal		External	

Figure 8.2 Internal and external implementation of supply chain management. (Reproduced with permission of Charles Poirier.)

Business Application \ Progression	Level I/II Internal Supply Chain Optimization Stage 0	Level III Network Formation Stage 1	Level IV Value Chain Constellation Stage 2	Level IV+ Full Network Connectivity Stage 3
Information technology	Point solutions ------------------ Inform	Linked intranets ------------------ Interact	Internet-based extranet ------------------ Transact	Full network communication system ------------------ Deliver
Design, development product/service introduction	Internal only	Selected external assistance	Collaborative design – enterprise integration and PIM	Business functional view – joint design and development
Purchase, procurement, sourcing	Leverage business unit volume	Leverage full network through aggregation	Key supplier assistance web-based sourcing	Network sourcing through best constituent
Marketing, sales customer service	Internally developed programs, promotions	Customer-focused, data-based initiatives	Collaborative development for focused consumer base	Consumer response system across the value chain
Engineering, planning, scheduling, Manufacturing*	MRP MRPII DRP	ERP – internal connectivity	Collaborative network planning – best asset utilization	Full network business system optimization
Logistics**	Manufacturing push – inventory intensive	Pull system through internal/external providers	Best constituent provider – dual channel	Total network, dual-channel optimization
Customer care*	Customer service reaction	Focused service – call centers	Segmented response system, customer relationship management	Matched care – customer care automation
Human resources	Internal supply chain training	Provide network, resources training	Interenterprise resource utilization	Full network alignment and capability provision

*Includes order management.
**Includes inventory management.

Figure 8.3 Supply chain management with application of e-commerce. (Reproduced with permission of Charles Poirier.)

shown from a different perspective and a slightly rearranged form to show how company departments might evolve through the process. Poirier suggests that this evolutionary process will follow these themes:

- The future belongs to the business network that satisfies specific customer demands through a seamless supply chain that establishes a sense of customization for those customers.
- The constituents can create enhanced market value by jointly creating profitable revenue growth through integrated interenterprise solutions and responses.
- The supply chain network will achieve its purposes and goals by being supported with leading-edge technology.

An important note is the variety of business functions/processes that are seen as supply chain components. This broad perspective inclusive of all contributing entities is referred to in this book as the supply chain network or extended enterprise. The term "e-commerce" as used here is not intended to describe only Internet-related or website buying. It is used to describe the impact of technology and modern technological tools used to facilitate and improve commercial relationships and transactions.

It is very important to understand the evolutionary process of supply chain management, both from the historical progress of technology and how technology has been applied within your company. A good understanding of where your company fits on the evolution scale gives strong hints of company and management culture. Companies that push the supply chain management envelope will encounter internal resistance unless the team truly understands the substance behind the plans. Enterprises that have grown through intimidation, raw power, and purchasing clout will not find it easy to trust a single-source vendor or provide confidential design information without feeling that the enemy might be at the door. Simply using a new name, "partners," instead of "vendors" will not suffice.

Supply-chain management evolution has not been an overnight phenomenon. The ideas have been around for many years, but the application of IT has greatly quickened the pace of implementation. One early example began 20 or more years ago as automotive manufacturers began to aggressively narrow their vendor lists. According to published reports, top-tier companies have gone from 5000 to 500 vendors in an effort to reduce costs. The thinking of many buyers changed from adversarial relationships to fewer and more cooperative relationships. Many factors account for this change, but two objectives stand out:

- Reduce paper and processing costs with fewer vendors.
- Larger suppliers could reduce costs by taking advantage of economies of scale.

Technology helped this trend along with new ideas for data exchange between companies and the then-new, engineering product-design tool, CAD. Another factor that drove this change was a new environment that allowed vendors to have greater access to product design information and the encouragement to submit cost improvement ideas. If a supplier could show cost reduction in the redesign, it was allowed to keep a portion of the savings and did not have to immediately share the information with competitors. The evolution of these ideas has brought us to where some newer companies do not even own manufacturing facilities, opting to outsource manufacturing as a service. The financial implications of not building facilities are obvious if the risk of vendor nonperformance can be resolved.

The benefits of improved supply-chain management have great potential, and as with most good ideas, the growth in importance has spread rapidly across every business sector. Supply-chain network partners have taken on responsibilities once assigned to their customer. The customer has been redefined to include the customer's customer and their customer on to the end consumer and the disposition or recycle of the product. Supply chain management is now a significant part of the strategic positioning of nearly every business. There are college-level courses on supply chain management, associations that focus on application of supply-chain technology and management techniques, and major multinational consulting companies with teams of professionals in computer science and business technologies to assist in systems design and implementation.

Supply chain management and its implications give rise to many strategic initiatives in nearly every industry.

- Locating supplier plants near the point of use is common, particularly in some areas of the automotive industry. In the bottling industries, the primary container (can) supplier frequently builds the manufacturing plant near or adjacent to the bottling plant. This greatly reduces inventory and inbound freight. With the long-term customer commitment, the vendor can develop shorter lead and manufacturing cycle times and become a true JIT supplier. There have been excellent cost reductions and service improvements.

- Automatic replenishment of maintenance and repair order of inventory stocks in manufacturing companies is frequently seen. This could include stipulations for local inventory storage or overnight shipment worldwide. The important fact is the commitment on both sides to an equally satisfactory, trusting business relationship.

- JIT delivery of finished components for higher-level assembly, such as seats to an automotive assembly plant, is very common. Very short lead-time commitments by the supplier can greatly reduce costs of inventory management. It is common in many industries for the customer to provide as little as 1 hour from order release to delivery requirement. In some instances, the vendor may have inventory appropriately staged for immediate use.

- VMI can also reduce inventory cost and place the responsibility for response on those best equipped to maintain appropriate stock levels.

- Postponed product configuration is a frequent strategy employed in the electronics industry. This allows a manufacturer to reduce inventory of fully assembled products by shipping partially configured units to be finished at a downstream location. The application of this by Hewlett-Packard Corporation in their printer delivery process was very effective in reducing the cost of the finished product.

- Dell Computer Corporation has built its business around effective, supply-chain strategic deployment, which allows management of a very large company with substantially reduced inventories. Some would call this JIT at its best.

Most of the examples shown here deal with downstream supply-chain issues. There are likely to be excellent strategic opportunities if we look upstream to our suppliers, their suppliers, and beyond. Think of each department or company that directly contributes to the development and manufacture of a product. Keep in mind also that in many companies, the largest financial component in cost of sales is purchased material. After spending many years wringing cost from in-house processes, many companies have gone to their suppliers for relief. Exerting downward pressure on supplier pricing is not new. That has been part of business since the beginning. The collaborative approach is to think beyond pure price pressure, to focus on at least three other areas of improvement from components within the supply chain.

- Provide an improved service that results in overall supply-chain cost reduction or an enhanced value for the customer.
- Improve nonadversarial information sharing and accuracy to eliminate or reduce costs associated with contingency planning.
- Share core competencies throughout the supply chain network.

We have all played the game where something is whispered to the first person and repeated to each person down the line. As the whispered words are passed down the line, we are always amazed at the change or the misinterpretation along the way. Are conversations between departments or between companies and their departments any different? We have all seen the cartoon in Figure 8.4. It may be funny but all too frequently this example is an apt description of information transfer between departments within companies. This misinformation is usually addressed by contingencies that always add cost.

The supply chain network consists of all the links that contribute to the value-adding processes of each stage in the product life cycle, links between companies and between departments within companies. The links begin with the initial concept of a product, the steps through design, the process of material acquisition, the value-adding processes of manufacturing and distribution, delivery to the end consumer, and from there through disposal or recycle. That is a lot of links and like any chain, weak links can occur.

There are obvious disruptions when weak links in the supply chain fail to meet the business objectives that were identified or assumed. This is most frequently seen in any or all of the following events, among many others:

- Late deliveries
- Product quality failures
- Failure of engineering change orders to reach all affected suppliers
- Incomplete order fulfillment from the distribution center
- Unusually high product-warranty costs
- Poor synchronization of material availability

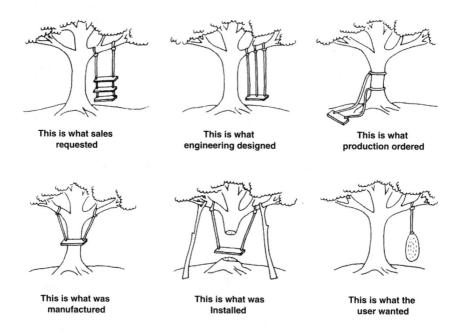

Figure 8.4 Results of interdepartmental misinformation.

- Questionable logistics control
- Unexpected process adjustments

How is your supply chain doing? Supply chain performance is frequently measured through benchmarking studies. Probably the most widely used performance measurement tool is the SCOR model available through the Supply Chain Council (SCC).

In 1997, the consulting firm, Pittiglio, Rabin, Todd, and McGrath (PRTM) and the manufacturing research firm, AMR Research, developed a business model to measure supply chain effectiveness. The development process included convincing a number of manufacturing companies to apply the model to gauge its effectiveness as a management tool in their facilities. The tool, called the Supply Chain Reference Operations (SCOR) model, was strongly embraced by the trial companies, resulting in the formation of the SCC. The SCC is a not-for-profit organization made up of over 800 manufacturing companies, suppliers of products and services, and academics that focus on supply chain performance. The SCC has gained wide acceptance with operations in the United States, Europe, Japan, and Australia. The Council's website is www.supply-chain.org.

The SCOR model (Figure 8.5) is a business-process reference model used to measure performance against a specific set of parameters within each of five top-level management processes: plan, source, make, deliver, and return (Figure 8.6).

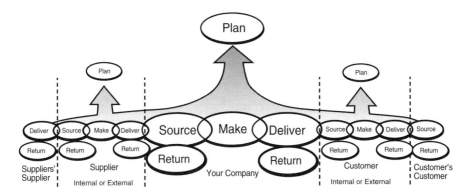

SCOR is Based on Five Distinct Management Processes

Figure 8.5 SCOR model.

> **Plan** includes those processes that balance aggregate demand and sup-
> ply to develop a plan that best meets the sourcing, production, and
> delivery requirements.
> **Source** consists of the processes that procure goods and services to meet
> planned or actual demand.
> **Make** includes the processes involved in the manufacture of products.
> **Deliver** includes processes used to provide finished goods and services
> to meet planned or actual demand, such as order management, trans-
> portation management, and distribution.
> **Return** is comprised of processes associated with returning or receiving
> returned products for any reason.

Within each of the above process categories there are three levels of
reference material (Figure 8.7). The top level describes the scope and content
for each of the five process categories. The second level includes a list of
core process categories a company can choose to describe their operations.
The third level defines the specific process elements within the company
used to measure process performance metrics and best practices.

The SCOR model, as a tool, has found wide acceptance as a measurement
of how successfully the supply chain is functioning according to standard
processes and metrics. The strengths of the SCOR model are:

- Use of standard processes and terminology
- Use of a structured review methodology
- Standard performance measures
- Easily understood operation activity metrics

The Performance Measurement Group (www.pmg.com), a subsidiary of
PRTM, provides benchmarking studies using metrics based on the industry
SCOR model. This assessment of your supply chain will provide insight for

Demand/Supply Planning and Management
▷ Balance resources with requirements and establish/communicate plans for the whole supply chain, including Return, and the execution processes of Source, Make, and Deliver.
▷ Management of business rules, supply chain performance, data collection, inventory, capital assets, transportation, planning configuration, and regulatory requirements and compliance.
▷ Align the supply chain unit plan with the financial plan.

Sourcing Stocked, Make-to-Order, and Engineer-to-Order Product
▷ Schedule deliveries; receive, verify, and transfer product; and authorize supplier payments
▷ Identify and select supply sources when not predetermined, as for engineer-to-order product.
▷ Manage business rules, assess supplier performance, and maintain data.
▷ Manage inventory, capital assets, incoming product, supplier network, import/export requirements, and supplier agreements.

Make-to-Stock, Make-to-Order, and Engineer-to-Order Production Execution
▷ Schedule production activities, issue product, produce and test, package, stage product, and release product to deliver.
▷ Finalize engineering for engineer-to-order product.
▷ Manage rules, performance, data, in-process products (WIP), equipment and facilities, transportation, production network, and regulatory compliance for production.

Order, Warehouse, Transportation, and Installation Management for Stocked, Make-to-Order, and Engineer-to-Order Product
▷ All order management steps from processing customer inquiries and quotes to routing shipments and selecting carriers.
▷ Warehouse management from receiving and picking product to load and ship product.
▷ Receive and verify product at customer site and install, if necessary.
▷ Invoicing customer.
▷ Manage Deliver business rules, performance, information, finished product inventories, capital assets, transportation, product life cycle, and import/export requirements.

Return of Raw Materials (to Supplier) and Receipt of Returns of Finished Goods (from Customer), including Defective Products, MRO Products, and Excess Products
▷ All return defective product steps from authorizing return; scheduling product return; receiving, verifying, and disposition of defective product; and return replacement or credit.
▷ Return MRO product steps from authorizing and scheduling return, determining product condition, transferring product, verifying product condition, disposition, and request return authorization.
▷ Return excess product steps including identifying excess inventory, scheduling shipment, receiving returns, approving request authorization, receiving excess product return in Source, verifying excess, and recover and disposition of excess product.
▷ Manage Return business rules, performance, data collection, return inventory, capital assets, transportation, network configuration, and regulatory requirements and compliance.

Figure 8.6 Description of five SCOR model processes.

where resources should be placed to gain the best improvement. Their benchmarking process provides the following deliverables:

Performance scorecard — Compares your performance in eight key "Level 1" metrics to median and best-in-class companies in a graphical representation.

Supply chain practice and IT assessment — Evaluates your organization's capabilities by assessing current and emerging business practices and IT support systems.

Data table — Compares your performance to best-in-class, median, and average companies for detailed supply-chain metrics.

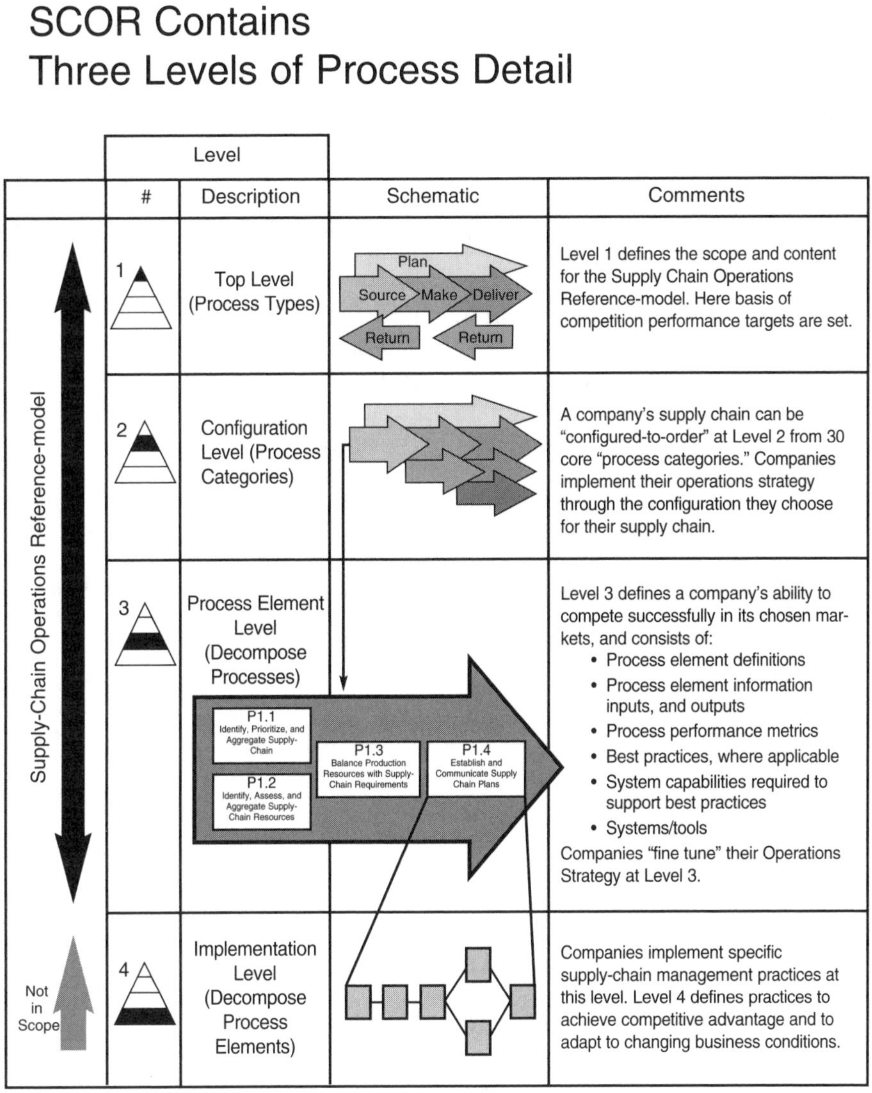
SCOR Contains
Three Levels of Process Detail
Level
#
Description
Schematic
Comments
Supply-Chain Operations Reference-model
1
Top Level (Process Types)
Plan
Source
Make
Deliver
Return
Return
Level 1 defines the scope and content for the Supply Chain Operations Reference-model. Here basis of competition performance targets are set.
2
Configuration Level (Process Categories)
A company's supply chain can be "configured-to-order" at Level 2 from 30 core "process categories." Companies implement their operations strategy through the configuration they choose for their supply chain.
3
Process Element Level (Decompose Processes)
P1.1
Identify, Prioritize, and Aggregate Supply-Chain
P1.2
Identify, Assess, and Aggregate Supply-Chain Resources
P1.3
Balance Production Resources with Supply-Chain Requirements
P1.4
Establish and Communicate Supply Chain Plans
Level 3 defines a company's ability to compete successfully in its chosen markets, and consists of:
• Process element definitions
• Process element information inputs, and outputs
• Process performance metrics
• Best practices, where applicable
• System capabilities required to support best practices
• Systems/tools
Companies "fine tune" their Operations Strategy at Level 3.
Not in Scope
4
Implementation Level (Decompose Process Elements)
Companies implement specific supply-chain management practices at this level. Level 4 defines practices to achieve competitive advantage and to adapt to changing business conditions.

Figure 8.7 Three levels of process detail in SCOR model.

One of the most important and applicable benchmarks is supply chain cost. Description of supply chain cost and methods used by the Performance Measurement Group (2001) to make this calculation follow. Details are included here because, when properly applied, this calculation will form the benchmarking baseline for supply chain cost improvement and return-on-investment calculations.

Total supply-chain management cost is the total cost to manage order processing, materials acquisition, inventory, supply-chain finance, planning, and IT costs, as represented as a percent of revenue. Accurate assignment of IT-related cost is challenging. It can be done using activity-based costing methods, or it can be based on more traditional approaches. Allocation based on user counts, transaction counts, or departmental headcounts are reasonable approaches. The emphasis should be on capturing all costs, whether incurred in the entity completing the survey or incurred in a supporting organization on behalf of the entity. Reasonable estimates founded on data are acceptable as a means to assess overall performance. All estimates should reflect fully burdened actual costs, including salary, benefits, space and facilities, and general and administrative allocations.

$$\text{Supply-chain management costs} =$$
$$\frac{[\text{Order management costs} + \text{Material acquisition costs} + \text{Inventory carrying costs} + \text{Supply-chain-related finance and planning costs} + \text{Total supply-chain-related IT costs}]}{[\text{Total product revenue}]}$$

Each element in the equation is described below.

Order management costs

1. **New product release phase-in and maintenance** includes costs associated with releasing new products to the field; maintaining released products; assigning product ID; defining configurations and packaging; publishing availability schedules, release letters and updates; and maintaining product databases.
2. **Create customer order** includes costs associated with creating and pricing configurations to order and preparing customer order documents.
3. **Order entry and maintenance** includes costs associated with maintaining the customer database, running credit checks, and accepting new orders and adding them to the order system, as well as making later order modifications.
4. **Contract/program and channel management** includes costs related to negotiating contracts, monitoring progress, and reporting against the customer's contract, including administration of performance or warranty-related issues.
5. **Installation planning** includes costs associated with installation engineering, scheduling and modification, handling cancellations, and planning the installation.
6. **Order fulfillment** includes costs associated with order processing, inventory allocation, ordering from internal or external suppliers, shipment scheduling, order status reporting, and shipment initiation.
7. **Distribution** includes costs associated with warehouse space and management, finished goods receiving and stocking, processing shipments, picking and consolidating, carrier selection, and staging products/systems.

8. **Transportation, outbound freight, and duties** include costs associated with all company-paid freight duties from point of manufacture to end customer or channel.
9. **Installation** includes costs associated with verification of site preparation, installation, certification, and authorization of billing.
10. **Customer invoicing/accounting** includes costs associated with invoicing, processing customer payments, and verification of customer receipts.

Material acquisition costs

1. **Materials (commodity) management and planning** include the costs associated with supplier sourcing; contract negotiation and qualification; and the preparation, placement, and tracking of a purchase order. These functions may be organizationally dispersed and/or decentralized, but we suggest that you group all related costs for purposes of this measurement study. Also, this category includes all costs related to buyers/planners.
2. **Supplier quality engineering** includes the costs associated with the determination, development/certification, and monitoring of suppliers' capabilities to fully satisfy the applicable quality and regulatory requirements.
3. **Inbound freight and duties**: Freight includes the costs associated with the movement of material from a vendor to the buyer and the associated administrative tasks. Duties are fees and taxes levied by governments for moving purchased material across international borders. Customs broker fees should also be considered in this category.
4. **Receiving and material storage** includes the costs associated with taking possession of material. This does not include inspection. Inventory-carrying costs are covered in a subsequent worksheet.
5. **Incoming inspection** includes the costs associated with the inspection and testing of received materials to verify compliance with specifications.
6. **Material process and component engineering** includes tasks required to document and communicate component specifications, as well as reviews done to improve the manufacturability of the purchased item.
7. **Tooling** includes costs associated with the design and development required to produce a purchased item, as well as the depreciation of the tooling.

Inventory carrying costs

1. **Opportunity cost** is the cost of holding inventory. This should be based on your company's own cost of capital standards using the following formula: Cost of capital × Average net value of inventory.

2. **Shrinkage** is the cost associated with breakage, pilferage, and deterioration of inventories.
3. **Insurance and taxes** are the cost of insuring inventories and taxes associated with the holding of inventory.
4. **Total obsolescence for raw material, work in progress (WIP), and finished goods inventory** are the costs for inventory reserves taken due to obsolescence and scrap. (Do not include reserves taken for field service parts.)
5. **Channel obsolescence** is the aging allowances paid to channel partners, provisions for buy-back agreements, and so on.
6. **Field service parts obsolescence** consists of reserves taken due to obsolescence and scrap.

Supply-chain-related finance and planning costs

1. **Supply-chain finance costs** include costs associated with paying invoices, auditing physical counts, performing inventory accounting, and collecting accounts receivable. It does *not* include customer invoicing/accounting costs. (See order management costs.)
2. **Demand/supply planning costs** are associated with forecasting; developing finished goods, intermediate, subassembly or end-item inventory plans; and coordinating demand/supply.

Supply-chain-related IT costs

1. **IT** costs associated with major supply-chain management processes.
2. **Development costs** incurred in process re-engineering, planning, software development, installation, implementation, and training associated with new and/or upgraded architecture, infrastructure, and systems to support the described supply-chain management processes.
3. **Execution costs** to support supply-chain process users, including computer and network operations, electronic data interchange and telecommunications services, and amortization/depreciation of hardware.
4. **Maintenance costs** incurred in problem resolution, troubleshooting, repair, and routine maintenance associated with installed hardware and software for described supply-chain management processes. Include costs associated with database administration, systems configuration control, and release planning and management.

Plan costs

1. **Product data management** costs include product phase-in/phase-out and release, post-introduction support and expansion, testing and

evaluation, end-of-life inventory management, and item master definition and control.

2. **Forecasting and demand/supply manage and finished goods** costs include forecasting, end-item inventory planning, distribution resource planning, and production master scheduling for all products and all channels.

Source costs

1. **Sourcing/material acquisition** costs include material requisitions, purchasing, supplier quality engineering, inbound freight management, receiving, incoming inspection, component engineering, tooling acquisition, and accounts payable.
2. **Component and supplier management** includes costs for part number cross-references, supplier catalogs, and approved vendor lists.
3. **Inventory management** includes costs for perpetual and physical inventory controls and tools.

Make costs

1. **Manufacturing planning** costs include MRP, production scheduling, tracking, manufacturing engineering, manufacturing documentation management, and inventory/obsolescence tracking.
2. **Inventory management** costs include perpetual- and physical-inventory controls and tools.
3. **Manufacturing execution** costs include MES, detailed and finite interval scheduling, process controls, and machine scheduling.

Deliver costs

1. **Order management** includes order entry/maintenance, quotes, customer database, product/price database, accounts receivable, credits and collections, and invoicing.
2. **Distribution and transportation management** costs include DRP shipping, freight management, traffic management.
3. **Inventory management** costs include perpetual- and physical-inventory controls and tools.
4. **Warehouse management** costs include finished goods, receiving and stocking, and pick/pack.
5. **Channel management** costs include promotions, pricing and discounting, and customer satisfaction surveys.
6. **Field service/support** costs include field service, customer and field support, technical service, service/call management, returns, and warranty tracking.

External electronic interfaces costs

1. **Plan/source/make/deliver** costs include interfaces, gateways, and data repositories created and maintained to exchange supply-chain-related information with the outside world.
2. **E-commerce initiatives** include development and implementation costs.

Note: Accurate assignment of IT-related cost is challenging. It can be done using activity-based costing methods or other approaches, such as allocation based on user counts, transaction counts, or departmental head counts. The emphasis should be on capturing all costs. Costs for any IT activities that are outsourced should be included.

The costs described here are the measurable costs of people and facilities directly related to the task of managing the supply chain. It is likely that this cost is significant but consider the additional real-cost impact hidden in operations. What is the cost of a material shortage occurring on the plant floor that affects production, or a less-than-complete order shipped to your best customer, or the cost of responding to defective products in the distribution pipeline? These are what make up the true costs and they add no value.

The above information on supply chain costs has been published with permission of PRTM and The Performance Measurement Group (PMG). PMG (a unit of PRTM Companies) provides consulting focusing on supply chain issues and can be reached at www.pmgbenchmarking.com. PRTM (www.prtm.com) also publishes a recommended magazine devoted to subjects on the supply chain and supply chain management. Frequently included in this publication are data on supply-chain management costs and trends among a large number of participating organizations.

In the end, of course, benchmarking will not change much by itself. It will or should show your company's performance relative to your competition or at least your benchmarking partner. The next step is to identify initiatives and begin the real work.

Whether you are planning to begin the process of supply chain management or to examine and revise current practices, the following ten steps are suggested by Schorr (1998):

1. **Top management leadership** — Whenever you are going to take on a project of this magnitude that changes the way a company is managed, you need to get top management to commit to leading the change.
2. **Vision/mission statement** — Once you have top management's leadership in place, you need to develop a clear vision/mission statement of what you are trying to accomplish.

3. **Communication** — Communicate that vision/mission both inside and outside the organization so that everyone understands what the company is trying to accomplish. If you want customers and both internal and external suppliers to agree to align themselves with the vision, you need to let them know what is expected of them.

4. **Preparation** — Get your own house in order first. Telling your customers and suppliers to do something you are not capable of doing will not work. Show them how it works.

5. **Identification** — Map out your entire supply chain. Identify the key suppliers and customers that need to be involved to dramatically improve performance throughout the supply chain. Initially this would include your immediate suppliers and customers, but eventually would spread to your suppliers' suppliers and your customers' customers.

6. **Benchmarking** — Benchmark yourself and your supply chain plans against the best supply chains in place today.

7. **Teams** — Develop cross-functional and cross-company teams to identify opportunities for improvement. These teams should include — at a minimum — the areas of demand management, forecasting, order entry, master production scheduling, material planning, supplier management, production management, distribution/logistics, and performance measurement.

8. **Measurement** — Develop the performance measurements to be used throughout the supply chain so that all supply partners will know what is expected and how performance is measured.

9. **Reinforcement** — Constantly reinforce the need to develop trusting relationships, valid partnerships, open and honest communication, and the sharing of benefits among all partners.

10. **Implementation** — Implement concurrent planning and execution technologies so that all resources of the supply chain are aligned to efficiently meet the needs of the ultimate customer quickly and profitably.

When you have all the best plans firmly in place and each supplier and customer issue correctly addressed, something will change. This change will be either through events external to your company or from within. In fact, keeping up with the evolution on just the technology front will be an arduous task. Supply chain management is no different from most managerial tasks in that we must continuously strive for the ideal. The ideal supply-chain management system has the following characteristics:

- The ideal supply chain will be or appear to be seamless.
- The ideal supply chain will have appropriate security measures.
- The ideal supply chain will be agile, able to respond to changes in demand in the shortest possible time.

- The ideal supply chain will be the most competitive group of companies within an identified market.
- The ideal supply chain will have well-designed relationship standards that can be coupled or decoupled easily.
- The ideal supply chain will have all partners operating in synchronized harmony.
- The ideal supply chain will maintain a continuous effort of performance metric measurement to ensure the best-in-class practices.
- The ideal supply chain will have closely linked partners using joint performance metric measurement to ensure the best-in-class practices.
- The ideal supply chain will have highly integrated information flows and access.

Ideals are what one strives for and it is unlikely that most company processes will meet each of the above characteristics; however, many companies continue to raise the bar on supply chain management, striving for the ideals. Collaboration is a tool that will reach new levels of performance for those companies willing to pursue the opportunities.

In this chapter, I have discussed what the supply chain is and provided an overview of where supply chain management fits in the collaborative enterprise. The SCOR model and the supply-chain cost calculation will help you determine some benchmarks from which to compare your company to others in the industry. These tools will also provide a point from which progress can be measured as new levels of performance are achieved.

References

Ayers, J.B., *Handbook of Supply Chain Management*, St. Lucie Press, Boca Raton, FL, 2001.

Brewer, P.C. and Speh, T.W., *Adapting the Balanced Scorecard to Supply Chain Management*.

Langenwalter, G.A., *Enterprise Resources Planning and Beyond*, CRC Press, Boca Raton, FL, 2000.

Lee, H.L., Creating value through supply chain integration, *Supply Chain Management Review*, September 2000.

Mann, P., A long time coming, *Manufacturing Systems MSI*, August 2001.

Performance Measurement Group, Measure Your Performance, white paper, Performance Measurement Group, Waltham, MA, 2001.

Poirier, C.C. and Bauer, M.J., *E-Supply Chain*, Berrett-Koehler Publishers, San Francisco, CA, 2000.

Reay, J.H., DoD Supply Chain Management Implementation Guide, Logistics Management Institute, McLean, VA, 2000.

Schorr, J.E., *Managing the Supply Chain*, John Wiley & Sons, New York, 1998.

Tarr, M. Benchmarking Global Supply Chains, white paper, KPMG International, 1999.

chapter nine

On-line, real-time data sources

The third leg of the collaboration process is on-line, real-time information from production and logistics activities that is used to confirm and track processes in compliance with collaborative agreements. This process is two-way communication. As demand information is provided to upstream partners, their commitment confirmation process comes back to the host. Information is generated and used by the processes to view two separate aspects of the collaborative process. The first is the general issuance of information to define the product, batch size, due date, batch recipe, shipment routing, warehouse location, bill of material information, and so on. This is the information that production managers require to get their job done. Along the way, other information is generated as a result of production, including quality assurance information, actual quantities produced vs. planned amounts, laboratory batch test information, storage location, shipment information, lot numbers, and so forth. The second use of this data is to confirm that production processes and quantities have occurred in accordance with expectations.

A fundamental business condition is revised through successful collaboration that changes the level of performance expectation from probably to absolutely. Historically, companies have protected themselves from nonperformance by their vendors through building safety factors into ordering and inventory calculations. The major impetus behind collaboration is the removal of these safety buffers, replacing them with time buffers or, better yet, event confirmation information. Much the same as a flight plan for aircraft is used to outline and later confirm the expected path of a flight as the flight progresses, so too is the production plan tracked to ensure that actual events are occurring according to the plan. The real-time confirmation data are the trust-building element that confirms adherence to the plan.

It seems safe to accept the premise that real-time events are the internal cogs that run the business, and maintaining management control of those events has always been based on having sound and reliable information. As manufacturing facilities get larger and more geographically dispersed, reliable information needs are even more imperative. They must be more rigorous due to greater investment and expanded distances. When thinking in terms of the supply chain network, the need for reliable, accurate, and timely information is at its greatest. Adversarial management suggests that everyone is on their own to find and make best use of whatever they can get. Collaborative management is precisely the opposite, based on the idea that the supply chain team is most effective when all partners have the latest applicable information that can support their value-adding contribution. This chapter provides a road map of where real-time, production-related information is located and also tell you how to gain access to it.

To add perspective, I outline the evolution of early concepts of production control techniques to computer integrated manufacturing, to the integrated packages and systems of today. Many system components within the production process will be identified and briefly described, including such sources as manufacturing execution systems (MES), supervisory control and data acquisition (SCADA), programmable logic controllers (PLCs), human–machine interface (HMI), data historian systems, and others. This overview of plant floor systems includes methods ranging from manual paper-and-pencil production control, manual data entry, PLCs used to control a process or machine, and computer integrated manufacturing execution systems. The emphasis is to illustrate the availability of *all* real-time data within process control systems, equipment control systems, stand-alone or integrated production-management systems, and manual data-entry systems. The focus is on the real-time and proactive aspects of plant-floor management tools and the value of these systems as internal information generators.

What are real-time data? What are on-line data? These are ambiguous terms to some people and the use of them in this text could be even more so. According to Edward Yourdon (1972), *an on-line system accepts input directly from the area where it is created. It is also a system that can return the output directly to the area where it is required.* Yourdon goes on to suggest other characteristics to support this definition:

- Remote access: the definition above implies that the input is delivered to the computer from a remote area.
- Files and data: the system works with an on-line database.
- People orientation: systems characterized as on-line are usually interacting with people or other immediate data input or requesting sources.

Some examples of on-line systems (Figure 9.1) include the following:

- Airline reservation systems
- E-business systems such as Amazon.com
- Credit card approval and acceptance systems
- Medical information systems
- Manufacturing execution systems

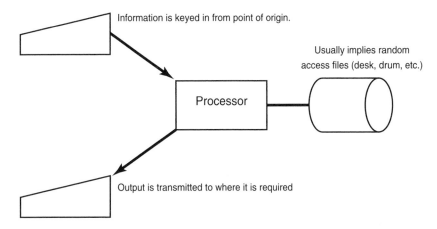

Figure 9.1 On-line computer systems.

Real-time systems as defined by Martin (1967) follow: *A real-time computer system may be defined as one that controls an environment by receiving data, processing them, and returning the results sufficiently quickly to affect the environment at that time.*

Examples of real-time systems include:

- Machine or process control systems
- Missile guidance systems
- Airplane autopilot systems

Our definition of a collaborative manufacturing system is one made up of many integrated or linked computer-system components and data sources that can receive and process data at random or programmed times. It is possible that a collaborative system would be required to process information at a real-time rate similar to a missile guidance system or a process control system, but would most often use these systems as data input sources. Collaborative manufacturing systems are on-line systems consisting of on-line and real-time components. Collaborative manufacturing systems are proactive, anticipatory, action- and people-oriented, computerized management tools.

The need for the collaborative manufacturing system and production management to have access to the supply-chain network information pool may be obvious, but presenting real integrated information, not just a lot of data, is a daunting task. The good news is that a vast amount of production information exists in every facility. The bad news is the information may be difficult to access, retrieve, and collate. This difficulty, more than any other factor, makes collaborative data exchange an evolutionary process rather than a giant leap forward.

The term "plant-floor production infrastructure" is used to describe and include all computer systems, electrical control systems, PLCs, and manual management tools used to manage and accomplish production. This collage has rarely been developed from an integrated vision, but instead is made up of individual methods, equipment, and software components implemented over the past 30 or so years of applying various stages of control equipment and data management technology. In many instances, plant-floor applications were developed or purchased, installed, and owned by a specific department or designed around and for a specific process. Examples include the installation of a quality-assurance data system implemented by and for the quality assurance department, or a PLC control system to control an injection-molding machine. This has brought us to the same "islands of automation" or just as bad, "silos of information" as discussed in earlier chapters. In the optimum production system, all data components within the production system are linked. Unfortunately, that is not the case since many of the disparate legacy systems — legacy systems being any control system, or data collecting, handling, collating, or information management system installed before today — may be based on obsolete technology, lack adequate documentation, and have limited functions.

For many years the three-level pyramid (Figure 9.2) was used to define and describe the hierarchical structure that illustrates how plant systems were applied. It is unlikely that there ever was a time when this structure suggested some level of importance or emphasis. More likely it fits because of the response time for each level of the infrastructure.

The full definition and explanation of planning-level systems were provided in Chapter 7. In this chapter, the execution/production system and the device control layer will be examined, both to suggest the availability of systems to assist in production and to illustrate the vast amount of data that exists within plant-floor systems (Figure 9.3). As the capability of these applications has evolved, the hierarchy is being redefined to suggest there are only two types of data systems employed in the production management infrastructure: on-line transaction processing (OLTP) and decision support systems. The difference in this definition from the pyramid view is that nearly *all* device-execution layer systems and control systems are included in the OLTP system definition. This definition suggests a broad view of the production-management infrastructure complex to include all computerized or manual systems, methods, and tools used to accomplish production.

The following outline of systems more closely matches how companies actually operate.

1. In most companies, large and small, planning systems ranging from a simple single-plant MRP system to the most modern ERP application are usually implemented and managed by the IT group. The view of these systems is a broad corporate perspective concerned with corporate-wide macro issues, such as financial planning, aggregate inventory data, human resource management, and customer relationship management. These systems are generally used to pro-

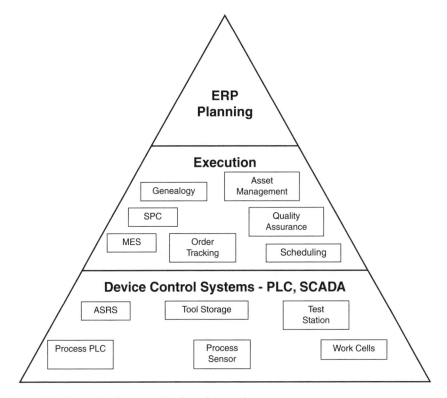

Figure 9.2 Three-level pyramid of applying plant systems.

vide decision support information or respond to events on an exception basis. The emphasis is on enterprise system standards and data roll-up functions, such as accounting and inventory. Consistent data presentation is a major thrust.

2. Plant-floor applications are just the opposite, operating in an on-line transactional processing world of optimizing and accomplishing current operational requirements within minutes, seconds, or milliseconds. The applications have been implemented on a system-by-system basis in response to requirements defined by department managers, manufacturing engineers, or equipment vendors. These systems have highly varied applications that include turning on a machine tool to make a specific threaded hole from a stored part program, measuring and adjusting an oven temperature on a minute-by-minute basis, changing a machine load schedule because received material did not meet quality requirements, or turning on valves to deliver liquid material in response to the product recipe. Most of these real-time events do not require human intervention but are executed with software logic. Real-time plant systems usually have a very granular functionality focus not found in planning-level applications.

Planning System Level
Material Requirements Planning - MRP
Manufacturing Resource Planning - MRPII
Enterprise Resource Planning - ERP

Because planning systems are usually batch operated and run on a planned basis, early versions of MRP, MRPII, and ERP systems can have operating cycles of one week or more. Modern ERP systems are designed with an architecture that operates with on-line response times.

Execution Level Plant Floor Systems
Manufacturing Execution Systems
Warehouse Management Systems
Quality Assurance Systems

Most plant floor management systems are online transaction processing systems that operate in minutes or shorter times. In most cases the frequency of transactions is few relative to typical computer systems applications.

Device Control Systems/Process Control Systems
Programmable Logic Controllers - PLC
System Control and Data Acquisition Systems - SCADA
Process Control Computer Systems

Systems in this category operate in milliseconds controlling processes and machine movements in real time.

Figure 9.3 Three types of system applications.

The vendor/technology community is structured along these lines. Although planning system suppliers are moving closer to the plant floor and plant-floor systems vendors are moving closer to planning system functions, the assumption of real-time event management by planning system vendors, or of plant-system vendors assuming the corporate view, is unlikely in the near future. The technology being applied is more than a little different. The issues viewed and the user needs are vastly different. Planning system implementations are frequently fully integrated to work with their own internal modules from a common database. On the other hand, the plant system infrastructure is made up of a wide assortment of legacy systems and manual methods that could not be discarded or quickly changed without extreme cost and disruption of production.

The dual approach is supported by good business and system design reasons:

1. Clear division of the systems into planning (decision support) and execution (transaction processing).
2. Corporate-wide information systems strategy separate from the requirements of localized production-facility systems.
3. Better environment for system improvement and upgrade at both corporate and local facility levels because of consistency and user perspective. Aside from the perfectly appropriate requirement of corporate IT standards, who really understands the requirements of an application better than the actual user?

In addition to the cultural and development history, there have been technical and practical reasons that have brought plant systems to where we are. The most significant roadblock to a seamless system has been the cost and complexity of the integration of various data sources and/or software packages.

The systems used in the execution and control levels are usually referred to as on-line and real time. In actual fact, they may not always meet the definition of real time, but are nearly always on-line transaction processing as opposed to decision support systems that are usually batch-operation oriented.

The development of managerial tools for the plant floor has also gone through continuous evolution. Early methods, from 1920 to 1970, were mostly manual record keeping. The tools used to manage production were very people-oriented, primarily based on written planning and control systems, including forecasting, operations planning, inventory planning and control, operations scheduling, dispatching, and progress control. Computer systems had very limited use for the manufacturing facility but certain planning applications, such as master scheduling and material requirements planning, were implemented late in this period. This is the era when assembly line concepts were begun, bringing with them new management opportunities such as assembly-line balancing, multiple-plant inventory management, and scheduling of various products produced by a single facility. Later, new computer-like devices called PLCs gained widespread use with their ability to maintain numerical control information for machine tools and processes. The general thinking behind production was based on master schedule forecasts, large lot sizes for economy of scale, building to a forecast warehouse inventory, and full production-facility utilization. New ideas included Phil Crosby's phrase "quality is free," work cells, and work-in-process storage at the point of use. The great system equalizer was building up inventory throughout the process to allow for production contingencies.

Computer integrated manufacturing arrived in the mid- to late 1970s and was a term in common use until the late 1980s. Computer integrated manufacturing was an ambitious idea with many definitions and variations. It also was an idea of great promise that frequently fell short of expectations. Manufacturing facilities were large and complex. Management had extended and maximized the tools of previous years and new ideas were being sought. At this time, improved PLCs and smaller, easier-to-use mini-computers were in widespread use. The pejorative term "islands of automation" was frequently heard describing the many improved production devices with no ability to tie them together.

The focus in the plant was cost reduction with a strong bent toward technology-oriented solutions. CAD systems were bringing significant improvements in the ability to produce and manage product information, including numerical control programs, improved bill of material definitions, and MRP tools to determine purchasing and inventory management directions. One of the major ideas supporting computer integrated manufacturing was the effort to define and develop very large, monolithic software systems that could manage many more points of manufacturing process integration. Unfortunately, this was the greatest weakness of the computer integrated manufacturing concept. Large monolithic systems were very difficult to develop and debug. The other criticism of this era was the term "hard automation." Because of the complexity of these systems, change was a very onerous task. Plant managers were generally and understandably skeptical of these projects for many reasons, including possible computer failure and general lack of flexibility.

During the 1980s, plant-floor production systems began to get serious attention from every level of management. The inexpensive personal computer became ubiquitous on the plant floor. Each department within the production infrastructure was able to develop and implement systems that fit their individual needs. The systems were relatively inexpensive and were applicable to specific functions within specific industries. A good example is a quality-control measurement system developed to meet the requirements of a particular industry or even specific company. Screens, information input, and report formats could be developed to fit the requirements of a single person. Systems could be large custom-developed implementations or "out-of-the-box" applications where users could simply load diskettes on their personal computers and get beneficial use within hours. Plant-floor systems tracked and managed orders through production, following product routings or process plant data where recipe information could be automatically downloaded to device control systems. Stand-alone industrial computer installations were everywhere and PLCs came close to computer functionality with the ability to store and manipulate data. MES made up of modules to track and manage work-in-process plant production orders were developed and applied primarily in discrete item manufacturing. Process manufacturing systems became more extensive as integrated multifunction controllers. The concept of the linked supply chain arrived, providing opportunities to improve management of inventory and logistics across the supply chain network. The application of the Internet and the idea of E-business grew explosively with a profound effect on manufacturing, requiring immediate movement toward make-to-order production. Product design and manufacturing had become global with component manufacturing done in various countries and shipped to the point of final assembly. Outsourced manufacturing services turned into a major business strategy, especially within the electronic equipment industries. Using the Internet and improved product-data management tools, design information can now be easily transmitted and reviewed anywhere in the world among supply chain partners. Collaboration regarding design for manufacturability is accomplished simultaneously around the globe with multitiered suppliers.

Many pundits are describing this new idea of collaborative manufacturing as one of the most significant milestones in business and manufacturing management — if done effectively. Collaborative manufacturing is based on the central theme of sharing information, both within and external to the supply chain network. It was originally begun in the electronics industry where off-site contractors frequently supply manufacturing services. Normal business activity includes the need to provide timely direction and manufacturing information, such as design drawings, engineering change order tracking, and supplier material delivery. It is also necessary to know and measure vendor performance. As this trend has grown, it has become important that supply chain partners work closely together to meet the common objective of providing the most effective customer service. This requires systems that can easily couple or decouple between different enterprise and plant-floor systems.

Collaborative manufacturing requires taking a whole new look at information availability and use. Plants are not just groups of people, machines, and control panels. Each plant has a unique production-system infrastructure made up of many linked subsystems, each having its own set of conditions and rules. The result is to cause events to occur or to respond to events that have occurred on some managed basis. When a controller on a machine tool completes the read of a line of code, certain actions occur. When the production planning department completes its work, there is a plan of what to make and where. When we remove the roof from the plant and look from above, we can see many seemingly disparate events taking place. In reality, each event was begun based on a previous event, generally creating data during the process. Much of the data is available and necessary for subsequent events and other production system components. Some may be provided to the enterprise planning system either electronically or through manual input. Some of the data is used only internally within the facility or enterprise, and some can be available for use by other legitimate interested partners.

For definition purposes, the production management infrastructure includes all *manual or computerized* off-line or on-line transaction-processing systems used to accomplish production. The following list is provided to indicate the broad range of system applications, devices, and data used to manage the production management infrastructure. The list is not a complete representation but is a good reference point. Many plants have similarly named applications with very different details.

Manufacturing Execution Systems

An MES describes a set of integrated functions within a packaged software system or it can also describe the accumulated functionality within the production management infrastructure. The term means many different things from one user company to another and even within the companies that produce and implement these systems. They were originally designed to replace the difficult-to-manage paperwork system used to track work orders through production.

MES come in many different forms and formats, with some packaged systems designed for specific industries. In other instances, the product design and functionality are the result of the capability and interest of the system vendor. The basic idea for MES grew in large part from the concepts behind computer integrated manufacturing. The major improvement since the computer integrated manufacturing era is the replacement of huge custom-designed software systems with smaller reusable components. The original idea was to have modular systems that could be reapplied in various industries, but the factors of individual user-company operation and continuous systems evolution have produced a wide variety of implemented functionality. Although these systems are in widespread use throughout many industries, they are not always described similarly nor are functions identical. An MES in use at an electronics facility is similar only in concept to one used in the food processing industry. The ideas behind the systems may be similar but industries have their own set of differences and terminology that make them distinctive.

MESA International, the trade association of MES vendors, offers the following list of functionalities that generally describe various areas of production management that might be included in a full MES implementation (MESA International, 1995).

> **Resource allocation and status** — Manages resources, including machines, tools, labor skills, materials, and other equipment, and other entities, such as documents that must be available for work to start at an operation.
>
> **Operations/detail scheduling** — Provides sequencing based on priorities, attributes, characteristics, and/or recipes associated with specific production units at an operation.
>
> **Dispatching production units** — Manages the flow of production units in the form of jobs, orders, batches, lots, and work orders.
>
> **Document control** — Controls records/forms that must be maintained with the production unit, including work instructions, recipes, drawings, standard operating procedures, part programs, batch records, engineering change notices, shift-to-shift communications, and edits as planned and as-built information.
>
> **Data collection/acquisition** — Provides a link to obtain the intra-operational production and parametric data.

Labor management — Provides the status of personnel in an up-to-the-minute time frame.

Quality management — Provides real-time analysis of measurements collected from manufacturing to ensure proper product-quality control and to identify problems requiring attention. Some systems can provide yield information and track rework requirements by serialized unit number.

Process management — Monitors production and either automatically corrects or provides decision support to operators for correcting and improving in-process activities.

Maintenance management — Tracks and directs the activities to maintain the equipment and tools, and to ensure their availability.

Product tracking and genealogy — Provides visibility of where work is at all times and of its disposition. Status information may include who is working on it; component material by supplier, lot, and serial number; current production conditions; and any alarms, rework, or other exceptions related to the product.

Performance analysis — Provides up-to-the-minute reporting of actual manufacturing operations results along with comparisons to previous and expected business results.

Very few systems have been implemented that are as broad as the possibilities presented by MESA. Another approach to define these systems can be found in McClellan (1997). Although my list includes the same system functions as indicated by MESA International, it is based on specific software divisions within a system and is described using outlines from currently available software system products (Figure 9.4). They are divided into core functions that are directly associated with managing the production process and support functions that are peripheral to the value-adding production process.

Core functions

Planning system interface — This describes the connection with the ERP system and defines how and what information is exchanged.

Order management — This function includes the accumulation and management of work orders in the system.

Workstation management — This function is responsible for implementing the work-order production plan, workstation scheduling, and the logical configuration of each workstation.

Inventory tracking and management — The inventory tracking function develops, stores, and maintains the details of each lot or unit of inventory.

Material movement management — The movement of material, manual or automated, is managed and scheduled through this function.

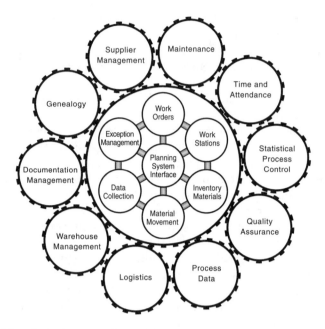

Figure 9.4 Manufacturing execution system.

Data collection — This segment acts as the clearinghouse and translator for all data that are needed and/or generated on the plant floor.

Exception management — This function provides the ability to respond to unanticipated events that affect the production plan.

Support functions

These identified functions are only a representation of possibilities and are not an exhaustive list of what is available or what will be on the market in the future. The long-range idea behind most system design is to provide the ability to plug and play whatever support systems may exist in the facility currently or any new product that might be acquired in the future.

Maintenance management — Maintenance management systems, sometimes called asset management systems, are used to manage production-equipment-maintenance–related issues, including predictive maintenance, work order and labor scheduling, procurement and storage of the repair parts inventory, and equipment record maintenance.

Time and attendance — Many software system products produce time and attendance information that can be used on a wide scale. Systems usually include clock-in/clock-out information along with labor data collection and employee skills data.

Statistical process control — Statistical process control (SPC) is a quality control method that focuses on continuous monitoring of a process rather than the inspection of finished products. The intent is to achieve control of the process and eliminate defective production.

Quality assurance — Quality assurance packages may or may not be tied together with SPC and/or ISO 9000 systems. Whether as separate or combined packages, they are frequent components of the production process.

Process data/performance analysis — Process data collection and management can be a standard package developed for specific applications, such as time/cost variance information or manufacturing process records.

Document/product data management — This can be a very large component of the manufacturing system used to create product drawing and process information. A modern view of this area is product life-cycle management, a system used to manage and record product data from design to disposal.

Genealogy/product traceability — Genealogy and traceability are similar functions designed to provide a complete history of a serialized item or a group of items. In addition to the in-house production data, most systems can include similar information on each bill of material item going into the finished product.

Supplier management — This is usually a custom-designed tool to communicate with suppliers. Data may include genealogy information, schedule information, quality assurance data, and logistics information.

Warehouse management — Warehouse management systems are primarily used to monitor and manage outbound inventory activities with some systems capable of inbound, raw, or purchased material management. Product location information and order fulfillment instructions are two of many on-line functions. Sometimes called supply chain execution systems, they can include logistics and other traffic management data.

In some companies, elaborate efforts have been made to include these or more functions into an integrated system. The important thing to remember is that systems identified as MES can have one or more of these components depending on the industry and the user company. Some companies have all of these systems and more, but do not use the term MES or manufacturing execution system. Some companies might call a single module, such as SPC, an MES. Other companies have an assortment of packages collectively referred to as an MES, but there is no tie among them. The MES descriptor does not have a broadly accepted meaning, especially among batch and process industries, but these plant-floor systems and their components do generate and maintain many data items that could be useful to supply chain partners.

The most interesting event in MES design is the advent of systems made of modules that can be added or deleted as necessary using a single database, similar to modern planning systems. One company has brought this new dimension to plant floor systems. Propack Data GmbH of Germany (www.propack-data.com) has developed a broad-reaching system that includes many or all of the plant management requirements using a set of modules tied together with a standard single database. The system is available as a complete integrated package or available by modules as required by the application. It is also capable of integrating with existing systems. The full system includes the following integrated modules:

Product data management

Master Data Management covers the creation, control, release, and version management of process data, such as production procedures, procedural descriptions, recipes, bills of material, routings, operations, and process-related master data. The data are archived in the system database and made available for inquiries, evaluations, and conforming documentation.

Production Data and Batch Archive includes report components for the technical and operational evaluation of the production process. The system operates on the basis of a SCADA system and uses a production monitoring board to integrate the data of all facilities relevant to the production process. The module incorporates a range of fundamental applications from individual production reports and failure or stoppage protocols, to quantity balances and variance comparisons. The module can collect, collate, and transfer operational information to other systems such as ERP.

Scheduling systems

The **On-Line Monitoring System** provides a representation of current production, giving production control the ability to see current schedule failures, predictable violations of dates, and planned idle times, as well as shortages of materials and resources.

Rough-Cut Capacity Planning is provided to plan orders for a certain period of time, such as a quarter or a month.

Personnel Placement and Training provides for administration of staff training plans, planning and execution of required training units, and documentation required by regulatory authorities. The module ensures compliance through qualification checks with every log-in to the system.

Process-related systems

The **Warehouse Management System** provides complete material control and traceability. The module includes full inventory management, including main and buffer warehouses for raw materials, auxiliary materials, work in process, and finished goods inventory. The batch-and packaging-units–related inventory management is based on storage sites, storage locations, and load carriers. Material is made available based on order-related, bill of material and business rules, such as allocation, conditional release, and processing up to a defined step.

Paperless Dispensing is used along with a step-by-step process for weighing materials in which the user is consistently guided. Information regarding order progress and the completion of weighing orders is directly transmitted back to the planning board. During weighing, labels are provided to identify material content at any time during processing.

Surveillance and Control of production is done through a line monitoring board that integrates all data from engineering, production, and quality assurance that are relevant for the manufacturing, filling, and packaging processes. This module is the central information point for the production process. Using continuously collected data from work centers and quality assurance, this module provides complete documentation of the production processes. Information received with the scheduled orders, including master data, calibration parameters, and production procedures is downloaded to the relevant point of use, such as scales and production equipment.

Electronic Batch Recording generates the order-specific production and packaging instructions with all order-related parameters for the respective processing facilities. The operator receives detailed processing instructions together with graphics or other visual data, planned defaults, and order-specific parameters. The batch record controls the user authorization and collects the actual data occurring in the course of the process. Through interfaces, the processing data can be acquired from machines and facilities as well.

Shop Floor Navigator is an information system that visualizes production processes with updates every minute. Reports, graphics, and statistics can be generated providing effective operation reports. The information is also available via local area network and the Web for outside locations. Current order data, such as actual quantity counters, efficiency, production, failure and stoppage times, as well as order master data, planned quantities, and item numbers can be displayed on the production monitoring board. Zoom functions provide access to detail information.

Monitoring provides continuous recording, monitoring, and documentation of environmental conditions. If recorded values exceed the value limits, an alarm is triggered.

Service modules

>   The **Web Gateway** module forms the link between remote locations and the plant modules. Using the abilities of the Internet, data of the processes currently running on the Web gateway can be compiled and made available as an HTML document. The data can be retrieved and edited by authorized individuals from anywhere within the company or external partners worldwide. The on-line presentation is done with standard browsers and is constantly updated.
>
>   **Maintenance and Repair** comprises the management of machine-specific data and machine maintenance with a running hour meter and a technical log. The module supports spare part logistics, repair planning, and scheduling of maintenance activities to fit in the operational process.
>
>   **Quality Management** supports the structure, maintenance, processing and evaluating of analyses, check plans, checklists, and sampling. The system-based documentation and evaluation of the quality data allows the detection of weak points, which can then be removed through both technical and organizational measures. Failures are not only discovered, but also avoided before they occur.

The system is designed with a uniform look and feel for all modules and is available with a multilingual and fully graphical user interface. This uniformity in the design will provide easier operator training across a broad range of functions within the plant and thus improve user acceptance.

The outline of this system is presented in Figure 9.5 to show how a fully integrated system can directly support the information needed for manufacturing collaboration. The information is first presented across the integrated business processes within the system itself, providing a full view of what is planned and occurring in production. Second, this consolidated information is available for internal use or to outside sources on an authorized basis through browser access.

Many plants have much of this functionality included in their production infrastructure even though system components may not be fully or even partially integrated. Most MES systems currently available have not developed to the extent envisioned a few years ago. There are many reasons for this, not the least of which is the problem of integrating legacy components into a full plant-wide system. These systems do, however, have an extensive amount of real-time data that can be used across the supply chain. In many companies, the information is still department owned, and it is not unusual to find substantially different versions of these applications within a plant or company. The underlying thought here is that much data are available in these systems but a thorough review is required to identify where and what data exist and how the data can be extracted.

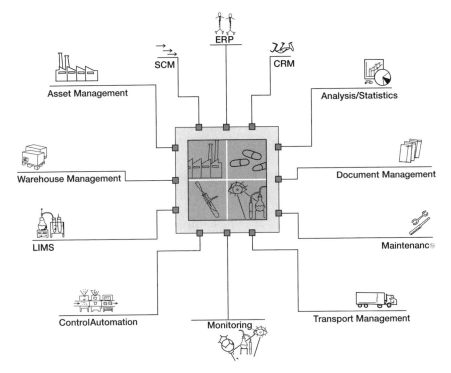

Figure 9.5 Seamless integration. (Reprinted with permission of Propack Data.)

The following list is representative of the systems in use in various industries, with a brief outline of the usual function.

Bill of material information and delivery — The bill of material lists the items (by part number) of material included in an identified component. This information usually is provided from the product data management system or it may be maintained in a product data library located in the ERP system. Information relating to the bill of material can include as-built information that shows details of items included in the assembly.

Boxing system — This is used to identify contents within a specific handling or shipping container. It can include parts within boxes within boxes within boxes, and so on.

Data historian system — This system organizes and maintains large amounts of data used to monitor and control process systems. These systems can collect data items from thousands of measuring points at a rate many times per second for each item. The data are often used in the control system to respond to variations in the production environment.

Device control system (DCS) — These systems are usually designed specifically to manage the functions of a device. One example is a

PLC programmed to run an injection-molding machine. DCSs can be extensive with the ability to collect data regarding such information as production quantities, downtime records, operator identification, and production orders processed.

Electronic signature requirement system — In regulated industries, such as pharmaceutical manufacturing and medical device production, it is frequently necessary to have a formal confirmation and recording of an event that follows Food and Drug Administration rules. Recent industry changes have allowed certification to be validated by data processing devices.

Engineering change-order tracking (ECO) — The tracking and management of product-engineering change orders can be part of other systems, such as a product data-management system or a separate package designed for a specific application. Basic functions manage work in process to identify and process change order requirements.

Genealogy reporting — Either as a stand-alone system or as an integral part of an MES, the purpose is to gather specific part source and process information for items on the bill of material. The information can be developed for a serialized part or lot and may include quality-assurance test results, serial numbers of each component along with their genealogy data, and any other information that would help identify the source and breadth of a product defect.

Graphical user interface (GUI) — The user interface is what operators use to view system information and to input data from their workstation. This is an excellent point to gather information regarding events as they occur, and is far better than writing information that is later manually entered into the system.

Human machine interface (HMI) — See graphical user interface.

In-process material tracking system — In-process inventory management usually includes tracking work orders and material through the process of being released from the raw material inventory to begin manufacturing to the finished-goods inventory stage. Systems that track work through production steps can provide substantial data, such as where the production order is in its process, deviations from process or production plans, data accumulated at workstations, schedule status, quality assurance and statistical process information, cost and yield variance from standard, current priority or work sequence position, component material status, and current physical location.

Interactive process instruction information delivered via video or audio — Operator information is commonly delivered or made available to workstations. Frequently, the production steps require interaction with instructions, and recording events and supporting data or variances. Some systems are rigid, providing specific steps that prevent the operator from taking alternative actions, while other systems provide a range of choices for the operator.

Inventory receiving — The receiving dock is a natural measuring point to begin or confirm source information, compare incoming material to the purchase order, begin or confirm product testing, recognize material shortage conditions, assign use priorities, collect source production data, and refresh inventory counts.

ISO 9000 — Frequently part of quality assurance or certification, ISO systems usually focus on identifying and tracking the process steps necessary to be in compliance with predetermined standards.

Kanban systems — Kanban describes the Toyota-developed inventory pull methods where an inventory buffer is managed by signaling for or allowing replenishment only when material has been removed. The idea is to identify a replenishment need and then pull material to fill the need as opposed to building to an anticipated inventory requirement that frequently results in more inventory than is needed.

Labor reporting — Labor reporting systems are used to identify the actual labor used on a shop order. With start and end times identified to the system for each work center or operation, the production times are accumulated throughout the in-process steps. From this data, variances from labor standards can be computed. In some systems, this information can identify the last operation and look forward to project the workload at downstream workstations.

Labor skills management — Some industries require that specific and sometimes licensed skills be applied at some workstations. The identification of the employee begins a search of the database to ensure that an individual's current credentials match the requirements of the operation on this work order.

Laboratory information management systems (LIMS) — In industries where product testing and analysis are done during the manufacturing process, LIMS are used to identify the analysis requirements, collect results, and include the information as a part of the product or lot history. One example is testing a sample in a steel production facility and including test data as a part of the lot history.

Logistics management — Logistics systems are used to manage material movement. Data can include shipper and shipping unit, dates, current location, estimated time of arrival, shipment cost, shipper performance, and inventory information.

Machine controllers — Devices and systems used to control equipment are excellent sources of real-time information. Most systems installed within the past 10 years are sophisticated enough to receive programs and other process information from manuals or automated external sources, store and manipulate data regarding the process performed, request and accept manual information from the HMI, display variances, and maintain history.

Maintenance and asset management systems — These systems are used to manage and record a range of maintenance information, including parts inventory, maintenance work-order information, asset maintenance requirements and history, and predictive maintenance schedules.

Manufacturing execution system (MES) — See discussion earlier in this chapter.

Material (inbound/off-site) inventory systems — Inventory management systems can include tracking and location information, warehouse data, logistics planning and execution, and process data.

Material handling systems — In-process material handling and storage systems, such as automatic storage and retrieval equipment, power and free storage systems, and assembly line conveyors, are usually managed with sophisticated computers or programmable controllers maintaining large amounts of data on location, progress, and status.

Off-site production monitoring — Many systems operate in upstream supplier facilities that can provide on-line information to track progress.

PC-based control — Much like PLCs, some programs are developed to run on a PC. The major difference lies in the increased ability of the computer over the PLC and the methods of programming.

Process automation — Process automation systems can range from a simple small PLC or PC to a very extensive system used to manage a refinery. These systems can provide a wide range of data but may require extensive data management to get specific answers. It is important to remember that a lot of data does not necessarily equal real information.

Process data historian — These are large database systems used to poll and maintain data from points of information generation within the process. Information sources can include sensor-based, real-time data and non–sensor-based data, such as time, events, state transition changes, messages and logs, instructions, and so on.

Processing recipe management and reporting — Recipes are the equivalent to the bill of material and routing information found in discrete manufacturing. The management of a recipe from its source to implementation can include adjusting process steps and inventory quantities. The Instrumentation, Systems, and Automation Society's (ISA) S88 and S95 establish some standards for recipe structure and management.

Product data collection — This is sometimes viewed as a simple data collection system or as a major component of the product life-cycle management process.

Product life-cycle management (PLM) — Sometimes a part of the ERP system or frequently a separate component, product life-cycle management is used to collect information throughout a product's life from design to disposal. The system can begin at design with the original CAD document and record events through manufacturing, engineering change orders, quality assurance, genealogy, customer data, and so on. PLM is used extensively in collaborative design applications.

Product test systems — Product test information may or may not be a part of the quality assurance system. In some industries where each individual item produced must be tested, a record of the results is or should be maintained. Actual test system criteria may reside here along with rules on how to respond to nonconformance test results.

Production control — Production control includes methods to track work in process to ensure conformance with the production plan. This information may be included in most MES or may be a manual handwritten system, using expediters to confirm performance on the plant floor. Systems may include work dispatch, order or batch priority assignment, workstation or process scheduling, and performance variance monitoring.

Programmable logic controllers (PLCs) — PLCs are used to control equipment and processes. Nearing the capability of computers, they can be an excellent source of real-time information.

Quality assurance systems and rework loops — Quality assurance systems are used to measure conformance to specified parameters for items being produced. These systems can provide substantial information regarding yield or deviation from standard. Rework loops are used to track nonconforming items through rework processes.

Receiving inspection — Whether a part of the ERP system or a stand-alone package, this process is used to monitor and manage inbound material through the receiving process. This can be designed to follow process routing information and production steps as outlined for the identified part number or vendor.

Regulatory compliance management — Certain industries, particularly food and life science industries, must meet regulatory requirements and gather data during the manufacturing process to confirm compliance. This can include manual confirmation and data entry, or confirmation by computerized systems with automatic data accumulation.

S88 or S95 standards automation systems — These are system design standards developed and published through the ISA to provide common automation and process control terminology and structure. A review of these standards will provide an excellent view of data availability methods. The systems installed in your plant may or may not follow these standards.

Safety and environmental systems — Critical issues may be associated with life-threatening or regulatory compliance that can affect the entire supply chain.

Supervisory control and data acquisition (SCADA) — This is a term applied in some industries to identify data collection and process control systems. These systems are usually application or company specific.

Schedule exception reporting — Scheduling exceptions are simply an easier way to monitor and react to events that will affect the manufacturing plan. Newer systems can expand this idea to include supply-chain supplier partners and logistics that enable early warnings and presumably responses to missed events.

Scheduling systems — Scheduling can be an extensive part of the planning system or it can be a simple set of sequencing rules for a workstation. Manual or automatic, enterprise or local level, these systems are the basis for how resources are assigned. As a source of real-time data, it is necessary to close the loop between the scheduling system and the plant floor, and to confirm that the schedule has been met or to identify what alternative actions must occur as a result of the schedule not being met. Some systems can be as simple as applying a priority number to each order, following one of many sequencing ideas, or responding to an advanced planning and scheduling (APS) system. Data availability and access to real-time information are necessary to any scheduling system.

Scrap reporting — Either as a tare allowance or actual measurement of scrap, this information reflects inventory or usage and can be used to identify production problems.

Sensors — Although many data items are collected through sensors located in the manufacturing process, information collected from an individual sensor is usually considered to be raw data and has little use by itself. Once the data item has been collected and applied within some broader application or production context, it has greater value and use in higher-level systems.

Statistical process control (SPC) — SPC is a quality control method that focuses on continuous monitoring of a process rather than the inspection of a finished product, with the intent to achieve control of the process and eliminate defective products.

Time and attendance — Time and attendance information is a legal requirement in nearly every industry with the obvious primary purpose of providing payroll information. This can also be a good source of genealogy information (who worked on what and when) and is critical to on-line resource scheduling.

Transportation management systems — Logistics, traffic, and freight management for inbound and outbound material movement is obviously critical information, particularly in companies using just-in-time techniques to support manufacturing. Information possibilities include product, supplier, physical source location, current location, estimated time to arrival, and cost.

Variance calculation systems — Most manufacturing facilities have established standards for their processes, and measuring actual variances against plan is very common. This has long been an accounting need, but some data have other uses. Variance from standard could be important to quality assurance and may affect yield considerations in production planning.

Warehouse management systems — Frequently considered a part of supply chain execution or fulfillment systems, they are a significant step in storing and selecting finished products. Although generally used for outbound order fulfillment, finished-goods inventory management, and stock rotation management, some systems are used to manage and control inbound raw material. Either application can provide data, such as physical location, date information, schedule, stock-outs, and quantities. Some systems can be global with the ability to define the best shipment point and some can provide processing rules and management for final point-of-shipment configurations.

A lot of space and time has been dedicated to explaining what is meant by the term "real-time data." The primary use of real-time information is to control processes and to view and manage events occurring within the manufacturing facility, such as equipment failure, production progress, yield/production rework information, work-in-process status, production bottleneck loading, current and planned capacity usage, inbound/outbound inventory issues, and so forth.

Real-time information generated in the plant management infrastructure and device control systems is extensive. The tools used to manage production are similarly applied in nearly every industry, but much consistency in the details is unlikely. It would be great if each system were made up of integrated modules but these are only now becoming available. The various standards programs being developed by industries will also facilitate progress. To gain an understanding of information availability, developing a map of information sources within the designated facilities will be necessary. Determining where the information is and how to access it can be a part of the design and implementation plan.

Some obvious rules behind designing a system that can provide precise and easily understood information rather than a lot of data follow:

1. The knowledge must be presented in a form that people can easily understand and work with.
2. The user should be able to view the rules and methods used to manipulate and present the data.
3. All results used for discussions among people need to be available to all participants.
4. Consistent and accurate information computed from actual events as they occur must be provided.

Information from the many sources within production processes is the primary tool to ensure that planned events are occurring. As John Kay of Daimler-Chrysler said, "If it is necessary to physically count inventory, the delivery date will already have been missed." It must be possible to rely on IT to provide information that tracks and confirms events as they occur. There is no substitute for the facts and the ability to confirm that most precious commodity in collaboration — trust.

References

Kennedy, J.P., New Ways of Using Information in Industrial Plants, white paper, OSI Software, 2000.

Martin, J., *Design of Real-Time Computer Systems*, Prentice-Hall, Englewood Cliffs, NJ, 1967.

McClellan, M., *Applying Manufacturing Execution Systems*, St. Lucie Press, Boca Raton, FL, 1997.

Melnyk, S.A. and Narasimhan, R., *Computer Integrated Manufacturing*, Richard D. Irwin, Homewood, IL, 1992.

Melnyk, S.A., Carter, P.L., Dilts, D.M., and Lyth, D.M., *Shop Floor Control*, Dow Jones-Irwin, Homewood, IL, 1985.

MESA International, MES Functionalities and MRP to MES Data Flow Possibilities, MESA International, Pittsburgh, PA, 1995.

Mize, J.H., White, C.R., and Brooks, G.H., *Operations Planning and Control*, Prentice-Hall, Englewood Cliffs, NJ, 1971.

Yourdon, E., *Design of On-Line Computer Systems*, Prentice-Hall, Englewood Cliffs, NJ, 1972.

chapter ten

Industries and data standards

If your company has suppliers or customers, you are part of a supply chain, and your supply chain can encompass a range of different industries employing a variety of different production strategies. This chapter will provide information regarding industries where collaborative manufacturing has application along with a description of different production strategies. There is an effort from many directions to develop industry standards regarding data transfer methods. Some of those standards and the associations behind them are presented.

Production or manufacturing is the value-adding process or processes of converting an inbound inventory into a higher-value product. In the context of this book, manufacturing and production are interchangeable terms. Distribution is the process of getting the product to the end customer and is generally made up of transportation or movement systems and storage systems.

Every industry with a manufactured product and a supply chain has both an opportunity and a need to apply collaborative manufacturing technology. A few examples include:

- Electronic equipment manufacturers
- Commercial and military aircraft manufacturers
- Automobile, truck, and farm equipment manufacturers
- Food products manufacturers
- Consumer goods manufacturing
- Pharmaceutical and medical products manufacturers
- Semiconductor and electronic components manufacturing
- Household appliance manufacturers
- Industrial equipment manufacturers
- Wood products suppliers and furniture manufacturers
- Chemical and petrochemical producers
- Primary metal producers
- Military equipment suppliers

- Government agencies buying from manufacturers
- Retail companies and product dealers
- Distribution and warehouse management firms

It is difficult to imagine any industry that cannot benefit from lower inventory, better supplier relations, improved product quality, reduced cycle time, simpler logistics, and a host of other benefits, some obvious and some not so obvious.

Although some of the most talked-about applications of collaborative manufacturing exist in certain consumer goods industries and electronic equipment manufacturing industries, the ideas did not start here. Collaboration may not have been the term used to describe the relationship, but collaboration has been around for many years and exists in nearly every industry. The new ground being examined here is a significantly more proactive version with a greater degree of openness and trust and the use of information technology to provide the immediate communication that has not previously existed. The other major difference from the past is the purposeful supply chain collaboration effort, intended to develop a competitive or collaborative advantage. To examine the breadth of these ideas, I begin with examples of manufacturing strategies within industries.

Although the financial objective has always been based on the best return on assets, there are many approaches to manufacturing strategies that are used to accomplish this. Strategies have evolved from the early 1900s when most manufacturing companies were highly vertical; as much of the end product as possible was built within manufacturers' own facilities. In the automobile business, this led Ford Motor Company to build steel mills to make its own steel and tire companies to own rubber plantations to ensure their source of rubber. Steel companies had their own mines, transport, and processing, and in some cases, company towns. Metal casting foundries were common as in-house departments, even though production volume may have been quite small. In recent years, petroleum companies have gone through cycles of building vertical capacity from exploration to drilling to pumping to transport to refining and marketing, only to return to more specialized areas of focus. In today's terms, this is described as focusing on core competencies.

Reasons behind the vertically integrated strategy were based less on the idea of earning more profit and more on controlling the manufacturing process. The thinking was to manage or control all processes, mostly to avoid relying on outside sources. In recent years, these ideas have undergone major change, where today some companies rely more on their core competencies, such as design or distribution, and include supplier partners with core competencies that center on the manufacturing process. This is most obvious in the electronic equipment industries where the supplier core competency is assembly and inventory management. It also fits when the production requirements are such that a company cannot effectively make use of full plant capacity and is better served by sharing a productive plant.

Companies such as Cisco Systems Inc. are rewriting the book on how to build a major product and service company, while relying on supply chain partners for a realigned contribution. Dell Computer Corporation is another example of a different approach to bringing product to market. Both companies are very aggressively collaborative in their relations with suppliers in ways that have produced complete shifts in ideas regarding capitalizing on strengths without carrying the liability of their weaknesses.

It is likely that within your supply chain there may be a variety of different manufacturing strategies being used. The most common manufacturer makes discrete things. These things are usually quite specific, such as a refrigerator, a cup, a rocket booster, a car, a fan belt, a wheel, and so on. Within the category of discrete item manufacturers, there are many approaches to managing the process.

> **Discrete item manufacturing** — Most manufacturing companies fall into this category. Making one or a million, discrete item manufacturing is usually related to things. Discrete items can be manufactured following one of two approaches:
> **In-line** — In-line manufactured items are built following a defined, consistent route to workstations, such as an assembly line.
> **Defined routing** — The workstations are not necessarily in a line. Manufacturing follows process steps outlined in a routing defined by work requirements that necessitate the movement of material to varying locations.
> **Discrete item build to stock/inventory** — In this category products are usually manufactured to a planned forecast and placed in inventory either at the manufacturer or distributor until a customer places an order for delivery. This includes products such as water heaters, bricks, kitchen sinks, tires, appliances, garments, hammers, shovels, nails, bathtubs, and so on. Manufacturing capacity requirements usually begin with the master schedule. The planning system determines the run quantities and appropriate lot sizes, calculates the material requirements planning, and issues production orders to the plant.
> **Discrete item build to order** — This business usually works with longer lead times but begins the manufacturing process only when a customer's order has been received. Although there may be purchased material in inventory, the finished product goes immediately to the customer. These products are frequently low-volume, highly customer-specific products built one at a time, such as aircraft, large trucks, special-application low-volume computers, and some furniture. There are many companies looking for ways to provide mass customization, the manufacture of a product individualized to a specific customer. While this will provide a build-to-order environment, management creativity will be required to accomplish this without increasing inventories or lead time. Synchronized inventories through closer collaboration will be a very useful tool.

Discrete item build to configure — In this category, manufacturing management processes are built around products that are made up of common components that can be configured into many similar but different end products. Examples include personal computers, certain household appliances, computer printers, and some automobiles. This is primarily an assembly process delayed as far down the distribution channel as possible.

Outsourced manufacturing — Outsourced manufacturing falls into at least two categories. One is the fully outsourced or turnkey concept where a supplier provides a completed product and ships to the buying customer in the name of the product manufacturer. Another facet of this category is full components built by a supplier of manufacturing services. In earlier years, this would have been called contract manufacturing. An example of this strategy is when Sears might contract the manufacturing of products built to their design specifications and carrying the Sears name. The item really is a Sears product even though it may have been built in a Whirlpool facility, information likely to be hidden from the end consumer. Another good example is Cisco Systems Inc., which has no production facilities, relying on others for manufacturing. The quickly seen advantages are a greatly reduced cost of facilities and production change flexibility. The obvious disadvantage is the question of supplier reliability.

Outsourced component manufacturing — In this instance, components are manufactured by an outside source to the design and specification of the supply chain host and shipped to an assembly point. This is common in the auto industry where items such as seats are supplied by external companies and delivered in exact sequence with the auto manufacturer's production schedule.

Engineer/build to order — This instance of manufacturing includes individually designed, usually low-volume products, such as industrial machinery products, mining machinery, and products that are designed for a specific function and built when an order is received.

Batch manufacturing — In this strategy, products are manufactured in identifiable lots or batches where the end product is or could be one of many like items, usually with a batch-identifying number but not a serial number. Products include many consumable products, such as food items, paint, tobacco products, toys, cosmetics, pharmaceuticals, textiles, and some metals. A batch could consist of a quantity of millions of items (cigarettes) or as few as one. Batch manufacturing uses discontinuous processes that are not discrete or continuous, but with characteristics of both.

Continuous process manufacturing — Process manufacturing is usually continuous and processes liquids or gas. Petroleum and chemical products are included in this category, identified by nonchanging or infrequently changing process parameters. Process manufacturers can be high-volume — truly continuous — or low-volume producers of smaller lots. In a continuous process, materials are passed in a continuous flow through processing equipment. Once established in a steady operating state, the nature of the process is not dependent on the length of time of operation.

Hybrid manufacturing — Consider a beer producer that processes liquids into individual containers with specific federal and state tax requirements and returnable-container identification requirements (e.g., the beer for Oregon with a specific state tax on returnable containers should not go to Kentucky). This begins with a liquid batch process and ends with very closely monitored discrete products. Steel manufacturing is another industry that begins with a process or batch strategy and results in discrete items.

Regulated manufacturing — Some industries, such as pharmaceutical and medical equipment producers, must comply with regulatory measures and be prepared to confirm compliance. This also applies to food manufacturers where health hazard prevention regulations must be met. It could apply to continuous processes, such as a milk production facility, or discrete items, such as medical equipment. Regulated manufacturing also includes atomic energy–related device manufacturing and certain aircraft components.

The primary characteristic usually found in discrete manufacturing is the use of routings that identify the path or combination of operations to be performed. During product design manufacturing engineers will establish methods and process steps to build the product most economically. The product design package will minimally consist of the product design and manufacture information, an assigned part number, the manufacturing process steps, and the bill of material. There could be many other items, such as test and quality assurance conformance standards, time standards, process information such as oven temperature, tool requirements, lot size determinants, worker skill requirements, and so on.

In most plants, production starts with a work-order release to manufacturing identifying the part to be manufactured, and the quantity and the date required. Routings and other information regarding the item to be produced most often are automatically retrieved from the product data repository and included in the planning and production process.

Part number — This is a unique number that identifies the item to be manufactured and/or the items on the bill of material.

Routing — This is a list of the manufacturing steps or operations required to manufacture the part number. Routings are usually made up of operations. The routing plus the operations defines a list of specific physical instances to make or move the item being manufactured.

Bill of material — A listing of the material (identified by part number) that goes into the part number being manufactured. The bill of material frequently is "indented" to identify levels of material that make up subcomponents. It is normal to have a bill of material with part numbers that have bill of materials that have part numbers with bill of materials, and so on. There is no limit to bill of material levels except what is required.

Batch or process manufacturing begins with a recipe that identifies the product; and defines the materials to be used, the quantities of each material, and the processing steps and parameters required for a specific batch. The following descriptions follow standards outlined in ISA 88, a standard published by Instrumentation Society of America to define common terms for batch and process manufacturing.

> **General recipe** — A general recipe defines raw materials, their relative quantities, and the processing required.
> **Site recipe** — The site recipe is derived from the general recipe but takes into account the geography of the site.
> **Master recipe** — Master recipes are derived from site recipes and are targeted at the process cell. A master recipe takes into account its equipment requirements within a given process cell.
> **Control recipe** — A control recipe is a batch created from the master recipe.

Modern batch manufacturing control systems can automatically accept the information from the recipe data and set the system controls accordingly.

In any type of manufacturing, the quantity to be manufactured is a fundamental part of the management process. In discrete manufacturing, this is referred to as the lot size. Lot sizes can be as small as one item or as large as thousands of items. Lot size is very industry dependent but is related to economics of the process, raw material on hand, and preferred finished-goods inventory levels. In batch and process industries, the term "batch size" is used to identify the finished product quantity.

Modern industry requires the ability to trace many products through their life cycle from point of origin. These data, usually referred to as genealogy information, are nearly always based on batch numbers, lot numbers, or serialized unit numbers. A given batch item, such as a can of soup, can be traced to a batch. The batch record is likely to have all related production information either in electronic or written form for possible retrieval. In discrete manufacturing, the lot number serves the same purpose as the batch number. The lot number may be made up of individual serial-numbered items. In some industries, the serialized end product can have genealogy information on each component back to its originating source. Production information is collected, maintained, and stored accordingly and may be electronic or written. Additional product information may be available to trace each item of raw material to its source.

Clearly, a lot of information developed during manufacturing could be used in many other areas of the enterprise. This information has proved difficult to use in other applications because of the many disparate forms of data, various system devices, and the inability to easily communicate between devices. The desire to provide communication links between enterprise-level systems and devices and processes on the plant floor has been on everybody's wish list for many years. With the wide variety of sources of real-time information on the plant floor and each requiring different data transfer methods, accessing this information has been difficult. Recognizing the need for this real-time information, certain industries have developed and are continuing to develop system standards to guide companies in their effort to design into equipment the ability for information access and transfer. This has been difficult to achieve but a lot of progress has been made.

Standards are usually initiated and developed by interested volunteer professionals working on committees within industry associations or consortiums. An extensive formalization process ensures the broadest and most accurate collaboration between the standards writers and potential users. Industry standards exist for thousands of products and methods across all industries and are most often adopted internationally. The information presented here serves as an indication of the effort and trend toward more accessible plant-floor information used and developed within the production infrastructure.

Standards development is most often an industry-by-industry process that leaves major gaps among different standards that have been developed for what appears to be a similar purpose. This book does not endorse any standard and those presented here comprise only an overview. They are presented to provide a background view of trends that assist in technology systems integration, the backbone of collaborative manufacturing efforts. Only an abstract or short overview is provided. The website address for the Business Process Management Initiative is provided for those wishing to learn more. Because most of this information was taken directly from these organizations, all of which have a technology bent, I apologize in advance for the computer-speak language.

Business Process Management Initiative, www.BPMI.org

The Business Process Management Initiative is an independent organization devoted to the development of open specifications for the management of e-business processes that span multiple applications, corporate departments, and business partners, both behind the firewall and over the Internet.

BPMI.org complements initiatives such as J2EE and SOAP that enable the convergence of legacy infrastructures toward process-oriented enterprise computing and initiatives, and that support process-oriented, business-to-business collaboration. Some examples are ebXML, RosettaNet, BizTalk, WSDL, UDDI, tpaML, and E-Speak.

BPMI.org defines open specifications, such as the Business Process Modeling Language (BPML) and the Business Process Query Language

(BPQL), that will enable the standards-based management of e-business processes with forthcoming business process management systems, in much the same way that SQL enabled the standards-based management of business data with off-the-shelf database management systems (DBMSs).

The Business Process Modeling Language (BPML) is a meta-language for the modeling of business processes, just as XML is a meta-language for the modeling of business data. BPML provides an abstracted execution model for collaborative and transactional business processes based on the concept of a transactional finite state machine.

BPML considers that e-business processes consist of a common public interface and as many private implementations as process participants. This enables the public interfaces for BPML processes to be described as ebXML business processes of RosettaNet Partner Interface Processes, independent of their private implementations.

In much the same way that XML documents are usually described, in a specific XML schema layered on top of the eXtensible Markup Language, BPML processes can be described as specific business-process modeling language layered on top of the extensible BPML XML schema. BPML represents business processes as the interweaving of control flow, data flow, and event flow, while adding orthogonal design capabilities for business rules, security roles, and transaction contexts.

Defined as a medium for the convergence of existing applications toward process-oriented enterprise computing, BPML offers explicit support for synchronous and asynchronous distributed transactions, and therefore can be used as an execution model for embedding existing applications within e-business processes as process components.

XML.org, www.xml.org

XML.org was formed and introduced in June 1999 by *OASIS*, the non-profit Organization for the Advancement of Structured Information Systems. Its purpose is to minimize overlap and duplication in XML languages and XML standard initiatives by providing public access to XML information and XML schemas. Today XML.org has grown into a centralized portal and has emerged as a valuable and leading resource to technologists, developers, and businesspeople developing purpose-built XML languages. XML.org attracts considerable traffic: 12,000 page views from over 3500 visitors a day.

XML, the next-generation of HTML, is now viewed as the standard way information will be exchanged in environments that do not share common platforms. Special-purpose XML languages and standards are practically announced daily; several hundred have already been adopted since XML 1.0 was released in February 1998.

The mission is to accelerate the global utilization and adoption of XML by providing an open and nonprofit industry portal that brings together all members of the XML community, including technologists, developers, and businesspeople.

Semiconductor Equipment and Materials International (SEMI), www.semi.org

SEMI is an international trade association with over 2400 members in the global semiconductor equipment, materials and flat-panel display industries. Since its inception in 1970, SEMI has played an increasingly vital role in industry expansion, visibility, and representation.

SEMI strives to foster growth and development of both member corporations and the professionals within them through business and technical education: workforce development, public policy initiatives, and its international trade shows. SEMI plays a significant role in the development of standards in the industry. The standard abstract shown below is one example of a series of standards dealing with manufacturing.

SEMI E96–1101, Guide for CIM Framework Technical Architecture **Abstract**: This guide describes technical architecture choices that enable application components to cooperate in a CIM environment and reduce the effort required to integrate those components into a working solution. The CIM Framework technical-architecture guide builds on publicly available specifications for distributed object computing. It defines manufacturing production systems' requirements for improved component interoperability, substitutability, and extensibility of the technical infrastructure. It provides guidance for specifying components and addresses options for using an underlying distributed object communication infrastructure. This document is intended for developers of components and applications, and integrators of MES systems that adhere to the CIM Framework specifications. It is also intended for system architects who contribute to the evolution of the CIM Framework architecture and guides, based on implementation experience. The guide focuses on software technologies that support the architectural goals for the CIM Framework rather than on manufacturing domain concepts that the CIM Framework encompasses. The technical architecture perspective complements SEMI E81.

Instrumentation, Systems, and Automation Society (ISA), www.isa.org

ISA is a trade association serving to advance and reinforce the arts and sciences related to the theory, design, manufacture and use of instrumentation, computers, and systems for measurement and control in various sciences and technologies.

ISA 95 enterprise-control system integration. The following description is provided by ISA: This standard is one of a series that will define the interfaces between enterprise activities — primarily ERP systems — and control activities. Part one provides standard terminology and a consistent set of concepts and models for integrating control systems with enterprise systems that will improve communication between all parties involved. The models and terminology emphasize good integration practices of control systems with enterprise systems during the entire life cycle of the systems.

This part of the standard defines the interface content between manufacturing control functions and other enterprise functions:

- Scope of manufacturing operations and control domain
- Organization of physical assets of an enterprise involved in manufacturing
- Functions associated with the interface between control functions and enterprise functions
- Information that is shared between control functions and enterprise functions

ISA 88 batch control, models and terminology. The following S88 information is taken from an article by Eddy Santos of S-S Technologies (Santos, 2001):The ISA S88 standard has been developed within ISA to establish predefined modules and common terminology for batch control systems development. The design standard is intended to provide a structural commonality between processes that allows easier access to control systems.

The S88 standard breaks down the manufacturing functions into categories, including procedural and physical models. The procedural model describes the following elements:

- **Procedure**: Strategy used to carry out a process, comprised of unit procedures.
- **Unit procedure**: Strategy used to carry out process activities and functions within a unit. A unit procedure is made up of one or more operations.
- **Operation**: Procedural element that defines an independent processing activity carried out by one or more phases within a unit.
- **Phase**: Smallest component of the procedural model in terms of process-specific tasks or functions.

The physical model is also a hierarchical definition of equipment used in manufacturing processes:

- **Enterprise**: Responsible for determining what products will be manufactured, at which sites, and with what processes. The enterprise is an organization that coordinates the operation of one or more sites. These sites may contain areas, process cells, units, equipment modules, and control modules.
- **Site**: Component of a batch manufacturing enterprise identified by physical, geographical, or logical segmentation within an

enterprise. It may contain areas, process cells, units, equipment modules, and control modules.

- **Area**: Component of a batch manufacturing site that is identified by physical, geographical, or logical segmentation within a site. It may contain process cells, units, equipment, modules, and control modules.
- **Process cell**: Contains all units, equipment modules, and control modules required to make one or more batches. It is a component of an area.
- **Unit**: Grouping of equipment modules, control modules, and other process equipment in which one or more process functions can be conducted on a batch or part of a batch.
- **Equipment module**: Functional group of devices that can carry out a finite number of minor processing activities. These activities make up such process functions as temperature control, pressure control dosing, and mixing.
- **Control module**: Lowest level of equipment in the physical model. It can carry out basic functions such as valve or pump control.

To further the model construction, the S88 standard identifies four types of recipes described earlier in this chapter: general recipe, site recipe, master recipe, and control recipe.

The standard also includes a description of the various functions required to manage batch production.

- **Recipe management**: Functions responsible for creating, storing, and maintaining recipes.
- **Production planning and scheduling**: Functions include methods used to produce production schedules.
- **Production information management**: Functions responsible for collecting, storing, processing and reporting production information and batch history.
- **Process management**: Functions include the creation of control recipes from master recipes and the initiation and supervision of batches scheduled for production. Additional process-management functions include the allocation of equipment and arbitration of common resources, and the actual collection of batch and equipment event information.
- **Unit supervision**: Refers to the functions associated with executing procedural elements within a control recipe. Also included are the complete management of unit resources and the collection of batch and unit information.
- **Process control:** Functions encompass the execution of equipment phases and the propagation of modes and states to and from any recipe procedure element and equipment or control module. They also cover the execution of I/O control on field devices and data collection from these devices.

The objective of the ISA committee is to provide a model that all companies can follow in their system design. The goal is to reduce costs through reapplied designs and to reduce application interpretation errors by providing a standard language for the system user and the system provider. The standard also helps to reduce the time to bring systems on line by using a modularity approach to system design.

Association Connecting Electronic Industries (IPC), www.ipc.org

The IPC is a U.S.-based trade association dedicated to serving members within the electronic interconnect industry. Among other functions, the IPC provides a process for producing various industry standards, one of which is *Electronic Interconnection Standards for E-Commerce,* developed primarily through the efforts of the National Electronics Manufacturing Initiative (NEMI), an industry consortium of electronics manufacturers.

The IPC Data Transfer Solutions Committee is developing this standard to support the industry need for standard communications protocols within an enterprise as well as between trading partners. The standard is made up a group of component standards to address a wide range of industry needs. The general goal is to improve interoperability of software used by manufacturing organizations that participate in the production of electronic interconnect products. When the standards are fully developed, they will help ensure plug-and-play operability between equipment in a production line, provide standards for managing the flow of material within a factory, and enable the development of virtual factories in which real-time control systems monitor the demand on factory resources and balance production schedules of transcontinental production lines. The IPC-2500 series (electronic interconnect standards) includes these standards with the breakout of information for 2570 as an example of the detail levels being addressed. A full description of these efforts is available through the IPC website at www.ipc.org or the NEMI website at www.nemi.org.

- IPC-2510 Product Data
- IPC-2520 Product Data Quality
- IPC-2530 Process Data (Standard Recipe File Format)
- IPC-2540 Shop Floor Communication
- IPC-2550 Execution System Communications
- IPC-2560 Enterprise Communication
- IPC-2570 Supply Chain Communication
- IPC-2571 Generic Requirements for Supply Chain Communication of Product Data eXchange
- IPC-2576 Sectional Requirements for Supply Chain Communication of As-Built Product Data

- IPC-2578 Sectional Requirements for Supply Chain Communication of Product Design Configuration Data
- IPC-2577 This standard will focus on product quality information exchange, providing a means for notification and acknowledgement of quality issues.
- IPC-257x This standard will focus on tracking work-in-progress.

The basic idea behind these standards is taken from the March 7, 2001 update of the committee's activities:

> The virtual enterprise envisioned by e-commerce technologies will enable companies to join into business relationships quickly and for short durations. A virtual enterprise may exist only for several months, in order to facilitate the production requirements for an original equipment manufacturer. The potential market described in these scenarios is only practical if business partners are interchangeable. The rapid creation of temporary business arrangements is only practical if all business units follow standard operating procedures.

Voluntary Interindustry Commerce Standards Association (VICS), www.vics.org

As shown in Chapter 3, the VICS has done a lot of work in the area of collaboration and could be called the leading nonprofit association in the field. VICS has led in developing the Global Commerce Initiative — a global standard for the implementation of CPFR guidelines and standards — in cooperation with ECR (Efficient Consumer Response) Europe. The VICS mission statement follows: The mission of the VICS Association is to take a global leadership role in the ongoing improvement of the flow of product and information about the product throughout the entire supply chain.

The Association's overall global objective (revised June, 1995) is to improve product availability to the consumer by providing leadership and encouragement in the identification, development and implementation of volunteer standards, protocols, guidelines, and other mechanisms which, when properly utilized, are expected to lead to better anticipation of, and reaction to, changes in consumer demand for these products with the subsequent optimization of production and carrying costs.

The Collaborative Planning, Forecasting and Replenishment Committee has been formed within VICS to promote the ideas of collaboration within the supply chain with the emphasis toward serving the consumer product retail industry. Collaborative Planning, Forecasting and Replenishment and CPFR are registered trademarks of VICS.

The mission of this committee is to create collaborative relationships between buyers and sellers through co-managed processes and shared information. By integrating demand- and supply-side processes, CPFR will improve efficiencies, increase sales, reduce fixed assets and working capital, and reduce inventory for the entire supply chain while satisfying consumer needs.

The VICS CPFR committee created the CPFR Voluntary Guidelines — now available on the VICS website — to explain business processes, supporting technology, and associated change management issues. Other papers published and available from the committee include:

- CPFR Guidelines
- Collaboration Data Modeling: CPFR Implementation Guidelines
- Collaboration Data Modeling: CPFR Implementation Guidelines from the Manufacturer's Perspective
- n-Tier CPFR: A Proposal
- Collaborative Transportation Management: A Proposal
- The Value Equation: Value Chain Management, Collaboration and the Internet
- CPFR Interoperability
- Global Commerce Initiative Collaborative Planning Forecasting and Replenishment (CPFR®) n-tier CPFR

The committee is made up of a number of companies representing consumer goods manufacturers, retail companies, and information systems providers and consultants, including Wal-Mart, Mars, Inc., Sherwin Williams, Oracle, Manugistics, Kimberly Clark, Smurfit Stone, and Logility. Most of the information in Chapter 3 on CPFR derives from VICS publications.

The work done by the committee is impressive. A significant amount of effort and thought has gone into the development of CPFR and the implementation guidelines and the results from their case studies after implementation indicate strong acceptance and success. The CPFR model has been developed with a strong orientation toward serving the retailer and is based on the premise of closer and more accurate order forecasting beginning with the retailer. Although the CPFR model includes manufacturers and their lower-tier suppliers, the model *ends at the point of order affirmation* by the supply chain partner and does not address or include the ability to track production processes. The production of the order according to necessary specifications, including quantity, quality, and shipment date is assumed. CPFR has history and implementation experience in many industries and can well serve as the beginning point for your collaboration effort.

The overview information on standards presented here is intended to give you an idea of the great amount of effort being invested to make the exchange of data from the plant floor easier and less costly to implement. The projects shown here are only a portion of those currently underway. As this book is being written in 2002, the standards effort is making an impact in many industries; however, the full answer to easy "plug-and-play" access to the real-time data being generated throughout the value chain has not yet been presented.

References

Chapman, L. and Petersen, M., Demand Activated Manufacturing Architecture (DAMA) Model for Supply Chain Collaboration, paper presented at International Conference on Modeling and Analysis of Semiconductor Manufacturing, Tempe, AZ, May 2000.

Santos, E., Understanding S88 batch control, *A-B Journal*, 8, , 2001.

Much of the information in this chapter was taken from the websites of the organizations named. Only an overview appears here. Details, along with much more information, are available at the organizations' respective websites.

chapter eleven

Collaboration and lean manufacturing

Every few years there is a new idea on how to fix or vastly improve business management and the process of manufacturing. These ideas are usually greeted with great fanfare, have their own set of acronyms, seem very mystifying to us common people, and require expensive consultants to help the uninformed find their way. For most of us, the acceptance process begins by sorting out the truth from the hyperbole, learning the details to see how the ideas might be applied, and having made the decision to proceed, going through agonizing implementation and retraining processes. Collaborative manufacturing does not fall into this category. This is a step in manufacturing management evolution, not a revolution. It is a significant step, but only a step. With collaborative manufacturing, nearly all the tools are already in place. The supply-chain management effort will be stretched a little and the resource planning–system connection will be relatively minor. Even the plant real-time information is likely to already exist. Collaboration requires a review of the objectives, some defined alignment with network partners, and tying the pieces together. This is hardly going to be an easy process, but the gut-wrenching system installations you have experienced or heard about should not be necessary.

As one looks back through the various recent management advances that range from a Gantt chart, or time-and-motion studies, to ERP systems, what is obvious is that real progress has been made. Those companies that do not keep up lose out to competitive advantages that are developed by their competition. Each hurdle leaves some companies out of the race and some companies much stronger.

This chapter describes two recent waves of manufacturing management innovation that provide a sense of progress and evolution. Collaboration is an outgrowth of earlier management ideas that progress from a very rigid systems approach in the 1960s and 1970s to openness and stakeholder involvement in the 1980s to lean manufacturing ideas built on close supplier ties and inventory management based on a "pull" or kanban in the 1990s.

Because lean manufacturing has become so popular and because many ideas behind collaborative manufacturing have a base in the close supplier relationships advocated in lean manufacturing methods, an overview of the basics is provided here.

Agile manufacturing was a term used in the late 1970s and early 1980s to describe companies that had taken major steps to be more responsive to their customers and reduce inventories at the same time. To be agile one thinks of being nimble and quick. In certain ways, that definition does apply but in others it does not. Agile manufacturing came after the MRP revolution when companies were given structured tools to manage their production process. These tools were very rigid and led to managing on a follow-the-system basis that tended to treat tasks as routines, not thinking processes. Applying MRP and economic lot sizes along with master schedules and annual forecasts was the model. The general order of the day was compulsory adherence. The term "agile manufacturing" was used to describe companies that were willing to think "outside the box" and consider how to run the business with less rigidity and greater participation of all stakeholders.

Agile techniques were rather radical at the time and were based on an idea of customer focus. Agile manufacturing was more of a philosophical approach that turned the focus outward to better serve the customer and at the same time opened up company processes some. Typical focus activities included the following.

Quality

Quality assurance became a real cause for manufacturing. In his 14-step quality improvement program, Phil Crosby's (1979) ideas, such as "zero defects" and "quality is free," were significant revisions to managerial thought at the time. Agile manufacturing suggested that quality was the necessary centerpiece for a manufacturing business. The prevailing attitude prior to this time was that some defective production items were normal and it was necessary to have elaborate inspection processes and rework methods, but alas, some bad parts were going to get through. The accepted practice was to have a staff of trained inspectors check the product quality of material from vendors and as it passed from one area of the plant to the next. The basis of this thinking was that production workers were so busy making things that they would make some that were not correct; thus, an evaluation by an independent third party was necessary. It was impossible to think that workers could or would check their work. This made for some interesting attitudes on the plant floor where quality assurance personnel were frequently seen as the enemy. The quality revolution changed all that by rejecting the idea that defects were a necessary part of life. Rather, it focused on the proactive idea that it was more profitable to prevent defects than to rework them, and getting production worker participation was crucial.

At the same time new tools, including quality circles and SPC, were being widely implemented. Another idea was to improve the design for manufacture, to remove or change processes that could negatively affect quality. The new approach placed the responsibility for quality squarely in the hands of the people who did the production, a major change in management and production worker thinking.

Inventory

Also included in activities at this time was a major effort to reduce inventory through the use of JIT material delivery. The idea was to reduce the inventory as well as the supporting costs, such as unnecessary movement and plant-floor storage space. Other inventory management improvements included:

- Improved plant-floor process layout to eliminate or reduce inventory movement.
- Synchronized processes to deliver subassemblies and component to match assembly needs.
- Lot size reduction and reevaluations of economic order quantity concepts. A frequently heard objective was to manufacture using a "lot size of one."
- Some effort to include suppliers in inventory and delivery discussions.

Change

A major change occurred in the management of people, particularly production workers. Ideas such as worker empowerment and quality circles became real production concepts with the recognition that production workers had a lot to offer toward improving production processes. Instead of confrontation and rigid production rules, the knowledge of the plant worker was actually solicited, bringing with it a new level of trust, appreciation, and a transfer of responsibility. In some companies, workers were given the ability to stop a production line whenever nonconforming product quality was seen.

Flexibility

Flexibility in manufacturing became an important part of production system design and plant management. The "lot-size-of-one" approach was aggressively pursued. The ability to change schedules to respond to customers' requirements more quickly and to rapidly introduce product design changes with IT tools, such as CAD and computer-aided manufacturing (CAM), became widely implemented.

Other concepts

Other concepts employed by agile manufacturers include:

- Cellular manufacturing — An idea of defining production cells to make products within a family. The idea is to have greater knowledge in operator skill and reduce inventory movement.
- Capacity planning — An early tool to determine the current plant capacity based on the order mix. Computer simulation is used to examine and optimize planned production.
- Paperless factory — The idea of using computers and plant-floor devices to track and mange production orders so as to eliminate plant-floor paperwork.

People

The general attitude toward production people changed. Since the 1930s when trade unions became a legal and powerful force, the relationship between the exempt and the nonexempt worker had become more and more adversarial. The "white collar" worker was definitely separate from the "blue collar." There were at least two major change agents:

- Japanese auto manufacturers were very strong during the 1980s and began building plants in the United States. Their attitudes were much more egalitarian, treating everyone, including supervisors, engineers, and production workers, as equals and each as an important part in the process. Maintaining nonunion status (not always successful) and maintaining a cooperative, we-are-all-in-this-together attitude, was an important part of management and a change for the American worker.
- As technology-oriented industries grew, they too operated on the basis of teamwork. Many of their workers were highly trained and hired for their intellectual abilities as well as their physical ones.

These were major changes in manufacturing management. Many companies took on a new mantra of dedication to the production worker. In many cases, companies became employee owned. The idea that an involved employee at any level could have ideas for improvement and could be seen as a company asset became common.

In *Agile Competitors and Virtual Organizations* (Goldman, Nagel, and Preiss, 1995), agility was described in these dimensions:

- Enriching the customer: An agile company is one that is perceived by its customers as enriching them in a significant way, not only the company itself.
- Cooperating to enhance competitiveness: Cooperation, both internally and with other companies, is an agile company's operational strategy of first choice.
- Organizing to master change and uncertainty: An agile company is organized in a way that allows it to thrive on change and uncertainty.

- Leveraging the impact of people and information: In an agile company, management nurtures an entrepreneurial company culture that leverages the impact of people and information.

The agile company was and is a general concept suggesting flexibility and a view that is external in nature. This was not an idea that gave away the company or abandoned realistic management processes but instead focused on an inclusive concept of greater stakeholder participation that included customers, suppliers, and employees. This was a major turning point in business and manufacturing management. It was the point where IT was introduced as a tool for manufacturing while at the same time business changes demanded a cooperative and participative manufacturing management process.

Another focused program dedicated to improving the production process is lean manufacturing. With many adherents and supporters, lean is an ever more common part of manufacturing management. Lean manufacturing is essentially an effort to adapt the Toyota production system — a system that has been strongly supported by collaborative relationships, used in Toyota automotive plants — to other industries. Lean manufacturing is somewhat more specific than agile manufacturing in that there is an actual outline of principles, a number of books on the subject, and a substantial amount of collateral information to explain and support the concepts. This overview of lean manufacturing is largely taken from two sources: *Lean Thinking* (Womack and Jones, 1996) and "Beyond Lean" by Flinchbaugh of the Lean Learning Center (www.LeanLearningCenter.com).

At first glance it might be appealing to look at a successful company and copy its methods. If those methods are simple and obvious, that may be possible; but to transfer the culture of a company is a completely different thing. Such is the case with lean manufacturing, which is not about simply copying a few methods. It is about reinventing your company along certain principles to follow a philosophy. The basis for lean manufacturing is comprised of these four rules:

- Structure every activity
- Clearly connect every customer
- Specify and simplify every flow
- Improve through experimentation at the lowest level possible toward the ideal state

The four rules contain the following five principles:

1. **Directly observe work as activities, connections, and flows**. Know the details and gain firsthand understanding of what is happening in the processes.
   a. *Structure, operate and improve activities, connections and flows*. Utilizing the four rules while designing, operating and improving

activities, connections, and pathways is where the bulk of lean transformation should be focused. Learn to talk about activities, connections, and flows; think in terms of them, and act on them. Activities must be structured to the minutest level of detail and relationships must be connected as binary customer/supplier links. All goods, materials, and information must flow through simple and specific pathways.

    b. *Understanding current reality requires deep observation.* Deep skill and commitment to understanding current reality are crucial in what makes lean system transformation different. Current reality does not mean using abstract measurements; it means direct observation of the activities, connections, and flows of the organization. That understanding of the current condition applies to broad company issues such as culture, but also applies to very detailed problems, such as why a certain tool isn't working or how to drive waste out of a process. Direct observation of activities, connections, and pathways is required to understand current reality. Observation done within the framework of the four rules provides the discipline of being thorough in understanding a current condition, and it provides the opportunity to be specific about what needs to change.

2. **Systematic waste elimination**

    a. *Connect to your customer and always add value.* Any goal beyond delivering the right product to the right customer at the right time at the right price is waste. Any activity that does not actually change the product being delivered is waste. All waste must be viewed as something to be reduced or eliminated. Organizations must connect all of their resources to the customer on a flow path designed to deliver value, and nothing else. The information required to deliver that value must flow through the same flow path. There must be clarity of what the customer values and how that is being provided. This includes internal functions, that is, customers within the company. Everyone has a customer, which means that everyone must find ways to add value for the customer.

    b. *Relentlessly pursue systematic waste elimination.* The definition of waste is anything that does not directly transform material or information to create value for the customer. If you can't eliminate the waste, begin with steps of reduction. If this is done relentlessly and daily for a long enough period of time, there will be a much higher ratio of value-added to non–valued-added work. Removing waste in the entire product process from design to delivery is the objective. Any of the following are candidates for waste removal:

- Overproduction
- Transportation
- Motion

- • Inventory
- • Waiting
- • Overprocessing
- • Product or process defects

3. **Establish high agreement on both what and how**. This high agreement should exist whenever coordinated action is required; therefore, for some activities, high agreement may be needed across the entire company, and in other situations, just between two or three people. The rest of the principle of high agreement calls out two specific categories: the what and the how. The what for the organization consists of goals and objectives, what markets to pursue, what costs are necessary, and so on. Without agreement on the what, an organization will work inconsistently and against itself. The second part of this principle is the how of the organization, specifically, how does the firm produce its results at the granular level of activities, connections, and flows. Seeking high agreement of the how provides not just dramatic daily performance improvement, but also the key to making those improvements sustainable. There are two elements to this principle:

   a. *Standardization is the foundation of continuous improvement: Create high agreement and no ambiguity.* Every improvement, every problem solved, and every process changed must be standardized. If it isn't standardized, high agreement on how things work does not exist. If there is no high agreement about how things work, then there is no strong operating system. Standardization applies to everything from what rules the senior management team will use to make a decision, to the pattern used to tighten bolts during the assembly process. Standardization is not just something you do. It is a continuous process of reaching a deeper and more detailed level of refinement. This is the process of continuous improvement, to be a little better each day.

   b. *Sustainable change happens only at the systems level. Lean is rules, not tools.* The system is the structure within the organization, which is made up of activities, connections, and flows, as well as mental models or ways of thinking. Detail at the systems level and system change make changes sustainable. The existing system is where the problems and opportunities lie; work on cultivating the capability of that system to solve its own problems.

4. **Systematic problem solving**. There are two elements to this principle.

   a. *See every problem as an opportunity to focus on the ideal state.* To have a world-class enterprise requires teaching everyone to adopt the attitude that every problem is an opportunity. A problem is not just when something goes wrong. A problem is any gap between current reality and the ideal state. There are many things that prevent people from viewing problems this way. Every barrier to adopting this attitude must be removed for a company to fully employ the philosophy that every problem is an opportunity to continuously improve toward the ideal condition.

    b. *Make decisions at the point of activity.* This principle will strengthen the organization for two reasons. First, no one person or team of people has enough time to solve all problems that the organization may face, and so we must engage everyone. Second, deeply understanding current reality is critical to effectively improving processes and no one understands those processes like the people who deal with them each day. Making decisions at the point of activity does not mean that the front lines solve all problems. The idea is to examine the problem from the lowest area of responsibility where the greatest knowledge exists.

5. **Create a learning organization**. Creating a learning organization at every level and through every activity is the most critical of the principles.

    a. *Create frequent points of reflection.* Be a learning organization. Reflection on how the organization works, thinks, and improves should be a daily activity integrated with your operating activities. Reflection should happen at every level of the organization and at different frequencies. The more points of reflection created, the faster, deeper, and more sustainable the transformation process will be.

    b. *Leaders must be learners and teachers.* As a company employs lean thinking the leaders will have new roles. As leaders, they must be learners. They must be open to changing themselves and involving themselves deeply in the learning and experimenting process. Leaders must also be teachers. If you cannot teach, you cannot lead. Leaders must also teach lean systems principles and rules to all involved and demonstrate how they will be used, starting with their own behaviors. Everyone from the CEO to line supervisors and workers are leaders. Leadership means understanding current reality very deeply and clearly, and having a vision for the ideal state with the understanding and ability to close the gap.

The five principles described above enable the effective application of the four rules. The four rules are the laws of lean transformation. The principles are the lens and the thinking to apply the rules and to help the process of lean transformation come alive. The principles and rules fit together as shown in Figure 11.1.

Efforts to reduce waste bring lean principles to the world of supply chain management. The ideas of supply chain collaboration or inventory synchronization are high on the list of opportunities to reduce waste (overproduction) by developing methods to address double forecasting or demand amplification. Synchronized scheduling must integrate the entire supply-chain network into a single scheduling system and deploy demand visibility

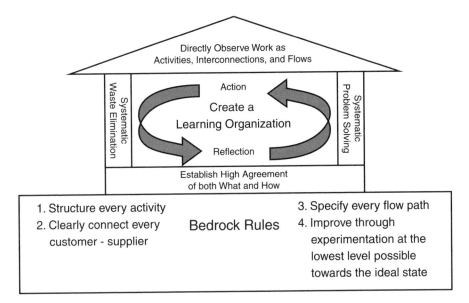

Figure 11.1 Principles and rules of lean transformation.

to all levels to achieve a "zero-waste" value system. To accomplish this, it will be necessary to provide demand visibility, process visibility, and appropriate time buffers. Each requires on-line, real-time collaboration.

In the current literature regarding manufacturing management techniques, some ideas appear over and over again. Mass customization, or the individualization of products, continues to be a general theme. Working more closely with customers and suppliers is a part of every presentation. Developing and maintaining flexibility and responsiveness are ever critical. Applying IT is the necessary supporting tool. Collaborative manufacturing helps to define specific objectives through the use of real-time information support.

Collaborative manufacturing concepts, while not a particularly new focus, add to any existing management approach. Whatever system is currently in use, the addition of improved supply-chain alignment and faster information availability will provide improvement. Collaboration is not a replacement of existing management approaches (with the possible exception of benign neglect). It is simply the next step in a long line of management system progress, from the craftsman as a one-person factory to the multinational corporation of today.

References

Crosby, P.B., *Quality Is Free*, McGraw Hill, New York, 1979.

Flinchbaugh, J., Beyond Lean, white paper, Lean Learning Center, Novi, MI.

Goldman, S.L., Nagel, R.N., and Preiss, K., *Agile Competitors and Virtual Organizations*, Van Nostrand Reinhold, New York, 1995.

Harmon, R.L. and L.D. Peterson, *Reinventing the Factory,* Free Press, New York; Collier Macmillan, 1990.

Lee, H.L., Padmanbhan, V., and Whang, S., Information distortion in a supply chain: the bullwhip effect, *Management Science*, 43, 551.

Maskell, B.H., *Software and the Agile Manufacturer,* Productivity Press, Portland, OR, 1994.

Taylor, D. and Brunt, D., *Manufacturing Operations and Supply Chain Management,* Thomson Learning, London, 2001.

Womack, J.P., Jones, D.T., *Lean Thinking*, Simon & Schuster, New York, 1996.

chapter twelve

Collaboration from the academic view

Collaborative manufacturing is little more than a cooperative strategy spread across the supply chain, and it is based on formal methods, a defined idea of trust, and more than an intuitive understanding of what is expected. Alliances, joint ventures, and collaborative efforts have been a solid part of business and society for centuries. During the past century, the academic community has done an extensive amount of work to examine and define the concept of cooperation among business entities. This study effort addresses motive and cultural issues, partner selection, management control, and other ideas to give some formal framework to the process. Although most study has been aimed at corporate-level alliances, many of the same issues have reference to the supply chain network and the objectives of collaborative manufacturing.

Cooperation has long been a hallmark of human success. The reason why we cooperate is usually determined by our relationship to some objective. Primitive man hunting in a group is one form of cooperative collaboration where individuals temporarily set aside their primary self-interest for the good of the group. Cooperation and competition have a way of getting in each other's way, and part of the relationship question is how much of a competitive edge is given up for the good of the collaborative effort. This balancing act is no less important in the application of cooperation for collaborative manufacturing, but there are reasoning processes that can provide some resolution to the challenge.

Cooperation is worthwhile only when there is a benefit to be gained. In business, cooperation can be very advantageous especially when linking with another company to fill resource or skill voids for the purpose of competing more effectively. In *Strategies of Cooperation*, Child and Faulkner (1998) have reviewed much of the literature on the subject and offer good insights on processes of cooperation. This book is recommended if you have an interest in theoretical and academic perspectives. The following ten ideas are presented in the introduction:

- Cooperative strategy is not new. It means working together to accomplish a specific advantage or goal. It is not passing orders down hierarchies.
- Commitment and trust are the key attitudes most strongly associated with success of cooperative alliances.
- Strategic alliances, including joint ventures, collaborations, and consortia, are all about organizational learning. However, many other types of cooperation, such as networks or virtual corporations, are primarily about skill substitution: that is, company A cooperates with company B because it sees that its partner can exercise a particular skill better than it can.
- Other forms of cooperative strategy, such as virtual organizations, networks, or outsourced corporations, are about capability substitution. Their strength lies in their specializations and their adaptability and flexibility, but not necessarily in the learning opportunities they afford.
- Cooperative enterprises (virtual organizations) do not do away with the need for intelligent purpose, a brain, and a central nervous (information) system if they are to achieve competitive advantage in relation to broadly integrated corporations.
- To cooperate does not mean to allow all proprietary information to pass unchecked to the partner.
- Issues of control need to be addressed, but more subtly than in hierarchies, as too great a degree of control in cooperative enterprises stifles innovation and motivation.
- A successful alliance is one that evolves into something more than was perhaps foreseen at the outset.
- The interface between the two or more company cultures is the crucible of potential achievement. Sensitivity to each other's culture is vital to effective operation. Its absence leads to a failed alliance, however great the potential economic synergies between the partners.
- Information technology makes the task of coordinating cooperative strategy that much easier, but it cannot and must not be allowed to substitute for bonding between cooperating company executives.

After study and examination of the narrower application of cooperation in collaborative manufacturing, the issues appear to be nearly the same as those listed above. The one significant difference is collaborative manufacturing is not about equals, as any customer/supplier relationship does have economic overtones. The academic view addresses cooperation in the broadest sense of joint ventures and alliances and their legal nuances. The view in this book is about cooperation to the benefit of the value chain partners.

Collaboration can be viewed from a number of perspectives, including economic perspectives, game theory, strategic management theory, and organization theory. For purposes of this book, I limit the review to economic perspectives.

- Market power theory is concerned with the ways in which firms can improve their competitive position by building a stronger competitive position. The collaborative advantage makes this possible.
- Transaction cost economics was discussed in Chapter 2. Closer relationships can reduce the cost of doing business.
- Agency theory is concerned with the ability of principals (buyers) to ensure that their agents (suppliers) are meeting their objectives.
- Increasing returns theory addresses the idea of companies forming alliances to achieve dominance in a market early in its development to avoid losing the dominant position to a competitor.

Trust has been mentioned earlier as a significant factor in collaboration and that is restated strongly by theorists. One definition of trust between cooperating businesses refers to the willingness of one party to relate with another in the belief that the other's actions will be beneficial rather than detrimental to the first party. This seems to apply as well to our purposes of collaboration.

To trust is to take risks. Uncertainty and expectations that may not be met always exist. One dimension of trust is calculative trust — what is expected and what are the downside issues. Another dimension of trust is shared understanding. Knowing the other party allows development of a mutual understanding. A third dimension is people sharing a mutual personal identity. Mutual respect, common goals, and mutual views of obligations can provide a sense of comfort and trust.

Trust can be built and fortified. There are processes to help trust develop between cooperating firms, but without trust the likelihood of alliance failure is certain. The need for trust is obvious and intuitive. There is no substitute.

Motives for collaboration go beyond what we might assume or take for granted. In *Cooperative Strategies in International Business*, Contractor and Lorange (1988) list some objectives for the formation of various types of cooperative arrangements.

- Reducing the time to bring a new product to market
- Risk reduction through broader partner involvement
- Achievement of economies of scale and/or rationalization
- Technology exchanges
- Co-opting or blocking competition
- Overcoming government-mandated trade or investment barriers
- Facilitating initial international expansion of inexperienced firms
- Vertical quasi-integration advantages of linking the complementary contributions of partners in a "value chain"

Other authors have identified external and internal factors leading companies to seek cooperative relationships. External factors include:

- Turbulence in world markets and high economic uncertainty
- The existence of economies of scale and/or scope as competitive cost-cutting agents

- The globalization or regionalization of a growing number of industries
- The globalization of technology
- Fast technological change leading to ever-increasing investment requirements
- Shortening product life cycles

Internal factors might include:

- To achieve economies of scale and of learning with one's partner
- To get access to the benefits of the other firm's assets, be these technology, market access, capital, production capacity, products, or labor
- To reduce risk by sharing it, notable in terms of capital requirements, but also with respect to research and development costs
- To help shape the market — for example, to withdraw capacity in a mature market

The process of selecting the right partners may be obvious based on your current relationships with major suppliers or it may not. We have discussed the reasons for cooperation, the issue of trust, and the motives and reasons behind businesses cooperating. In most instances, the cooperation being anticipated in a collaborative manufacturing relationship will be based on close historical experience between two or more companies. The existing relationship is the primary impetus toward collaboration, but there may be instances where a closer examination of the prospective partner is in order. Porter and Fuller (1986) identify six areas of evaluation for a collaborative partner:

- Possession of the desired source of competitive advantage
- Complementary or balanced contribution
- Comparable view of strategy
- Low risk of being or becoming a competitor
- Preemptive value in relation to rivals
- High organizational compatibility

There are many other criteria that might fall into this area of choice, but these form the fundamental bases for decisions. In this day of third-party manufacturers serving multiple major clients, new concerns may arise regarding capacity, scaled growth potential, cost management (current and future), and management compatibility. There is also the objective of easy engagement and disengagement in structuring relationships. Once having reviewed and satisfied the qualifications of the partner, some basis for the collaboration will depend on negotiation and the value established by the partners. Once again, Child and Faulkner (1998) have addressed the issue and offer the following negotiation guidelines.

- The creation of a perceived win/win situation leads to a more effective alliance

- The benefits and not just the costs should be considered in valuing assets to be put into or used in the alliance
- The strength of need of the partners will influence the value negotiations
- The uniqueness of a particular asset, such as a brand name or technology, creates a premium value determinable only by negotiation
- The valuation range of an asset will be somewhere between its existing value and the assessed value of future benefits to the alliance
- The position in the valuation range will depend on the relative strength of the partners, their possible alternative courses of action to the alliance, uniqueness of assets, and negotiating ability and forebearing or hard attitude of the partners

The question of control should be treated openly and up front to avoid false expectations that will require future adjustment or bring failure. It has been stated that a win/win environment is necessary to avoid stifling of innovation. The relationship must be equally satisfying to each party in the area of control, but that will vary depending on earlier values given to participants. If the value chain host has three vendors for each major supplied item and this is acceptable at the outset, the win/win feeling may exist but control might not be the same. However, the exercise of control both in style and content is a greater issue in collaboration, particularly when viewed across a supply chain network. If a supplier provides 25% of its output to one customer that has ten other reliable sources, the relationship and the mechanisms to manage and control will be different. This is obvious when studying relationship control but much less so when actual negotiations are in progress. If the 500-pound gorilla customer makes a request, the tendency to say yes comes very easily.

The literature suggests a gatekeeper role on both sides to facilitate communications between partners. The relationship requires certain personality qualities that are positive and supportive. This is not a place for confrontational personalities. Project team leaders will have a continuing role in the relationships similar to the gatekeeper to provide stable direction and leadership during development of the collaboration detail agreement and after implementation and start-up.

Other considerations affecting collaboration include the partners' cultures and how the organizations will learn and grow. Issues of culture and learning are more than just passing concerns. A hard-driving company that responds quickly with product changes will not do well with partners that do not respond equally. Vendor relationships are a possible point of cultural dissension. Another point might include currency of information technology systems and their responsiveness. The ability to learn and grow toward higher performance levels could be another point of contention.

The last consideration that should be defined up front is exit strategies. What is the process for withdrawal and disengagement? The academic literature does not give much guidance on the subject of withdrawal, probably due to the usual condition of expected continuation of agreements. In collaborative manufacturing alliances, conditions do suggest and expect the coupling and decoupling of partners within the supply chain network, either with the host choosing other sources or the supplier choosing alternative opportunities. This is obviously an area of potential conflict when considering proprietary information exchange and retrieval, be it product design information, operation methods, or market and pricing data. The collaboration agreement should also contain information that addresses the exit arrangement with details that include inventory, tooling, and drawing disposition, proprietary information handling, employee issues, and dispute resolution.

Much has been written on the subject of alliances and collaboration; however, the subject in this book is applying collaborative concepts to the supply chain network. The primary difference with collaborative manufacturing appears to be the inclusion of economic buy/sell relationships between the partners, whereas most alliance research looks at relationships at a joint venture level where parties invest in the combination for the purpose of a success that may or may not include intercompany trading. In collaborative manufacturing, the alliance is based primarily on the supplier/customer relationship and advantages that can be gained through something other than the historic arms-length business process. This seems to be an alteration of participant roles, but not something that should cause managers to disregard what has been learned about managing business relationships. If the objectives of collaborative manufacturing relationships are solid, it is likely that experience gained in the past is just as applicable in today's environment.

References

Child, J. and Faulkner, D., *Strategies of Cooperation*, Oxford University Press, Oxford, 1998.

Contractor, F.J. and Lorange, P., *Cooperative Strategies in International Business*, Lexington Books, New York, 1988.

Porter, M.E. and Fuller, M.B., *Coalitions and Global Strategy*, Harvard Business School Press, Boston, 1986.

Porter, M.E., Ed., *Competition in Global Industries*, Harvard Business Press, Boston, 1986.

chapter thirteen

Automotive industry collaboration

The automotive industry is a very large and complex global industry made up of the largest multinational corporations with a range of products that includes automobiles, trucks, and mass transit busses. Top-level companies include General Motors Corporation, Ford Motor Company, Toyota, Nissan, Daimler-Chrysler, Volkswagen, Volvo, Honda, Kia, and others. These companies are usually referred to as original equipment makers (OEMs). The multitiered supply chain is made up of very large companies that may or may not be global in their reach. First-level vendors are referred to as tier-one suppliers and their suppliers as tier-two suppliers and so on through the hierarchy. Some suppliers serve only one OEM while others serve a variety of customers. Although supplier relationships are not permanent, they do not change at a rapid pace. Investment in facilities and production capacity is high and margins are always thin and based on high volume. The original equipment customer is only one side of the market, as after-market replacement part sales can continue for many years.

The industry is in a constant state of change to react to a variety of issues ranging from product design to meet changing market demands, to globalization of production facilities and political swings in the many countries in which they operate. This is a multitiered industry with a very broad supply-chain network of production material and production equipment suppliers.

Product cycle times are generally considered long term, with some models lasting years. Development periods can be lengthy, taking as long as 36 months or more from approval of a design to the time that production begins and the car is available to the market. The product life cycle is affected in the short term by frequent annual changes to the product and the production facilities.

The industry has been in a multiyear transition, moving from very vertically integrated production processes to focusing more on core competencies and outsourcing component manufacturing and services. At the same time, industry consolidation has brought a mixed bag of supplier relationships and overcapacity. The industry is huge in any measurement scheme. There are over 30 primary producers and over 2000 direct suppliers of products and services.

The industry is being driven to further change for many reasons. Today's issues include:

- **Improved time to revenue** — The time required to bring a product to the market can be extensive. With a total cost for a new product launch estimated to be in the range of $1 billion plus, reducing the time to begin generating revenue is a significant objective. Down from 60 months only a few years ago, progress is being made but there is room for improvement.
- **Improved part traceability** — The liability and warranty issues in this industry require improved methods of component traceability. The objective is to provide for most major components a product history that identifies the complete sourcing and production history from any origination point within the supply chain to the end user.
- **Design for manufacture** — The area of product design has been an area of supplier collaboration for some time. Collaborative product development includes design for manufacturing input from supply chain sources that examine reduced assembly times and easier production complexity.
- **Modularization** — There has been continuing movement of outsourcing by the OEMs to larger components called modules, where vendors assume responsibility for a fully functioning module and the correct delivery of that module to the assembly line in accordance with the build schedule. The OEM sets the meta-design rules that are used to guide the supplier in product design and development, shifting the responsibility for supply-chain product design and production coordination to the tier-one supplier.
- **Mass customization** — As the market looks for individualized vehicles (built to order versus built to a dealer inventory), the variety of product availability is increasing. This will require reexamining supplier arrangements and new ideas of inventory availability and transport. A current industry objective is to reduce lead times to produce a finished product from 30 days to 5 days from receipt of a product order.
- **Quality** — Current quality objectives are to reach reject levels of 2 parts per million.
- **Logistics** — The industry has set some objectives for suppliers to meet. They include shorter order lead times — as low as 2 hours in some instances — to match the assembly line schedule. On-time delivery of 98.5% and higher is the norm.

Many of these issues are currently the focus of collaboration among automotive manufacturers and their suppliers. Collaboration has been a part

Product Development: Definition
The complete set of extended enterprise activities required to support the manufacturing of new products
which includes advanced development through launch and life cycle support

Activities

Figure 13.1 Definition of product development. (Reprinted with permission of OESA.)

of the industry practice for some time. There have been some bumps in the road, many of which relate to information systems and data transfer. Progress is being made in this area with the work of the Automotive Industry Action Group (AIAG) and the Original Equipment Suppliers Association (OESA). AIAG is an association of companies within the automotive industry that focuses on enhancing business processes and practices involving trading partners throughout the supply chain. The association has published standards that address nearly every sector of the business. OESA is an association made up of suppliers to the industry and has many areas of interest, particularly in the area of e-commerce issues, such as manufacturing collaboration and product development collaboration.

The industry is embarking on product life-cycle collaboration with very high ambitions. In product design, the focus is on bringing together multiple decision makers early in the process. In Chapter 6, an outline by the OESA presents the business case scenario for the use of collaborative design tools. As a part of the education process, the Association is pursuing an effort to define external collaborative product design between customers and suppliers (Figure 13.1). The OESA's definition of this activity follows: The complete set of extended enterprise activities required to support the manufacturing of new products, which includes advanced development through launch and life cycle support.

According to a report from AMR Research (O'Mara and Prouty, 2002), if design collaboration is executed flawlessly, the 10-year payoff could exceed savings of $1600 per finished vehicle. Flawless execution is not to be assumed a *fait accompli,* as there are many issues to address before the payoff is reached. Some of their estimates offer very interesting possibilities.

- Over 75% of the product cost is set up front in the conceptual design phase.
- If products can be brought to market 50% faster, expenses associated with new vehicle programs can be cut 20% to 30% and the risk of missing the customer demand window is reduced.
- Design reuse can reduce vehicle program expenses through lower warranty costs; faster engineering time; and better tooling, testing, and documentation. It can also reduce errors in all these functions.

In the same report, AMR identified some specific areas of savings opportunities:

- **Engineering labor efficiency** — Engineering labor hours are estimated to be as low as 30% efficient. By reducing meeting, travel, document search, error correction, and other non–value-adding time in engineering, efficiency will double to 60%.
- **Engineering IT support costs** — Dedicated IT personnel attached to engineering functions could be reduced with superior CAD integration tools and less hand integration to product data management (PDM) and other systems.
- **Engineering travel expenses** — By allowing engineers on development teams to manage design meetings via the Web, travel expenses can be reduced by more than half.
- **Warranty expense** — Increased design reuse will reduce warranty costs using more proven parts and components.
- **Tooling expense** — Increased design reuse will reduce tooling costs by using more existing parts.
- **Assembly labor expenses** — Better design for manufacturability through the integration of CAD, BOM, and CAPE systems will reduce labors hours per vehicle.
- **Direct materials cost** — Increased design reuse, platform reuse, and part count reduction will allow lower cost sourcing by reducing the variability of demand to suppliers, purchasing leverage, and purchasing process costs.
- **Feature-driven revenue** — Faster and more comprehensive sharing of design concepts across engineering, manufacturing, and marketing will allow more value-added features to be cost effectively included in the final design, supporting higher, final net sales prices.
- **Finished goods inventory** — By extending vehicle platform reuse, postponement strategies will allow higher rates of manufacture to order, which will reduce finished goods inventories.

The area of product design collaboration appears to offer significant opportunities to improve the product and the cost structure, not only at the design phase, but also through the life of the product by including field information from the customer. There are a few obstacles in the way as noted in the AMR report (O'Mara and Prouty, 2002), including the resistance to change and intellectual property issues. It will not be easy, but the opportunities appear to be well worth the effort. (See Figure 13.2.)

Production/inventory synchronization in this industry is known as demand collaboration. The goal of demand collaboration is to move the planning system BOM explosion process out from behind the four walls of the OEM into an industry portal (public marketplace). Here, an OEM would publish its demand, the material requirements explosion would occur, and

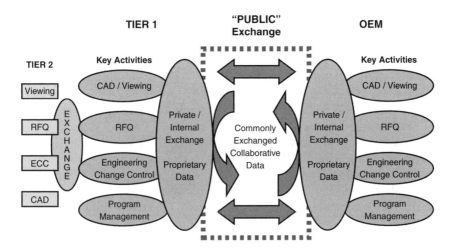

Figure 13.2 Process map for collaborative process development. (Reprinted with permission of OESA.)

the suppliers would then review the demand and respond as to whether they can meet it. If somewhere in the supply chain a supplier cannot meet the demand, the customer can then act accordingly to source additional parts from a competitor, move the demand forward in the schedule if additional capacity at the supplier exists, and so on. The goal is to identify bottlenecks and smooth out forecasts before they affect the process.

There are, however, significant challenges to demand collaboration. For demand to be properly calculated, everyone in the supply chain must update inventory, shipments, receipts, usages, and yields using real-time information both to identify and to confirm the current actual condition, all prior to the BOM explosion. If this information is not current, results of the requirements explosion will be incorrect and the collaboration process will be more of a data entry exercise to update the demand manually.

The OESA is working to address opportunities in this area through its Supply Chain Management Study Group. The study group (OESA, 2001) lists the following items as requirements:

- Create visibility throughout the supply chain.
- Automate activities.
- Provide alert messaging to support management by exception.
- Supplier electronic communication.
- Be able to collaborate electronically through the use of technology tools that:
  - Improve information velocity
  - Provide information visibility
  - Provide information aggregation
  - Enable vertical collaboration

In distribution/order fulfillment, the CPFR guidelines are starting to gain traction. Many of the OEMs have already begun to implement VMI programs. While most of these implementations have focused on stores items (nuts, bolts, gloves, offices supplies, etc.), implementations are starting to occur for purchased parts and raw materials. Some companies are now using VMI systems to communicate updated inventory status on an hourly basis.

One problem in this area is that information being communicated to the supplier is frequently not current, as many companies maintain the perpetual inventory data in their enterprise resource planning systems, the primary information source for VMI applications. Because many companies do not yet report shop-floor information on a real-time basis (production numbers are usually reported at the end of a shift or run), the data in the enterprise resource planning systems may not be current. Effective manufacturing collaboration requires on-line data from the production processes to ensure that all systems are working with current information.

Another complication of collaboration is the suppliers' requirement to subscribe to multiple software systems, either through an application service provider model or by investing in an enterprise user license. Depending on which system their customer is using, suppliers will need to use the appropriate front-end applications to receive and process the data. If the software system on the buyer's side is different from what the supplier has in place, the cost to transfer the information can be quite high and beyond any value to the supplier.

Suppliers are working together through the AIAG, and are looking at ways to reduce these costs. Their goal is to get the software vendors together to develop a common data format using XML. This common format is a major key to allow these disparate applications to talk to one another. Trying to get the numerous companies to work with each other and agree on a common format is going to be a significant challenge, but there seems to be mutual agreement among vendors that this must occur.

A collaborative competitive advantage can be gained when suppliers join together for a defined project and length of time to jointly develop and build a particular module. Similar to contract manufacturing in the electronics industry, automotive OEMs are starting to require their tier-one suppliers to become full-system suppliers by accepting the responsibility to design and build a module and each of its components. Each of the next-tier suppliers will then be responsible for making their component and providing it to the tier-one supplier to assemble and ship. This use of collaboration can be seen with Daimler-Chrysler and some of their suppliers at their truck plant in Brazil, where Dana Corporation provides one of 17 different rolling chassis designs to the assembly plant within a 2-hour lead time. At this same plant, Lear Corporation provides an interior module that includes seats, carpet, sun visors, and back panels. These are long-term commitments to collaboration that require on-line, real-time information systems to maintain synchronized production and inventory information between the two immediate companies as well as other suppliers.

Although standards have been developed, electronic data interchange (EDI) tools have not been implemented very deeply in the supply chain. One of the concerns in this industry is how lower-tier suppliers will react to the requirement for closer collaboration through electronic connections. To gain an understanding of the perception that usage was bottlenecked at the second-tier level, a study was done by the AIAG (Cornell, 2001) to determine what barriers were keeping companies from embracing this technology. The study found technology and cost barriers, as well as trust issues, such as the following:

- Unstable relationships with higher-tier customers
- A lack of confidence in industry initiatives
- A concern for upper-tier process inconsistency
- Little information as to future plans and strategies provided to most lower-tier suppliers
- A lack of loyalty by upper-tier customers to their suppliers

The ideas behind closer information transfer appear to be cost effective, but the trust environment presents considerable weight against investing in something that is not embraced by the broader range of supply chain partners. Another negative effect has been data integrity, as available information has not been reliable. The result is that suppliers are still making telephone calls to get the "real information."

New technology and the Internet are seen as important new tools to improve information availability and enable closer supplier integration. By automating manual activities and by developing the ability to collaborate electronically with real-time information from the production processes, the supply chain network is improved. The industry has been a magnet for information system ideas that would provide improvement. This has resulted in systems being custom developed for specific applications that were very expensive and not very reliable. The industry is looking for improvement but, like most industries, well-defined solutions that have evolved to a level of performance, reliability, and cost that ensure successful use by all levels of the supply chain are necessary. A wide consensus exists that software systems in general have not yet matured to the point that suits the broader issues of this industry. As companies extend to a global reach looking to increase their customer base, they must be able to implement best-of-breed systems and adapt their current business processes accordingly.

The expectation is that the supply chain network will evolve to a pure hub-and-spoke model to meet the varying needs of the automotive industry. This model, shown in Figure 13.3, will provide the ability to accelerate electronic communications, share information collaboratively, build industry leadership, drive technology solutions, develop automotive industry standards, and be an important step toward the 5-day car.

The future holds interesting challenges. One of these is the trend from nonmodular to modular design, building, and shipping of components. The

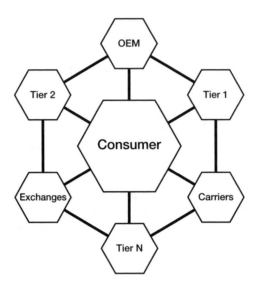

Figure 13.3 Pure "hub-and-spoke" model. (Reprinted with permission of OESA.)

nonmodular approach has made it relatively easy for an OEM to switch suppliers. Modularization will require suppliers to have a greater investment in dollars and knowledge, making it more difficult for an OEM to replace a supplier, and thus increasing the supplier's bargaining power. Another challenge is the move toward the build-to-order or x-day car that is going to lead a major transition from just-in-time parts delivery to build on demand/order to delivery, giving greater impetus to modularization.

With Internet-mediated procurement, and rapid, low-cost dissemination of information, suppliers' relationships with the OEMs are likely to change. The relationship is expected to become less personal with real-time information systems as the main conduit for production-requirements demand information, and plant-floor systems as the source of information that confirms the virtual inventory is available according to plan.

The full impact of the Internet has not yet been determined. The benefits, such as speed, accuracy, and improved communications, are necessary to support the numerous initiatives of the OEMs. The expectation is that companies that can adapt technology changes most rapidly will be the ones to grow and increase market share as improved production results through applied technology can be the differentiator among competitors.

The automotive industry, especially Toyota and Chrysler, has defined early collaboration relationships. As the industry moves through consolidation to reduce overcapacity, works to reduce the time and cost to bring a new product to market, and reaches toward the 5- or even 10-day car, the need to employ closer collaboration with all of their partners will be a cornerstone of their progress. Supply chains are likely to become closer and more identifiable as competing units, requiring tighter and more accurate information management to ensure that each process of the system is in proper synchronization with every other process through delivery to the customer. Collaboration is alive and well in the automotive industry and still has a long way to go.

References

Cornell, K., Why EDI Is a Tough Sell to Lower Tiers, AIAG VOLT Project white paper, Automotive Industry Action Group, Southfield, MI, April 2001.

Fine, C.H. and Raff, D.M.G., Internet-Driven Innovation and Economic Performance in the American Automobile Industry, E-business white paper, Reginald H. Jones Center for Management Policy, Strategy, and Organization, The Wharton School, University of Pennsylvania, Philadelphia, PA, 2000.

Green, J., Manufacturing revolution underway in Brazil: companies build emerging market templates, *Ward's AutoWorld*, August 1998.

Helper, S. and MacDuffie, J.P., E-volving the Auto Industry: E-Commerce Effects on Consumer and Supplier Relationships, white paper, Reginald H. Jones Center for Management Policy, Strategy, and Organization, The Wharton School, University of Pennsylvania, Philadelphia, PA, April 2000.

O'Mara, K. and Prouty, K., What Is the Return on Design Collaboration in Automotive?, white paper, AMR Research, Boston, MA, 2002.

Original Equipment Suppliers Association, Collaborative Product Design Study Team Findings and Recommendations, OESA, March 2001.

Original Equipment Suppliers Association, Supply Chain Management Study Team Report, OESA, March 2001.

Veloso, F., The automotive supply chain organization: global trends and perspectives, white paper, Massachusetts Institute of Technology, Cambridge, MA, September 2000.

chapter fourteen

Life science industries

The life science industry includes a broad range of manufacturers with products ranging from bandages to pharmaceuticals and hospital equipment. Companies range in size from global giants, such as Merck, Johnson & Johnson, Aventis, Pharmacia, and General Electric Medical Systems, to small, fewer-than-20 employee companies developing their products or serving supplier functions for larger firms. This is a manufacturing industry with global supply chains and global distribution. The significant, most unique factor is the regulation by governmental agencies, such as the U.S. Food and Drug Administration (FDA) and equivalent agencies in other countries.

This business domain is comprised of a wide range of companies and products, but for purposes of this text, three major sector categories will be discussed. The categories include manufacturers of pharmaceutical products, biotechnology products, and medical devices, such as x-ray machines or MRI scanners, and body implant products, such as pacemakers or stents used to repair blocked blood vessels. Drug products can range from prescription products to over-the-counter products, such as aspirin or cough drops.

The following issues form the daily perspective of business managers in this industry.

- Of paramount importance is compliance with procedures issued by government agencies that measure every element of the product life cycle. Beginning from the initial concept of a product through the full product life cycle, companies must follow detailed rules and processes that cover nearly aspect of development and manufacturing processes.
- New pharmaceutical product development costs are estimated at over $800 million and can take 10 to 15 years. Only three out of ten new compounds get through the clinical trial process. Managing and improving the time to develop and bring a new product to market are obviously critical concerns.

- Merger and acquisition activities have been and are expected to continue as a general condition of the industry. The acquisition strategy is aimed at company growth and new products as companies buy technologies at the development stage and apply global resources to bring them to market. This consolidation has left many islands of information and disconnected business processes across nearly every enterprise. Connecting the various facilities and their business processes with usable information is an industry need of paramount importance. The activity drivers here include multiple compliance environments, many legacy point solutions with difficult interconnection capability, and the need to provide clean and accurate data to business systems and supply chain partners.

- A similar area of collaboration consideration is the growing use of third-party contract manufacturers. The focal point is on product and quality-assurance information transfer from supply chain partners and internal facilities that can comply with the requirements of the FDA's 21 Code of Federal Regulations Part 11 concerning electronic records and electronic signatures.

- The use of CPFR and other distribution tools are being applied across many areas of the delivery side of the supply chain to meet the needs of the retail industry in pharmaceutical prescriptions and over-the-counter products. Vendor-managed inventory methods are in common use to serve hospitals and other medical-service delivery processes.

- Mass customization is seen as an important wave of the future. The idea of generating a drug or a medical device in response to a patient-specific formulation or a patient group–specific formulation is expected to grow. While some argue that this is only an imaginative idea which may someday be viable, others see it as a near-reality, result of converging medical sciences.

- Collaboration in most companies is a matter of sharing information. In regulated industries, the idea of sharing information takes on additional considerations, particularly when normal electronic tools such as the Internet are included in a network. Certain items of information must meet FDA rules as spelled out in the FDA's 21 Code of Federal Regulations, Part 11, which concerns electronic records and electronic signatures. Electronic records are defined as any combination of text, graphics, data, audio, pictorial, or other information in digital form that is created, modified, maintained, archived, retrieved, or distributed by a computer system. Electronic signatures are defined as a computer data compilation of any symbol or series of symbols executed, adopted, or authorized by an individual to be the legally binding equivalent of the individual's handwritten signature. Most manufacturing process information and the transfer of information must meet these regulations. Information generation, transfer, and storage sources such as MESs must also meet these standards.

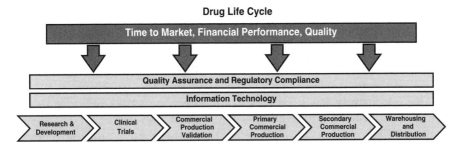

Figure 14.1 Drug life cycle.

Most major players in the industry have long and arduous product development processes that usually take many years, very large budgets, and teams of people (Figure 14.1). It is not always enough to just have data. In this industry data must be properly managed to protect product safety and quality and to comply with government guidelines. This requires systems to provide comprehensive management of production procedures and product information, including the creation, control, release, and version control of process data, such as production procedures, standard operating procedures, procedural descriptions, recipes, BOMs, routings, operations, and process-related data. As a product is developed, the process for manufacture is as much a matter of record as the actual ingredient recipe or BOM item. The definition of the manufacturing processes is called good manufacturing practices (GMPs). The GMPs along with the actual process information for the specific batch forms the batch record (BR). The BR will generally contain process data, quality assurance and environmental information, and information from decision points in the process. Part of the batch record information will include confirmation signatures by management to verify compliance with GMPs.

As the BR information is developed and maintained, security that ensures the data is correct and not susceptible to tampering is an absolute requirement. The end result is a record of information that includes the process steps, the results for a batch having passed through the process steps, and the identification of persons who confirm compliance and data integrity. The result is a validated BR, an information wrapper for the specific batch. The validated BR will include a roll-up of the compliance confirmations of each supplier.

A production schedule may be an important bit of information but it may not be a part of the BR. The transportation method may or may not be a part of the BR, but environmental considerations during manufacturing processes are likely included. The combination of BR data existence and accuracy should make collaboration easier. Modern MES that are built with seamless integration between modules and with built-in connections to external systems, including ERP and supply chain partners, provide an excellent information-support platform.

Collaboration is a major factor in the pharmaceutical industry to manage clinical trial information. Clinical trials involve a well-managed series of tests over extended time periods on a broadening group of users to test a new drug product. These tests can involve various sources of technical information, inventory, and processing at multiple site locations anywhere in the world, and individualized and personalized product identification.

A clinical study starts with the need to determine the efficacy of a drug in humans in different dosage forms. Parameters such as number of patients, number of countries, multilingual label texts for these countries, types of drugs used (including primary drug and comparator drugs), dosage forms and strengths, and so on are defined. A material and capacity check is then performed at all sites based on the requirements of the study. If the study is to be conducted across multiple continents or if material needed for study is in excess of what one site can supply within a reasonable amount of time, all sites can get involved in packaging supplies for the study.

Data such as item master, recipes, routings, BRs, and procedures can be defined by one site and shared across all sites involved in the implementation. Furthermore, a simple inventory check from one site to the other sites' warehouses can enable the site to pull materials from other sites and make them available relatively quickly for study.

Listed below are some benefits that can be derived from the deployment of a collaborative system across multiple sites.

- **Information gathering**: The data that need to be collected and documented in support of a clinical study can be enormous. Every study requires a definition of new items, recipes, and procedures, unlike conventional manufacturing where the same items, recipes, and procedures are normally defined and used for several years. Label design is a very crucial aspect of clinical studies, where each container packaged must have the right patient number and the correct drug and dosage form. Therefore, each box gets a different label for which all parameters, such as directions for use, federal caution statements, storage restrictions, warnings, and so on, have to be appropriately defined in all relevant languages. Finally, other data, such as study details, randomizations, patient kits, and so forth, have to be defined. Data gathering and documenting are very time consuming, and broadening the global reach through multiple process sites requires collaborative systems that can easily interact and share information. The idea of a fully accessible data repository is central to realizing this requirement.
- **Control of creation and modification**: In support of regulatory requirements, the collaborative system offers the ability to control the creation and modification of objects, such as items, recipes, and electronic signatures, to monitor the activities in the system and track user actions. This creates a high degree of accountability and therefore leaves less room for mistakes. Universal user groups can be

defined, made up of users from all sites to facilitate interapproval of objects between locations. For example, objects defined by one site can be approved by the appropriate users at other sites in the event of the absence or unavailability of resources due to other reasons. This allows organizations to proceed with the necessary approval processes with minimal delays.

- **Site sharing of manufacturing and packaging**: Visibility into the organization's global clinical supply warehouses helps management make key strategy decisions for planning resources and capacity among sites to fulfill study requirements. This is a huge advantage over the past methods of zero visibility and a more or less independent packaging environment. Delays caused in supplying material for studies have been nearly completely eliminated by the new collaborative manufacturing environment. The organization can now realize its primary prerequisite for product success — speed to market.
- **Material traceability on all batches produced on the shop floor**: This comes in the form of backward- and forward-tracing reports that any user can print, either as part of regular reporting procedures or, in case of an emergency, at the clinical center. Pharmaceutical organizations must provide a report of all batches that were used in patient kits supplied for a study. Also if, in the middle of a study, it is discovered that a product is unsafe, the backward tracing report can be used to determine what drug components were used in making the product. Then a forward tracing report on these drug components can be used to determine what other products shipped might need to be recalled.
- **Expiration dating of drugs**: When a drug is manufactured, there are two critical dates associated with the drug — retest date and expiry date. Retest date is the date after which the drug needs to be re-assayed to determine efficacy and safety. Expiry date is the date beyond which the drug cannot be used, either because efficacy is known to be lost or for safety reasons. A collaborative system helps track retest and expiry dates of drugs shipped to clinical centers. With the help of a simple report, it is easy to check which drugs are either due for re-assay or are getting close to their expiry dates at clinical centers. The drugs can then be recalled and destroyed and resupplied if necessary.

One example of synchronized supply chain collaboration in this industry has been well deployed by Cosmed Group, a provider of ethylene-oxide sterilization services for medical devices and pharmaceuticals. Ethylene oxide sterilization is a highly toxic process that must conform to environmental and process rules, causing many manufacturers to choose to outsource this service. Customers ship pallets of manufactured products to the Cosmed facility where the palletized products are received and staged for entry into the sterilizing vessel for a three-step process consisting of preconditioning, sterilization, and aeration. This is a continuous process performed within the vessel that is monitored and controlled through each step, where each customer's product may have a unique process recipe that requires validation of parameter conformance and recording of BR information.

The process is managed by a manufacturing execution system that provides secure Internet links allowing customers to enter orders, browse schedules, and review performance information. The execution system has fully integrated scheduling, batch process control, quality assurance, statistical process control, preventative maintenance, instrument calibration, and customer service functions. Customers receive automatic e-mail notification when loads are received, sterilized, and shipped. Immediately following each sterilization process, the customer receives a preliminary sterilization record for review.

The alignment process with one customer includes a secure website that allows entry of orders from their location. The information entered includes the customer-designated tracking number (i.e., load identifier). Additional information includes product descriptions, number of pallets, date and time the product left the manufacturer, and estimated arrival time. The customer indicates the sterilization process number and can include special circumstances or information regarding the load. Once the information has been submitted and accepted by the Cosmed system, the order is shown as in transit. The customer can review these data to see all loads in transit along with their accompanying information. Processing data that become part of the BR and visible schedules gives everyone, including the inbound and outbound logistics providers, information they need to manage their tasks most effectively.

Service is what Cosmed provides and a major service factor is to turn loads around as rapidly as possible to meet the customer demand requirements. Synchronized inventory and process management is accomplished through highly visible collaborative information processes.

The use of product life-cycle management systems is widespread. Although seen most frequently in medical device suppliers, these applications are gaining in other areas of the broader industry. Application examples include an orthopedic implant manufacturer that has 17 plants with over 1000 users with access to the system to facilitate collaboration activities. In another example, a surgical equipment manufacturer cites gains including 80% reduction in engineering change-order cycle time and an 18% reduction in the new product introduction process. Another company points to a 75% reduction in the time to prepare FDA submission documents. Other typical benefits cited include:

- Improved change control and audit capabilities for compliance with 21 CFR Part 11
- Single-product information and document repository
- Maximized reuse of product information
- Extended product information and decisions across the enterprise

- A single tool to manage information associated with device master records, design history files, nonconforming material reports, and validation plans and reports
- Reviewed and remotely approved contract development projects by sharing data interactively among interested parties
- Product change collaboration across the supply chain through a defined information-sharing-and-tracking methodology with data security assured through encryption technology
- An automated process of managing nonconforming material receipts.
- A method to manage the process of medical-device reporting compliance

Issues ranging from global manufacturing to support clinical trials to meeting regulation reporting requirements to collaborative product development and supporting manufacturing process management are at the top of most industry agendas (Figure 14.2). Because of the life-affecting nature and the high cost of new products of this industry, collaboration takes on new meaning of importance as a modern enterprise management tool.

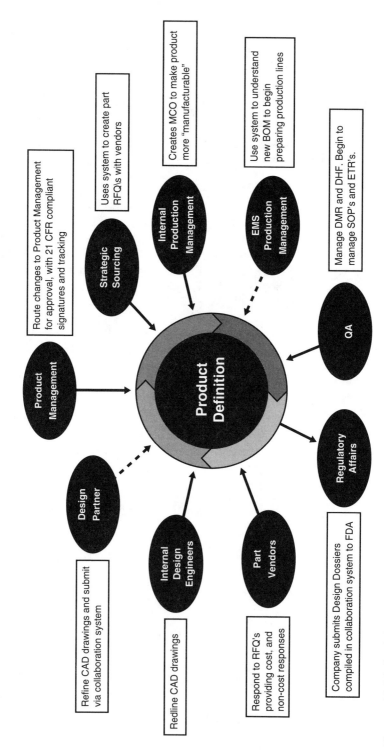

Figure 14.2 Medical device product collaboration.

References

Agile Software Corporation, Product Collaboration in the Medical Device Industry, white paper, Agile Software Corporation, San Jose, CA, 2001.

Artlinger, M., Enabling Collaboration in the Pharmaceutical Industry, white paper, eRoom Technology, Cambridge, MA, 2001.

Engel, S., $802 million: this is how much it takes to develop a new prescription drug today, *PharmaBusiness*, January 2002.

Kodama, D., CPFR advocates cite benefits despite early stage of adoption, *Managing Automation*, July 2001.

Propack Data, Electronic Records; Electronic Signatures, Final Rule, white paper, Propack Data, Cary, NC, 2001.

chapter fifteen

Electronics industry collaboration

The U.S. electronics industry is made up of more than 2500 companies, and annual sales are estimated at over $550 billion. The industry ranges from computer manufacturers to government electronics to consumer products and telecommunication equipment manufacturers and their suppliers. The industry is pervasive, affecting our lives wherever we are. There are more than 400 million Internet users worldwide and over 500 million cellular subscribers. It is difficult to imagine how the world economy would function without computers and communication systems that we now take for granted. It is obvious that this is not a monolithic industry where everybody is doing the same thing, but there are some business issues that do appear to be consistent or at least widespread.

Electronics is a global industry with manufacturers on every continent with supply chains and design teams that are operating 24 hours every day 7 days per week. A major trend in this industry is the greater emphasis being placed on volume manufacturing plants in regions such as Central Europe and Asia, particularly China. This brings the requirement for product and process portability across continents as volume manufacturing is moved from new product introduction facilities to volume plants in these regions. This portability requires additional collaboration with respect to product and process data between plants.

Product life cycles can be very short. Time to market for a new product is a critical measurement for nearly every company. Products that once had a life cycle of 18 months now have an average profit life cycle of 6 months. As innovations reach the marketplace, consumer prices are slashed and profits almost eliminated. According to one study, improving time to market by 1 month can improve profits by 11.9%. Tools that can shorten the time for design and manufacturing ramping are in strong demand.

Design and engineering changes are especially important in the electronics industry. The importance of design collaboration in electronics is realized by the emerging RosettaNet standards for high technology design and manufacturing. The RosettaNet cluster 2C for "Product Design Information" contains the following six definitions of Partner Interface Processes or PIPs:

2C1   Distribute Engineering Change Status
2C2   Request Engineering Change
2C3   Distribute Engineering Change Response
2C4   Request Engineering Change Approval
2C5   Notification of Engineering Change Order
2C6   Notification of Engineering Change Implementation

Many companies are outsourcing manufacturing to reduce capital investment and focus on core competencies of design and marketing. One example is the estimate that over 50% of all semiconductor products will be outsourced to third-party packaging and foundry houses by 2010. Doing so will require product content information to be shared, modified, and managed across a global value chain network. This also requires third-party manufacturers to provide close collaboration networks with customers to maintain confidence that production is in line with expectations.

The inventory pipeline, which is estimated at 1 year of sales, can have multiple versions of a product in process between initial vision and customer delivery, all of which are very susceptible to engineering change and market demand variables.

The bullwhip phenomenon can have a devastating effect that contributes to false shortages of material and erratic ordering patterns. Demand information collaboration for supply chain synchronization is becoming an integral part of industry relationships. In early 2001, collaborative manufacturing was brought into focus when Alan Greenspan remarked,

> The same forces that have been boosting growth in structural productivity seem also to have accelerated the process of cyclical adjustment. Extraordinary improvements in business-to-business communication have held unit costs in check, in part by greatly speeding up the flow of information. New technologies for supply-chain management and flexible manufacturing imply that businesses can perceive imbalances in inventories at a very early stage — virtually in real time — and can cut production promptly in response to the developing signs of unintended inventory building.

Many companies have used acquisition strategies to build market share and to gain capacity. Integrating the various facilities into coherent manufacturing process pipelines is a continuous and unrelenting effort.

Collaboration is alive and doing very well in this industry. Examples are the activities of the National Electronics Manufacturing Initiative (NEMI) described earlier and NEMI's effort to develop industry-led standards to provide easy inter-operability and transfer of data to and from production facilities NEMI's Plug-and-Play Factory Project was created to develop an open, vendor-independent environment for electronics assembly, inspection, and test equipment. The project addressed the issues of how to quickly integrate new pieces of electronics assembly equipment into a shop floor line management system and how to manage the vast amounts of data available in today's electronics manufacturing environment. It also addressed issues relating to the collection of shop floor data from disparate pieces of equipment and how that data could be transferred between remote locations via a Web browser. Activities focused on three areas:

- Definition of standards for a software framework that will allow interoperability among software and equipment produced by different vendors
- Development of process-specific machine communication interface standards for surface mount equipment
- Establishment of a test bed to prove the concepts developed by the project

Central to the plug-and-play effort was development of a software framework based on XML (extensible mark-up language), the universal format for structured documents and data on the Web, which encodes data into a format that is both human- and machine-readable. This platform-independent and vendor-neutral framework provides a common interface among all the hardware components on a printed circuit board manufacturing line, enabling equipment and software from various vendors to work together in a seamless fashion. It also allows data to be collected from all the machines on the line — regardless of vendor or location — and be displayed inside a Web browser.

Three standards of XML (CAMX) were developed by NEMI's Plug-and-Play Factory Project to facilitate interoperability among hardware and software components used in the manufacturing process (Figure 15.1). Based on XML, these standards provide a common interface among all the hardware

Standard	Title
IPC-2541	Generic Requirements for Electronics Manufacturing Shop-floor Equipment Communication Messages (CAMX)
IPC-2546	Sectional Requirements for Shop-floor Equipment Communication Messages for Printed Circuit Board Assembly
IPC-2547	Sectional Requirements for Electronics Manufacturing Test, Inspection, and Rework Equipment Communication

Figure 15.1 NEMI standards.

components on a printed circuit board manufacturing line. They also leverage GenCAM, the industry standard that defines how product data for printed circuit boards should be described, including information needed for tooling, manufacturing, assembly, inspection, and testing requirements. These standards are available at www.ipc.org.

PLM systems have been deployed extensively in this industry to manage the flow of engineering and product information across the supply chain. As the product life cycle continues to shorten and the supply chain broadens, there is more information that must be shared with more partners over wider distances faster. Some of the daily issues include:

- Ensuring that the precise current definition of the product is being communicated to all internal and external partners in real time.
- Knowing the current cost of the product and the effect of changes in development, production, or procurement.
- Reducing the time for new product introduction and the time to implement product changes.

Early collaborative product-development tools centered on the storage and management of engineering information and the maintenance of a central repository that was accessible to those with proper credentials. This trend has matured where today's applications include extensive abilities to manage change across the extended enterprise and gain real-time feedback from manufacturing resources to confirm the as-built information. Some of the broader impacts of the current state of the art can be seen in the following examples:

- With engineering facilities located in the United States and manufacturing facilities in China, Honeywell was able to reduce its scrap rate by 50% through reducing time to effect product changes faster and avoiding the manufacture of nonconforming products.
- Verifone was able to reduce its product change–cycle time from 25 days to 2 days across 11 engineering and manufacturing facilities.
- Microsoft was able to take advantage of a product life-cycle collaboration system to develop its Xbox console by sharing information among 200 suppliers. "Anytime a change occurred, we used the system," said Todd Holmdahl, Xbox hardware general manager. "This enabled us to communicate information to all parties involved in a vigorous formal way whenever something changed on the motherboard. The last thing you need when you're doing something as fast and as complicated as Xbox is to have compatibility problems with your technology, or not to have someone in the communication loop. Collaboration technologies are important in that they give you a formal way to communicate."
- Another example of state-of-the art manufacturing systems in today's collaborative environment is Nokia Networks, a part of the Nokia Group with headquarters in Espoo, Finland. Nokia Networks is a

leading infrastructure supplier for the mobile Internet. According to Jouni Juvonen, Team Leader, Nokia Information Management, Nokia Networks, the Production Line Control and Monitoring (PLCM) system controls the entire execution of shop orders and makes real-time manufacturing data visible on company's internal web. The PLCM project addressed several critical needs in the areas of new product introduction, manufacturing agility, and information systems integration. The PLCM platform helps the company fulfill its goal of being a leading global network infrastructure provider. Some of the main benefits of PLCM include enabling lot size of one manufacturing, recording complete product build history, providing real-time process monitoring, and managing quality data.

- Ericsson Radio Systems AB of Sweden has demonstrated effective supply chain collaboration. They produce radio base stations, devices used to make up cellular telephone system infrastructure. The order lot sizes can range from 1 to 500 for any one of 3000 different product permutations. Typical customers include AT&T, Vodafone, and other telephone service providers.

The system, originally implemented in 1999, is used to manage and track customer orders from order receipt to fourth-tier supplier authorization. The capable-to-promise decision can be determined within 10 seconds of a request based on a current view of capabilities within the supply chain. The order information is then sent throughout the extended enterprise to the currently connected 25 first-tier suppliers, 10 second-tier suppliers, 1 third-tier and 1 fourth-tier supplier.

Pontus Andersson, vice president of the Customer Configuration and Logistics Centre, offers these comments regarding the system and its development over the past 2 years:

"It was necessary to rely less on forecasting and, instead, focus on tools for operational control."

"The tools that were implemented allowed members of the supply chain to optimize themselves for the benefit of the entire supply network."

"Event-driven execution solutions could take a company or an entire supply chain a giant step closer to a frictionless flow of material through true supply chain collaboration."

"The system was not designed to be a window into our suppliers' world to serve as a means by which we could control and second guess them. Instead, the system serves as a window into Ericsson's world for each of the suppliers. They are provided with real-time demand information and parameters for replenishment."

Figure 15.2 presents statistics on the differences between the traditional supply chain and the full supply chain vision.

Traditional Supply Chain   Full Supply Chain Vision

	Traditional Supply Chain	Full Supply Chain Vision
Order Lead Time	15 days	2 days
Inventory turns	5	80
On Time delivery	20%	99.9%
Total Indirect Cost (Relative)	100	80

Figure 15.2 Traditional supply chain vs. full supply-chain vision.

A major driver of collaboration activities is the rapidly evolving practice of contract manufacturing. Many companies, large and small, are turning to sources of manufacturing expertise to help develop, manufacture, and ship their products to the end user. A typical contract manufacturer can serve as many as 50 different companies from one facility, providing services that range from simple assembly of shipped in components to full-product responsibility that includes design for manufacturability feedback, material sourcing, product test and record management, packaging, and shipment to the end user.

From the perspective of the contract manufacturer, one might imagine the tasks necessary to maintain management control over incoming inventory, scheduling, product changes, customer shipment information, and quality assurance. What started as a simple assembly process for test or overflow capacity has become a deep collaborative effort among companies with global multifacility manufacturing capability serving many different customers, such as Intel, Sun Microsystems, or Cisco Systems.

Companies in this business recognize the need to use collaborative tools from a number of perspectives:

1. Internal processes to maintain their own management control systems must be above typical standards. The argument made by the contract manufacturer is that they can do a better job by focusing on a core competency of manufacturing. Since that is the primary value they bring, the ability to perform is the center of management effort. The contract manufacturer must be everything and more than a company might expect from their own facilities.
2. The relationship with a number of high-level customers, each with their own set of suppliers, engineering changes, and varying end-user customer requirements suggests an environment with many continuous touch points and an anticipatory posture that effectively deals with every contingency before the moment of crisis on the plant floor.
3. Issues of culture and trust are just as real in this industry as any other. The ever-present concern of "How do I know my product is being produced correctly and on time?" is pervasive and must be accommodated.

The answer to trust issues is total openness and complete electronic connection for everyone. Collaboration is at the center of this industry: ERP systems linked in real time. Product life-cycle management systems installed with like systems or extensions at contractor sites, supplier locations, and customer location are common. Engineering change-order management systems that can affect different lots within the manufacturing pipeline are the norm. On-line assembly and test data are available to a variety of secured observers. And in some cases, cameras are in place allowing customers to actually see their products being assembled and tested.

Equally as important as the in-house management functions is the view for the customer. New product introduction requires information exchange and engineering change orders on a frequent basis, sometimes many times each day. It is not unusual to expect order, assembly, test, packaging, and delivery of $100,000-plus customer orders within 3 days with supply-chain response time of 2 hours from order placement to material delivery. Keep in mind that this is not an exception but is normal operating procedure in many parts of the electronic equipment industry. The requirement for real-time processes and results information to be on-line and available to the customer is obvious.

The question is how to provide the sense of security that everything is happening according to plan every day. The answer is total openness and complete connection electronically for everyone. One company uses an extensive PLM system to link every node, including customers and suppliers, into a real-time network. If a customer or a supplier does not have a system in place, this company will furnish it as an extension of their own. If the customer has a noncompatible system, the company develops a link to its PLM system so that information can be transferred bilaterally. The PLM system is set up with product and process information relative to each facility since plants in China and California may have different processes. This allows each production facility to see and manage processes on a local basis.

As indicated in Chapter 10, the idea of collaboration has had a major impact on this industry. The efforts by NEMI to provide easy "plug-and-play" connections for manufacturers in a supply chain have already brought significant rewards. As the electronics industry continues to focus more on core competencies of design and development and deals with ever shorter product life cycles, collaboration with a wide range of supply chain partners seems to be the obvious direction to take. With major companies such as Intel, Sun Microsystems, and Cisco Systems leading the way, other organizations in the industry will be pressured to keep pace.

References

Andersson, P., Automated Collaborative Execution and the Real-Time Supply Chain, white paper, Educational Society for Resource Management (APICS), Alexandria, VA, 2001.

Cartwright, J. and Goldstein, B., Virtual factory: improving supply chain communications, *Circuits Assembly*, September 2000.

Dugenske, A., Fraser, A., Nguyen, T., and Voitu, R., *International Journal of Computer Integrated Manufacturing*, 13(3), May–June, 2000.

Electronic Industries Alliance, *Electronic Industry Primer*, Electronic Industries Alliance, Arlington, VA, 2002.

Kodama, D., Speeding communications, *Managing Automation*, December 2001.

Shah, J.B. and Serant, C., Microsoft's Xbox sets supply chain standard, *EBN*, 11 March 2000.

Substantial information in this chapter was furnished by Andrew Robbie and Alan Fraser of Teradyne, Inc. They have long been active in standards development groups such as NEMI and RosettaNet to improve information access and transfer within production facilities.

chapter sixteen

Process industry collaboration*

This chapter will focus on collaborative manufacturing in the continuous segments of process industries such as pulp and paper, refining, mining and metals, and chemicals. These heavy industries personify the uniqueness of process manufacturing: added value by physically converting raw material (feedstock) into an intermediate or finished product. This industry group is characterized by heavy processing assets, long periods of continuous operation (3 to 5 years), absolute conformance to the physical laws, and very strict health and safety regulations. Beyond this environment, process manufacturing has two fundamental differences from discrete manufacturing. The first is in the nature and distribution of capital assets and costs. A typical process manufacturer has up to 75% of its capital assets invested in manufacturing assets, and approximately 65% of its costs occur in manufacturing operations. The high cost of manufacturing assets and their associated maintenance usually position process manufacturing as a high volume/low cost operation that makes return on assets (ROA) a primary measure of financial performance. The second difference is in the supply chain model that each employs. Discrete supply chains tend to be convergent, combining multiple suppliers' components, with a defined specification into a finished product. Process supply chains are divergent, V-type, processing a limited range of materials into many products defined by many diverse specifications. A classical example is in the pulp and paper industry where a pivotal part of the business model is to build the mill at the source of its feedstock in the middle of the forest where it produces hundreds of grades of kraft paper and fiberboard.

---

* David Woll of ARC Advisory Group has provided this chapter. He is a vice president of consulting at ARC Advisory Group and has been associated with defining and applying process automation for over 35 years. Dave has been a long time participant and thought leader in process manufacturing with Bristol Babcock and Foxboro Company, and is now with ARC.

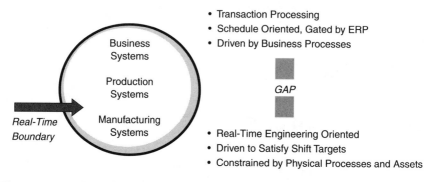

• Transaction Processing
• Schedule Oriented, Gated by ERP
• Driven by Business Processes

GAP

• Real-Time Engineering Oriented
• Driven to Satisfy Shift Targets
• Constrained by Physical Processes and Assets

Figure 16.1 Traditional manufacturing focus.

Process manufacturers continue to capitalize on the proven advantages of collaborative supply chain management; however, the issue of true collaboration between business processes and plant work processes is only now beginning to be addressed. Refining is a good example of the industry's sophistication. On the supply side, in order to optimize cost, integrated oil companies may refine as little as a third of their production and, depending on market conditions, sell up to two-thirds of their competitors' product under their name through their outlets. This model works because products are diverse, but specifications are similar. Collaboration is critical because trading is conducted in real-time, and a number of factors come into play. These factors include prices that are continuously in play, matching crude assays to processing assets (refineries), logistics systems that include multiple logistics modes (tanker, pipeline, barge, truck), and storage options that must be optimized. With respect to collaboration in demand-side planning, we don't need to look any further than the smart pumps at our gas stations. This capability has allowed refiners to keep their finger on the users' pulse: this is ultimate collaboration. In most cases, refineries are in the production planning loop with ERP systems but are not utilizing true collaboration.

The collaboration interface of concern is between business operations and plant operations. In the process industries, there has been a traditional gap between businesses and manufacturing. The biggest difference has been that business has been transaction based because MRP/ERP is transactional, and manufacturing has been real-time because the process runs in real-time. As a result, the boundary at which people needed to react in real-time was much closer to manufacturing than business. (See Figure 16.1.)

Looking forward, collaboration is critical; production systems will no longer be schedule driven. These are real-time systems focused on the real business issues of capacity and product mix. They are driven by market opportunities and empowered with a view from suppliers to customers.

In this picture, something has also changed in manufacturing. The luxury of shift-to-shift planning is gone. The real-time boundary has moved to the business systems, and plants are asked to make capable-to-promise and

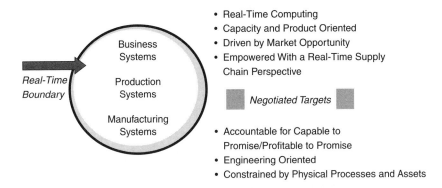

Figure 16.2 Collaborative manufacturing focus.

profitable-to-promise commitments in real-time to capture market opportunities for capacity and product mix. (See Figure 16.2.)

Process industries' production planning is almost exclusively accomplished using ERP planning facilities, and SAP is the dominant ERP supplier. Most of the major process manufacturers continue to be preoccupied with getting their financials on the new systems, and have not yet turned to formally integrating their business and plant systems. However, some have been able to take advantage of the high-level, well-defined interfaces such as PPPI (Production Planning for the Process Industries) offered by SAP and associated interfaces available from most automation suppliers. Evidence of the value of using real-time production information is shown in the table in Figure 16.3. These results were realized in the recent integration of a legacy process automation system and a SAP R/3 in a chemical plant.

Using real-time information to align assets and processes is the key to collaborative process manufacturing. It has been shown that the best, and maybe only way, to synchronize and align a process manufacturing enterprise is by ensuring that everyone always has the same information. Eliminating barriers to information and ensuring that everyone shares common information is at the heart of collaborative manufacturing. The key to extraordinary performance is when people are supportive because they see

Benefit Description	Improvement
Conversion Efficiency	5–15%
Asset Utilization	10–20%
Recycled Reduction	15–20%
On Spec	10–20%
On Schedule	60–90%
Inventory Turns	5%

Figure 16.3 Typical benefits from real-time ERP integration (chemical).

their role as part of an overall objective and are synchronized through the use of common information.

Utilization of best practices and continuous improvement is a procedural dimension of properly using information. One of the largest and most successful world-class process manufacturers recently completed a process plant performance study using Six Sigma methodology. The results showed that most process plants are underperforming. In fact, they were operating at less than four sigma, and transitioning states can draw that performance down to as low as two sigma. However, when empowered with accurate information, proven best practices, and a culture of continuous improvement, most process plants have the capability to approach six sigma during steady state and to sustain minimal upsets during state changes.

Synchronizing manufacturing and business is a hollow statement. It does not specify how synchronization is accomplished, either within manufacturing or between manufacturing and business. The only real way to synchronize the enterprise is to empower every user with the same information. When this information includes targets and performance against targets, the enterprise can become a mutually supportive and synchronized environment.

Data management in process manufacturing has had a checkered past. Typically, data was locked in disparate devices and proprietary data sources, and was only available on a point basis through an intermediary repository. While necessary in the past, this approach introduced complexity and compromised performance and security. In terms of cost to implement, this approach was cheap and easy, but in terms of maintenance and support, the cost can be high for the performance received. A centralized database approach brings ease of expansion but creates issues associated with redundant data. It also introduces the need to synchronize the data, because a central database is separated from its source. State of the art publish/subscribe technology is now being used in the process industries to facilitate global collaboration access to data and to eliminate barriers to information.

"If you cannot measure something you don't understand it and cannot improve it." This perspective is fundamental to improving manufacturing performance and critical to collaboration. Prior to the concept of collaborative manufacturing, process plants could run with the understanding that if targets were not met on this shift, the next shift would pick up the slack because the product mix was predictable. As we move into the collaborative manufacturing era, this will be considered a poor use of assets. The current reality is that most plant managers cannot see their plants' performance until the following day when the accountants present it to them. Most operations managers do not understand the condition of their processing assets or the actual available capacity. Finally, an understanding of actual process performance vs. theoretical performance is just a guess. In order to achieve the promise of collaborative manufacturing in the process industry, these and other performance parameters need to be visualized routinely as a standard part of business and manufacturing best practices. Activity-based costing

systems need to display performance information to the plant manager in real-time so he has the opportunity to take corrective action before a shift ends. Predictive maintenance and capacity modeling facilities need to present these parameters to operations management so that they are capable of satisfying promised commitments. Finally, process modeling and reconciliation facilities need to present process performance in order to make valid profitable-to-promise commitments.

In the process industry, the measure of financial performance has become return on assets. This is primarily because the preponderance of capital assets are manufacturing assets. Return on assets is the primary measurement along with profit margin and asset turnover (throughput). These ratios reveal how to use collaboration to increase financial performance. Profit margin is a target because higher efficiency as a result of collaboration increases margin short term. Asset turnover is a target for collaboration because the higher the sales it can drive, the higher the return on assets even if margins are tight. The objective in process manufacturing is to bring in enough sales to cover fixed costs. Incremental sales then fall straight to the bottom line.

Return on assets should drive a company's manufacturing strategy. A clearer understanding of the basis for a healthy return leads to a discussion of how to achieve it and how collaboration facilitates performance. The manufacturing strategy for a particular company is a function of its unique requirements, but the following is an example of how a manufacturing strategy can work with a well conceived marketing strategy to enhance a company's performance.

The first step is to consider the potential gain of higher manufacturing throughput on either a single product or a suitable mix of products on specific manufacturing assets. This higher throughput will maximize profit as volume exceeds the break-even point. Manufacturing needs to be able to capitalize on this improved asset turnover opportunity by making increased capacity available along with an enhanced ability to utilize this capacity. High asset availability must also be in place in order to support asset utilization. From a net margin perspective, manufacturing should focus on increased productivity and, ultimately, profitability by supporting a reduction of fixed assets and associated costs as a result of doing more with less. Improved energy utilization, leading to reduced energy costs and again higher profits, must also be a focal point. (See Figure 16.4.)

Another interesting strategy to increase asset utilization is emerging. Earlier discussion revolved around using collaboration to capitalize on available demand to absorb unused capacity. A new strategy attempts to create demand by reducing market cost, which in turn absorbs excess capacity, reduces average operating costs, and enhances return on assets.

Standards are playing a critical role in the emergence of collaborative manufacturing in the process industry. There is a new breed of process automation emerging that is based on a blend of information technology and proven control technology, which provides the functionality and availability necessary to satisfy the requirements of process manufacturing.

Benefit Description	Improvement
Increased Capacity	5–7%
Capacity Utilization	3–5%
Unscheduled Downtime	40–50%
Productivity	7–10%
Fixed Cost Reduction	10–15%
Energy Utilization	5–7%

Figure 16.4 Typical benefits from real-time collaborative manufacturing (refining).

Figure 16.5 provides a functional view of the direction collaborative process automation is taking. This is a distributed-processing, single-model implementation. At its core, it utilizes Internet technology to provide common data and a common infrastructure. In the context of network standards, it utilizes Ethernet — TCP/IP as the common infrastructure, and the Network Time Protocol for common time. The platform supports process control anywhere in an open sensors and actuation environment. The user has the option of selecting which supplier's equipment best satisfies the requirements. Logical control is focused on those networks that provide the richest logical control functionality, and both process and logical control are transparent to each other. There are no proprietary barriers; however, the benefits of structure at the real-time control and events level is introduced by the S88 Standard.

Collaborative production management applications are an integral part of the automation platform, sharing the same common data, infrastructure and system services. Finally, the manufacturing work processes and business work process engage within the structure provided by the S95 Standard,

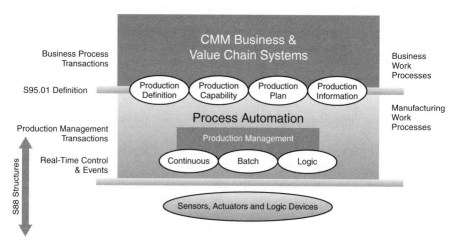

Figure 16.5 Process automation functional view.

which is the current implementation of the Purdue Reference Model that depicts process manufacturing work processes. (See Figure 16.5.)

A logical discussion of process automation involves more detail. Process control utilizes the functionality of the Foundation Fieldbus H1 standard to provide process control anywhere. It takes advantage of the common function block structure and Foundation Fieldbus services, which are optimized around process control. It also uses the publish/subscribe facility to support peer-to-peer and peer-to-host communications. Logical control utilizes the functionality of the Profibus, Devicenet standard buses, and similar standard buses to provide logical control.

The Foundation Fieldbus HSE standard binds all the buses, providing a high bandwidth Internet technology-based common infrastructure, which also serves as the common infrastructure for production management applications and third party Web-enabled integration. Third party Web-enabled application will be utilized where these third parties have a deep understanding of manufacturing operations or of the physical process and can bring value to the user. Application-specific appliances associated with major equipment will also tie directly into the common infrastructure.

Future automation will be presentation agnostic and will support information presentation through scalable devices, including browsers through thick clients. Business systems will also be a logical extension of the automation platform utilizing the TCP/IP common infrastructure and sharing a common protocol stack.

In order to maximize operational efficiency, it is not sufficient for each part of the enterprise — marketing, sales, engineering, production, customer services, suppliers, and suppliers' suppliers — to be efficient. The way in which they all interact over the lifetime of the product must also be optimized. Adding the concept of collaboration provides a means to begin applying the principles of feed forward and feedback control to the steady stream of sequenced, distributed, and interconnecting processes that comprise the manufacturing enterprise. In order to impose this kind of control, new information must be made available, measurement and analysis tools must be put in place, and business process automation across site and enterprise boundaries must be put in place. These are the building blocks for collaboration.

Collaboration offers many benefits to enterprises. Simply sharing information among users enables companies to synchronize operations. Enabling users to have direct access to their partner's information can improve this process by eliminating the need to coordinate activities, but the biggest gains are expected when process models extend from the production floor to the business systems and include automatic, collaborative workflows that can drive efficiencies across the entire extended enterprise. (See Figure 16.6.)

A collaborative manufacturing framework, when designed to fit within the context of the processes that drive production methods, provides an orchestration that will measurably improve the overall production process. When stand-alone systems are connected, existing and inherent flaws in

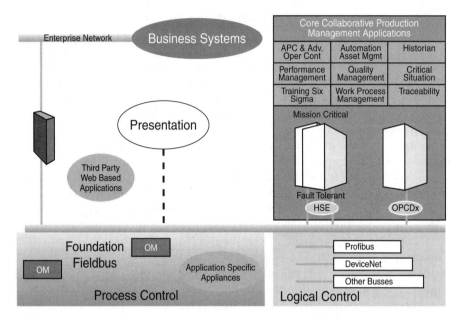

Figure 16.6 Process automation logical view.

underlying processes are exposed and manufacturing planners are presented with the opportunity to re-engineer processes and optimize them in ways not previously attainable.

Collaboration requires the sharing of information according to the agreed rules and business processes involved in creating and delivering customer-focused solutions. It also involves collaboration in product and solution design. As orders are received, they must be properly distributed throughout the value network and then driven through the appropriate plants and fulfillment processes. As orders are produced, information about progress and quality must be globally accessible in a secure way.

Process manufacturers are constantly striving to drive cost out of their production systems, and, in turn, drive down the cost of the delivered product. Leading-edge companies increasingly perceive a collaborative environment as a means of fostering efficiency throughout the product life cycle by combining functionality, reducing redundancy, and rendering all systems less expensive to execute and support.

Manufacturers are implementing collaborative solutions to improve their ability to rapidly respond to market opportunities. They seek faster responses in the order-to-fulfillment cycle as well as in their time-to-market capability. Factors such as new product introductions, speed of delivery, time to deployment, and maintaining market share are typically cited by process manufacturers as primary reasons for going forward with a collaborative strategy encompassing the entire value chain. Changing market conditions can mean different things to manufacturers depending on their product and sector, but the common denominator is that speed and response times are tied directly to the degree of integration, and subsequently, to the collaboration between systems.

Many manufacturers see a collaborative environment as a means of accomplishing process improvements. Issues such as inventory visibility with suppliers, asset management, process improvement, and improving customer relationships are all contributing factors.

chapter seventeen

Summary

Most of the media information and software systems vendors discuss collaboration as e-commerce or, even worse, c-commerce. This is not a correct view. E-commerce or c-commerce, if the terms still have any meaning when this book is published, usually identify business done over the Internet, such as Amazon.com and Dell Computer. Collaboration is the process of companies or business units working closer to provide improved inter-enterprise information synchronization. It is the value of closer information ties that makes collaboration a worthwhile business initiative. The Internet (e-commerce) can be one of the enablers, as are personal computers, cell phones, supply-chain management software, logistics management systems, CAD systems, and a host of other tools.

Collaboration is a modern business idea that uses technology, but one that is the product of our times. Ideas that are real in today's world include contracted manufacturing; intercompany, global, product-development teams; and point-of-sale information processed in near real-time. These ideas are not about technology, but rather business culture and the continuous evolution toward ever better processes. As surely as business has gone through previous transformations, there will be others in the future.

Collaboration appears to be different, but so too was the "quality-is-free" idea when originally advocated by Phil Crosby. Actually, collaboration is different, not because of technology, but because these ideas bring together a broader group of people working toward identified common goals, as in product definition collaboration where more minds are brought together simultaneously to collectively enhance a new product's features and reduce cost. In inventory management, collaboration is an inclusive tool allowing a broader group of minds to work to reduce demand fluctuation and the resulting increased cost and inconvenience. In enterprise collaboration, the task is to improve support for business processes by bringing more people closer through consistent and current information, reducing errors caused through misinformation or information lateness, and improving trust by using facts to make decisions and commitments.

Collaboration has some weaknesses. Collaboration is based on the elusive concept called trust. Inherent in trust is vulnerability. Vulnerability can leave people uncomfortable, which is what made the adversarial business process what it is. To make collaboration a success, this vulnerability must be satisfied with truth or facts — the real-time information as events occur in the business process.

Trust is the commodity that replaces backup inventory or just-in-case inventory. Trust is what replaces adversarial and costly business relationships. Managed trust allows more people to review proprietary information. The ideas do not range so far as to avoid normal business common sense. It would not be prudent to allow credit for a person or company that is not creditworthy. It would also not be wise to abandon supplier selection criteria in the expectation that everyone in this new world has evolved to sainthood. Business is still business.

Culture can also be considered a weakness, as it seems inherently easier to work against openness and trust than to embrace it. We have been so long infused with the idea of protection in business and of guarding against mishap. Murphy's Law, which states "if something can go wrong it will and at the worst possible moment," has been the mantra that has supported many successful people and companies. Management has spent years designing methods and systems to plug gaps where Murphy's Law can affect them and their company. Although collaboration may be seen by some as a process of stripping them of these protective methods, that is certainly not the primary intent. The intent is to replace these protections with something even stronger — real-time information facts, truth, understanding, and awareness across a broader spectrum of participants.

In the early days of airplanes when mail delivery was the only paying business, there were no elaborate flight-tracking radar systems or schedules. When it was time to leave, the pilot threw some bags of mail in the airplane and departed. If the weather along the route was bad, the pilot landed and waited for improvement. At that time, if the airplane got to its destination a day or two late nobody really cared. It was a miracle that the plane made it at all. Today every commercial flight has a flight plan with continuous tracking that confirms progress and/or any deviation from the flight plan. Business is headed in the same direction with processes that ensure the anticipated activities are on course. Collaboration provides the current focus of activities toward that objective.

What makes collaboration different is the positive and proactive nature that supports two basic ideas:

- Collaboration works toward the idea that all who should know will have access to the correct information.
- Collaboration processes provide the tools to track and confirm events that build the element of trust through current knowledge.

It appears that collaboration will be a major business improvement opportunity, but there will be leaders and laggards with firm convictions on each side. The current consensus seems to be that collaboration can be a high-stakes win/win idea. A report by the Yankee Group (Derome 2001), suggests that three areas of cost can be dramatically affected by collaboration:

- The cost of interaction
- The cost of goods sold
- The cost of inventory

The Yankee Group estimates this cost savings across 26 industries in the United States to be $83 billion annually by 2005. This is not a bad contribution for a concept that has been around since the first time two people got together to plan how to catch dinner.

References

Derome, J., The collaborative commerce value statement: a $223 billion cost-savings opportunity over six years, report, Yankee Group, Boston, 2001.

Fraser, J., Collaboration: at the heart of a revolution, *APICS Magazine*, October 1997.

Greene, A., Beyond superficial collaboration, *Industry Directions*, November, 2000.

appendix A

Hierarchy of supply-chain software systems

Many sources of information can be used in developing collaboration links, ranging from planning systems across the supply chain to global positioning systems that can track a truck on the way to deliver material to the plant floor. Although a lot of information is likely to exist in systems already in place, there may be a need to look at upgrading in some areas. Figure A.1 illustrates the current array of computer system applications used within the production environment of the supply chain. They are shown here to provide a brief overview of the many facets of this complex world. Each application listed has a number of vendors, with each package likely to be different from the rest. The systems audit of the current condition will identify data items and information processes that will be the base for building collaborative bridges. The hierarchy and description of the individual components derive from information published in *MSI Magazine* in February 2002, and are reused with permission.

Trade exchanges are website portals that combine transactions, services, and content to optimize and automate buying, selling, and fulfillment processes. Enterprise commerce management (ECM) describes the next generation of collaborative business systems that combine applications and services in an Internet technology environment that extends systems integration to customers, suppliers, and a wider range of employees than ever before. Devised by AMR Research, the concept suggests guidelines for companies managing disparate investments in enterprise, buy-side, sell-side, supply chain, and other types of business applications and manufacturing systems.

Collaborative product development combines advances in computer-aided design (CAD) with what has come to be called collaborative product commerce (CPC) — the means to share product-related data of all types with the larger community of interested parties. Solutions use Internet technologies to permit individuals to collaboratively develop, build, and manage products throughout their life cycles. Collaborative product development can, for example, collapse the time it takes to turn intellectual property into

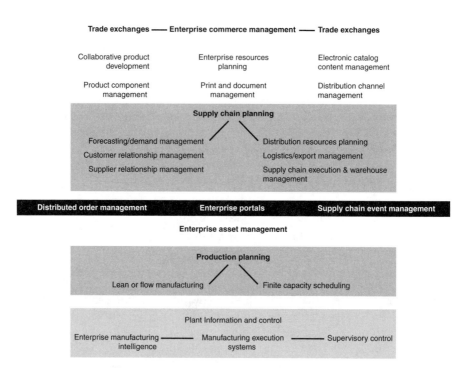

Figure A.1 Major and emerging supply chain applications.

deliverable products. The same tools allow manufacturers to work more closely with suppliers and others to ensure rapid ramp-up of production for new products. In the absence of a common data model, open, object-oriented interfaces from one application's data management system can be used to reference relevant data to another application. Other elements of a solution might include secure portals for conducting business and group collaboration, and as a means for viewing and marking up CAD drawings and other technical documents. The term "product life-cycle management" is similar to CPC in its connotations.

Enterprise resources planning is the current generation of the manufacturing resources-planning systems installed in many manufacturing plants. The term "enterprise resources planning" was coined to reflect the fact that these computerized systems have evolved well beyond their origins as inventory transaction and cost accounting systems. The software has become the means to support and speed the entire order fulfillment process and to automate and integrate both business and production process management. By recording transactions, that is, the computerized record of events (e.g., the receipt of inventory or issue of a work order), the ERP system tracks resources — such as materials and labor — used in financial, manufacturing, and distribution management.

Systems planning methodology uses material requirements planning (MRP) and master production schedule (MPS) to calculate requirements for materials, make recommendations to release replenishment orders, and reschedule open orders when due dates and need dates are not in phase. Many of today's ERP systems also take into consideration capacity constraints when planning production. But, unless equipped with advanced planning functionality, they do so only serially. ERP is increasingly seen as a transaction backbone and data source for ancillary decision-support systems.

In addition, functionality has more recently been introduced to support the specific needs of vertical industry segments, such as consumer packaged goods or automotive manufacturers, as well as special operations, such as demand management, an essential feature for better management of supply chains. ERP systems have begun to incorporate functionality for customer interaction and managing relationships with suppliers and vendors, making the system less inward looking.

Electronic catalog content management solutions aggregate, transform, cleanse, update, and publish product content via Internet trade exchanges or other on-line means.

Product component management systems combine information about components, suppliers, designs, and processes to facilitate supply-chain information sharing and limit component proliferation.

Document and print management allows enterprises to better manage, view, distribute, and print business and technical documents. The latest solutions use Web-based technologies to support document distribution and collaboration. Solutions from vendors in this space vary, but what they have in common is their relevance to processes, such as engineering change and product development, which increasingly take place in a multi-enterprise environment.

Distribution channel management, or partner relationship management, facilitates sell-side e-business, while at the same time forging a community of partners involved in product sales and distribution. Channel management solutions must be flexible enough to deal with the multiplicity of arrangements attendant on sales — for example, sales through a central commerce site, with fulfillment through channel partners; or conversely, establishment of partner-branded commerce sites that feed sales into a central underlying commerce engine. Channel management also ensures timely delivery of qualified leads and marketing information, and automates dealing with contract and warranty issues, compensation, and reimbursement.

Supply chain planning is the generic term for software applications used by manufacturers to decide what products to build and when to build them, based on forecasts, current orders in-hand, and availability of needed resources. It also can be used to plan product distribution through networks of warehouses and other transit points, and to design such networks as well. Supply chain planning — unlike earlier generations of planning tools such as material requirements planning — makes use of advanced planning and scheduling (APS) technology, which allows for plan generation based on multiple constraints, including materials and capacity. However, some forms of planning, such as most finite scheduling packages, make use of simulation technology rather than APS.

Forecasting/demand management integrates supply and demand information so as to optimize operations. Forecasting applications — which predict activity over a weekly or monthly time horizon — remain central, but demand management is today a broader activity that can include replenishment; sales and operations planning; and integration with marketing, order, and customer management systems.

Traditional time-series forecasting averages past performance of a demand stream to anticipate further demand. More sophisticated systems take into account factors beyond historical demand, employing statistical methods to remove biases. These more complex forms of forecasting determine and predict the effect that "causal" or "event-driven factors," as well as macro-economic indicators, have on demand. Recent advances in forecasting have focused on gauging the impact of pricing and promotions, product introduction and obsolescence, intermittent demand, and product proliferation.

Customer relationship management ranges from off-the-shelf contact management solutions to high-end interactive selling suites that combine sales, marketing, and executive information tools. These include product configuration, quote and proposal management, and marketing encyclopedias. Some systems include functions for complex pricing, promotions, commission plans, team selling, and campaign management. Enterprise solutions for large companies with hundreds or even thousands of users have capabilities for call center/help desks, field service, forecasting, and spend-and-profit analysis.

Logistics/trade management solutions focus on managing the movement of goods. Logistics software primarily refers to transportation management solutions, although other applications — such as inventory management and optimization packages that look at inventory issues across the supply chain — also can be seen as logistics management solutions. International trade logistics (ITL) software handles specific aspects of global trade, including regulatory compliance, export/import management, regulatory compliance, and restricted party screening. ITL solutions also aggregate content about regulations and restrictions.

Supplier management allows companies to integrate with their most important suppliers to streamline order management, replenishment, and fulfillment; inventory management; and engineering change management. It has been suggested the term "strategic sourcing" denotes everything that precedes the signing of a contract, including spend analysis, identifying potential suppliers, request for quotation and contract negotiation, and monitoring and improving suppliers.

Supply chain execution and warehouse management automates workflow within warehouses and distribution centers using a transactional information system. Simple storage and retrieval of materials have been superseded by strategies to increase throughput and productivity by managing the full range of warehouse resources to direct activities that include receiving, put-away, picking, shipping, and inventory cycle counts.

Sophisticated techniques, such as cross-docking or flow-through distribution, allow fast-moving products to go immediately to shipping upon arrival. Users configure the systems with descriptions of the facility floor and the rules they want to govern material movement and worker activity.

The lines among warehouse management, distribution, and transportation systems are blurring as more warehouse systems handle logistics functions, such as load planning and building, shipment scheduling, and yard management. This trend led to the coining of the term "supply chain execution" or "fulfillment systems" to connote their more holistic role.

Fulfillment management combines multi-enterprise order management, event management, inventory management, supply chain execution, and logistics management. In some cases, these suites are meant to support commerce initiated on private trade exchanges. The market, however, is fragmented, involving enterprise, supply chain planning, execution, and event management vendors, that is, both transactional and decision support.

Enterprise portals are Web-based user interfaces and information repositories for collaboration. A portal can be partitioned to provide roles-based views, and may include workflow, alerts, and the use of key performance indicators. While an enterprise portal can serve internal users via passwords and security, it may also serve as a customer- or supplier-facing portal. Internet-based trade exchanges use portal software as a user interface, but portals typically are seen as a subset of a trade exchange solution.

Supply-chain event management (SCEM) collects real-time data from multiple sources across the supply chain. The software converts the data into information that gives business managers a clear picture of how their supply chain is performing. If a problem requires immediate attention, the application can launch workflows and issue alerts to relevant parties via e-mail, phone, fax, personal digital assistant, or other device. The introduction of SCEM represents the coming together of two kinds of functionality: analytics, formerly accomplished by data warehousing; and workflow, accomplished by means of integration tools.

Enterprise asset management is used by maintenance management software vendors to connote the wide-ranging functionality that their systems include, such as inventory management and financials.

Production planning is a subset of supply chain planning, a generic term for software applications used by manufacturers to decide what products to build and when to build them, based on forecasts, current orders in hand, and availability of needed resources. Vendors have established supply chain suites that include demand, transportation, supply chain, and production planning — each attacking these problems at different operational levels and granularities of detail within a pre-integrated environment.

Lean or flow manufacturing is essentially a mixed-model production method that operates on production lines that manufacture up to a specific quantity of a particular product each day. These lines also must have the ability to produce unlimited variations of that base product on any given day. Take, for instance, a production line dedicated to building manual car transmissions. A flow line for that product might have the capacity to build 30 transmissions per day. It also would be able to produce the appropriate mix of three-, four-, and five-speed transmissions needed to fill specific customer orders every day of the year. Flow lines achieve this precise level of mixed-model production because they are designed to ensure that each product is built within a specified amount of time. Once the total time it takes to build a product is determined, equal slices of that time are allocated for the performance of each operation along the line. In this way, each product moves through the production process at a steady rate from beginning to end without stopping. When executed properly, this single-unit manufacturing style enables product to move smoothly, precluding the need for excess inventory and preventing unnecessary queues and bottlenecks from forming on the shop floor. This syncopated movement of the product between workstations, also known as the "drum beat," must be maintained so that the total time to build a product stays within the limits necessary for all product to be delivered on time.

Finite capacity scheduling is scheduling software that takes into account that manufacturing resources, such as production capacity, are finite. Other constraints might include personnel, regulatory pressures, or materials, as in traditional MRP II. Applications may also be called dynamic scheduling or advanced planning and scheduling systems.

Plant information management and control furnish aggregation points for data generated by control automation or process control systems, or for work done on plant floors. Control, in this sense, refers to solutions that manage plant data, rather than process control itself. This diverse space includes applications for supervisory control, enterprise manufacturing intelligence, and manufacturing execution system solutions. Thin clients, portal technology, and Web-enabled devices have changed plant information management in ways that weren't foreseen until recently — providing functionality for automating, monitoring, and controlling plant-floor operations, as well as for establishing bi-directional data transmission throughout the enterprise. All this points to convergence of information technology, and specifically of production management, with plant automation.

Enterprise-manufacturing intelligence solutions are closely related to plant portals, which consolidate data taken from a wide range of computing sources — on plant floors, enterprise systems, and elsewhere — and organizes that data into meaningful, roles-based information, aggregating the data from disparate sources for analysis and reporting. EMI solutions typically stress applications for analysis, rather than simple monitoring or visualization of trends.

Manufacturing execution systems were described earlier in the text.

Supervisory control began as operator interfaces for industrial processes controlled by programmable controllers. Over time, in addition to process monitoring and data acquisition, they've become increasingly involved in managing production and manufacturing execution. Process control itself is more typically accomplished by means of a programmable logic controller (PLC). The increasing use of software-based logic — so-called soft control or soft logic — performs the same functions as the PLC, but does so within a PC-based environment. At present, it is said that this option is best used when the application involves considerable memory use and information management. Further, the use of component-based software promises to make the design and implementation of supervisory control applications easier, less expensive, and functionally richer than ever before.

appendix B

Enterprise resource planning system: an example

Enterprise resource planning systems have taken on an increasingly significant role in the management of most large companies. PeopleSoft Inc. has been kind enough to share information on its PeopleSoft 8 system to provide an overview of the current breadth and complexity of a modern system implementation. Other major system suppliers will have similar capabilities, although the names of, and terms used to describe, the modules may differ.

As shown in this example, enterprise resource planning systems typically have a range of applications from customer requirements planning to financial to supply chain/manufacturing to human resources. The systems are designed in a modular form that allows companies to deploy only those functions they see as necessary. The deployment can begin with nearly any single module and expand to fit the requirements of the business or as they can be absorbed by the organization. Incremental deployment allows the user to grow into acceptance rather than being forced to undertake a massive retrofit in one giant leap.

PeopleSoft groups its products into the following business process categories:

- Customer relationship management
- Enterprise performance management
- Enterprise service automation
- Financials
- Human resources management
- Portal solutions
- Supply chain management
- Trading exchange services

Each of the business process categories is discussed along with a brief description of each product module. This is not a complete or a detailed presentation of the system, but it will provide a sense of the managerial impact that these tools can provide. As you read through this material, consider how the information may be used to support improved collaboration, either as a source for information or as a user of information from other sources, including real-time process information.

Customer Relationship Management (CRM) provides seamless integration among customer, financial, supply chain, and employee management systems. You gain closed-loop management of all sales activities, complete functionality for managing marketing programs, and a comprehensive customer support system, plus all the tools required to integrate both field service and help desk operations. In addition, there are built-in analytics to monitor all enterprise data constantly, revealing the relationships between customers, products, channels, and profitability. Access can be through a Web browser.

> **CRM Field Services** improves the efficiency of internal and third-party field service organizations. It tracks service-level agreements, entitlements, warranty coverage, and return material authorizations. Service orders can be automated and product configurations can be stored here.
>
> **CRM Help Desk** provides a single access point for call tracking, problem management, and problem resolution. The system captures and displays information about a company's IT and telecommunications infrastructure. It also captures and displays information related to system status, trouble tickets, known product defects, and other data to assist staff in resolving problems consistently and effectively.
>
> **CRM Interaction Management** aggregates customer information from multiple systems and sales channels into a comprehensive customer history. Because it integrates tightly with CRM Support, it keeps customer information readily available for call center agents responding to customer needs. From one easy-to-navigate screen, agents can access multiple databases, configure and enter orders, check status, resolve bill inquiries, log service issues, and retrieve product information. Interaction Management can also be integrated with Help Desk and Field Service to help trap and track all interactions and transactions with your customers.
>
> **CRM Marketing** empowers the enterprise to plan, target, execute, and refine marketing activities. The solution's tools enable the creation of targeted multiwave, multichannel campaigns while reducing campaign management expenses. Closed-loop business processes drive effective leads for sales force execution. Analytics provide executive management with campaign insight and control.
>
> **CRM Portal Pack** provides a view of your CRM application data and transactions via a set of prebuilt pagelets. Displayed on your Enter-

prise Portal homepage, Portal Pack pagelets provide CRM application functionality, reports, and related content.

CRM Quality Management is a comprehensive system for managing quality processes across your organization. By improving your ability to track and resolve product defects and product enhancement requests, CRM Quality Management helps you to deliver the world-class products and services required to acquire and retain profitable customers.

CRM Sales enables strategic and tactical management of the entire sales process while providing a 360-degree view of the customer across the enterprise. Sales managers benefit from powerful forecasting functionality and pipeline-, quota-, and territory-management tools.

CRM Support automates call routing and tracking, entitlement processing, workflow, credit authorization, and problem resolution.

CRM Telemarketing expands the functionality of your marketing organization to include outbound telemarketing campaigns.

CRM Warehouse provides the tools and technology needed to manage a complete view of your customer for analytic reporting and analysis.

CTI Integration is an integration application to the Genesys CTI Framework.

Customer Behavior Modeling uses enterprise-wide customer data integrated with behavioral metrics and demographic information from third-party providers. With these data, you can define and select populations of customers, use data mining to build predictive models, and score your customers based on relevant criteria.

Customer Scorecard facilitates the measurement and communication of customer-centric objectives throughout your enterprise. Customer Scorecard tracks key performance measurements and communicates progress against CRM-related goals.

Enterprise Warehouse provides the tools and technology to manage enterprise-wide information for reporting and analysis.

Mobile Sales for WAP Phones enables remote sales teams to stay connected to customers, the company, and critical information. With a wireless phone, sales representatives can manage opportunities, schedule meetings, or access company information anytime, anywhere.

Enterprise Performance Management (EPM) is a tool to gather, analyze, and report on all types of organizational data. With this information, you can manage and communicate progress to achieve strategic objectives.

Activity-Based Management enables you to analyze the costs and profits of your business activities for better present and future cost and profitability management.

Analytic Forecasting provides a systematic process for creating quality forecasts that enable you to optimize business planning and supplement historical data analysis with collaborative efforts to drive both tactical and strategic business planning. An audit facility even alerts you if current forecasting methods are producing values that are outside user-defined levels of acceptance.

Asset Liability Management provides modeling and simulation functionality so that you can manage uncertainty, make better investment decisions, and synchronize business strategy across organizational units.

Balanced Scorecard is an Internet solution that measures performance using multiple perspectives, such as financial, customer, internal processes, and learning and growth indicators. Balanced Scorecard draws information from all your systems into a single strategic framework that provides performance data across your entire organization.

Business Planning and Budgeting Solution delivers top-down strategic planning with continuous forecasting and bottom-up budgeting. Seamless integration between Business Planning 8.3 and Budgeting 8.3 facilitates collaborative processes.

Customer Behavior Modeling uses enterprise-wide customer data integrated with behavioral metrics and demographic information from third-party providers.

CRM Warehouse provides the tools and technology you need to manage a complete view of your customer for analytic reporting and analysis.

Customer Scorecard facilitates the measurement and communication of customer-centric objectives throughout your enterprise. Customer Scorecard tracks key performance measurements and communicates progress against CRM-related goals.

Enterprise Warehouse provides the tools and technology to manage enterprise-wide information for reporting and analysis.

EPM Portal Pack provides views of your EPM application data and transactions via a set of prebuilt pagelets.

Financials Warehouse provides the tools and technology to manage financial information needed for analytic reporting and analysis.

Funds Transfer Pricing enables you to calculate margins and align management decisions with current market conditions and asset liability committee objectives (ALCO). You establish the rules for determining internal charges and credits to your business units based on instrument characteristics such as risk, repricing, and optionality, then distribute information to anyone, anywhere, in the format you define.

HRMS Warehouse provides the tools and technology to manage workforce information needed for analytic reporting and analysis.

Risk Weighted Capital calculates economically appropriate charges for expected losses and capital, and then reports the effect on customers, products, channels, business units, and time.

Supply Chain Warehouse provides the tools and technology to manage supply chain information needed for analytic reporting and analysis.

Workforce Planning helps you answer critical questions related to key competencies essential to your organization, such as how your workforce compares with your competency needs and what competency needs will fulfill your organizational strategy.

Workforce Rewards helps you determine the overall value of your compensation package, and then puts that information in the context of the overall marketplace.

Workforce Scorecard couples the strategy management techniques espoused by Robert Kaplan and David Norton to provide an effective, automated mechanism for managing and measuring human resources (HR) performance.

Enterprise Service Automation: Operating costs — your expenses incurred from contracted services and internal projects — are the largest hidden costs facing business today. Service automation gives you the tools to manage these costs.

Billing allows you to customize, calculate, and submit invoices in multiple currencies and languages. You can manage bill cycles and streamline processes to create a billing system that reflects the way you do business.

Contracts can accommodate virtually any billing request and still satisfy your own revenue recognition requirements. Integration with other modules enables you to manage your contracts, revenue, and billing for products and services from start to finish.

Expenses helps to control your expenses by providing flexible payment options, versatile data entry methods, the ability to set up user-definable control data, and integration with other applications.

General Ledger offers a comprehensive Internet solution that goes beyond traditional ledger functions, providing reliable financial control, flexible data collection, comprehensive global processing, and readily accessible information.

HRMS Warehouse provides the tools and technology to manage workforce information needed for analytic reporting and analysis.

Mobile Time and Expense is a fully detachable nomadic application that works independently of network connections. Business travelers can simply download information to their PCs, enter project time and expense reports in a detached mode, and then reconnect via a Web browser to submit reports for approval.

Mobile Time and Expense for Palm enables you to capture time entries and expense receipts on a handheld device — anywhere, anytime. Time and expense entry on a Palm means convenience for your mobile workforce, reduced transaction costs, and increased accuracy and productivity.

Payables enables you to manage cash disbursements efficiently, while both accelerating your enterprise workflow and maintaining good vendor relations.

Projects provides a centralized repository for financial and distribution information related to individual projects, whether the end product is a fixed asset or a service deliverable.

Resource Management is an Internet solution that automates resource scheduling and enables staffing collaboration and planning. Resource Management helps match the right people to each project, taking into account project requirements and employee competencies, preferences, and availability.

Services Procurement automates the process of procuring and managing contract services. This solution enables you to procure both requisition- and project-based resources, aggregate service suppliers, and optimize business processes.

Travel is an integrated self-booking tool that enables employees to book air, hotel, and car reservations for corporate travel. The confirmed travel bookings are stored within My Wallet™ in the Expenses module and are used to automate expense entry for reimbursement.

Financials: Financial data reporting is at the center of ERP systems, providing detailed accounting and money management for the total corporation down to and through individual business units and departments. Due to widespread use and financial reporting ramifications, the key words in enterprise systems are consistency and accuracy. Information presentation must follow uniform input and display processes and be steadfastly reliable. To accomplish this, modern systems are made up of fully integrated application modules.

Activity-Based Management enables you to analyze the costs and profits of business activities for better present and future cost and profitability management.

Analytic Forecasting provides a systematic process for creating quality forecasts to optimize business planning and supplement historical data analysis with collaborative efforts to drive both tactical and strategic business planning. An audit facility alerts you if current forecasting methods are producing values that are outside user-defined levels of acceptance.

Asset Management provides comprehensive financial and tax accounting functions.

Balanced Scorecard is an Internet solution that measures performance using multiple perspectives, such as financial, customer, internal processes, and learning and growth indicators. Balanced Scorecard draws information from all your systems into a single strategic framework that provides performance data across your entire organization.

Billing allows you to customize, calculate, and submit invoices in multiple currencies and languages. You can manage bill cycles and streamline processes to create a billing system that reflects the way you do business.

Budgeting supports company objectives by creating an interactive and collaborative budget process. It also fully integrates with Business Planning to create a complete planning and budgeting solution, aligning your top-down strategic planning with continuous forecasting and bottom-up budgeting.

Business Planning and Budgeting delivers top-down strategic planning with continuous forecasting and bottom-up budgeting.

Cash Management provides rapid collection and consolidation of information through automation, manages cash flow requirements, quickly accesses and captures enterprise and third-party information, and provides relevant cash position reporting.

Deal Management handles debt and investment transactions in a broad range of financial markets, streamlines and improves treasury deal processes and also reduces costs through automated deal initiation, administration, settlement, and position monitoring.

Deduction Management automates the deduction management process and integrates with other solutions, such as Receivables and Supply Chain.

eBill Payment provides a fully integrated electronic bill presentation and payment package for both B2B and B2C transactions. eBill Payment tells your customers everything they need to know about their accounts. Customers can monitor their account status, view recent transactions and invoices, and make payments over the Internet.

Enterprise Warehouse provides the tools and technology to manage enterprise-wide information for reporting and analysis.

Expenses helps control expenses by providing flexible payment options, versatile data entry methods, the ability to set up user-definable control data, and integration with other applications.

Financials Portal Pack provides a view of your Financials application data and transactions via a set of prebuilt pagelets. Displayed on the Enterprise Portal homepage, Portal Pack pagelets bring the Financials applications' functionality, reports, and related content you need to move your financials business processes more rapidly to the Web at the lowest possible cost and risk.

Financials Warehouse provides the tools and technology to manage financial information needed for analytic reporting and analysis.

General Ledger offers a comprehensive Internet solution that goes beyond traditional ledger functions, providing reliable financial control, flexible data collection, comprehensive global processing, and readily accessible information.

Grants enables you to better handle the many administrative tasks associated with sponsored research.

MarketPay is a business-to-business electronic bill presentment solution for on-line marketplaces.

Payables enables you to manage cash disbursements efficiently, while both accelerating your enterprise workflow and maintaining good vendor relations.

Projects provides a centralized repository for financial and distribution information related to individual projects, whether the end product is a fixed asset or a service deliverable.

Purchasing streamlines the procurement process by using automated sourcing of requisitions, workflow approvals, exception-based workflow notifications, and electronic commerce, including XML, electronic data interchange (EDI) transactions, e-mail, automatic faxing, and sourcing of items through electronic catalogs.

Receivables is both an accounts receivable and a credit management system.

Risk Management allows you to capture your overall treasury performance and check the valuation and analysis of your portfolio of transactions and exposures.

Travel is an integrated self-booking tool that enables employees to book air, hotel, and car reservations for corporate travel. The confirmed travel bookings are stored within My Wallet in the Expenses module and are used to automate expense entry for reimbursement.

Human Resources Management (HRMS) lets you manage HR business processes — from recruitment to retirement — with Internet applications.

Benefits Administration can build and manage a comprehensive benefits system tailored to the particular needs of your organization, from automated enrollment and billing to the selection of multiple benefit programs.

Directory Interface helps you reduce IT costs by automating the time-consuming process of profile maintenance. Directory Interface automatically triggers changes in user profiles when business events occur in HRMS.

eBenefits offers employees self-service benefits transactions, including open enrollment, plan changes, dependent and personal data maintenance, and life event processing.

eCompensation empowers employees with a collaborative application that shows their complete compensation package in an intuitive format and provides the tools to plan their financial futures.

eCompensation Manager Desktop enables managers to make fast, informed compensation decisions, and then act on them all on-line. Managers gain easy access to total compensation information as well as third-party benchmarking and salary surveys.

eDevelopment is a collaborative application that supports the personal and professional development of employees. Functionality includes training management and delivery, skills and competency management, and career and succession planning. And with its global architecture, eDevelopment supports multiple currencies and languages as it helps meet the training and development needs of organizations around the world.

eEquity is a Web-based collaborative application that delivers information to employees, optionees, and managers about your company's stock option plans and stock purchase plans. You can track grants and associated vesting; view stock option and stock purchase activity; model gross and net gain based on value and taxation assumptions; and report sales on-line to the organization.

EPay helps your employees make better decisions about their earnings. ePay is a collaborative application that gives your employees immediate access to their personal payroll data.

eProfile is a collaborative application that enables employees to maintain their own profiles. eProfile ensures that data changes comply with your organization's requirements.

eProfile Manager Desktop is a collaborative application that gives managers greater control over employee information. Managers can manage employee status and review employee demographic information in an intuitive Web environment.

eRecruit enables applicants and employees to collaborate in real time and use intuitive, role-based homepages.

eRecruit Manager Desktop transforms the complex task of recruiting into a streamlined experience for hiring managers and recruiters. Managers and recruiters can search the talent pool, screen applicants, perform background checks, or manage on-line job postings across the Internet.

Flexible Spending Account Administration (FSA) allows U.S. and Canadian companies to administer health-care and dependent-care FSA claims.

Global Payroll supports worldwide operations with streamlined application maintenance, easy global deployment, and easy management across borders.

HRMS Portal Pack provides an intuitive view of HRMS application data and transactions via a set of prebuilt pagelets. Displayed on your Enterprise Portal homepage, Portal Pack brings HRMS application functionality, reports, and related content.

HRMS Warehouse provides the tools and technology to manage workforce information needed for analytic reporting and analysis.

Human Resources offers comprehensive HR solutions, from recruitment to compensation to workforce development.

Payroll for North America provides the tools to efficiently calculate earnings, taxes, and deductions; maintain balances; and report payroll data while minimizing the burden on IT managers and payroll staff.

Payroll Interface enables the seamless transfer of employee data and updates from Human Resources Management to the payroll system.

Pension Administration is used to manage multiple, complex, defined-benefit plans with a single Internet solution that can be configured to match your unique plan rules. It automates tasks ranging from pension calculations to tracking service credit, producing reports, and providing critical information to use when counseling plan participants.

Resume Processing helps the organization process and respond to resumes as quickly as possible. It automatically extracts data from resumes and enters it into data fields.

Stock Administration is an Internet solution for establishing, managing, and administering multiple, complex, stock option plans; employee stock purchase plans (ESPPs); and ESPP programs for your workforce. In addition, the eEquity collaborative application works with Stock Administration to provide extensive self-service administration for employees, optionees, and managers. Finally, you can value and report stock-based compensation plans in accordance with FAS 123.

Time and Labor provides a global solution with a single repository. Time and Labor enables the organization to record labor details, summarize time, present analyses to time reporters and administrators, and make adjustments to time that has already been paid through a single point of entry. Time and Labor supports a range of business functions, including payroll, financial and cost accounting, project management, employee benefits, and organizational administration.

Workforce Planning can answer critical questions related to key competencies essential to your organization, such as how your workforce compares with your competency needs, and what competency needs will fulfill the organizational strategy.

Workforce Rewards helps you determine the overall value of your compensation package, and then puts that information in the context of the overall marketplace so that you can drive a competitive compensation strategy.

Workforce Scorecard couples the leading-edge strategy management techniques espoused by Robert Kaplan and David Norton to provide an effective, automated mechanism for managing and measuring HR performance.

Portal Solutions are a unification framework for every type of system and content your users need. A customized, role-based homepage provides the single gateway to all your critical information, such as eBusiness applications, databases and applications from other vendors, external content, and more. Unlike portals from earlier-generation vendors, Portal Solutions provides a complete infrastructure solution, with the tools, open integration framework, and platform to speed your migration to eBusiness with a single technology.

Enterprise Portal seamlessly connects customers, suppliers, employees, and partners to business processes on-line and in real time.

Through a common Internet browser, you can unify Internet-based applications, client/server and legacy systems, knowledge management suites, user productivity and collaborative services, and partner sites for universal access.

The role engine automates the identification and delivery of information relevant to specific roles within — and outside — the organization. Parameters include user-specific workflow, analytic alerts, and pre-built application access (including self-service functionality). The Portal Packs deliver application functionality to the Enterprise Portal via prebuilt, plug-and-play pagelets.

Supply Chain Management (SCM) solutions are designed for the collaborative enterprise. With fully integrated, end-to-end solutions, you get real-time information. From order capture, collaborative planning, and fulfillment to service and measurement, information can be accessed anytime, anywhere through a Web browser. Solutions are comprehensive to suit any organization's supply chain needs, big and small.

Activity-Based Management enables the analysis of costs and profits of your business activities for better present and future cost and profitability management.

Billing allows you to customize, calculate, and submit invoices in multiple currencies and languages.

Bills and Routings provides accurate, reliable bills of material (BOMs) for important tasks, such as planning, allocation of materials to production, and cost roll-ups. Bills and Routings also provides control over routings, work centers, and resources to build and manage the product life cycle. In addition, Bills and Routings offers important revision control, substitute items, and master routings functionalities.

Cohera Catalog Management System is a high-performance, Web-based solution for integrating and managing catalog content.

Collaborative Supply Management provides strategic planning, inventory, and replenishment information from back-end ERP systems. The information is made available to your suppliers in real time, improving business collaboration, supplier response capability, and employee productivity. By sharing the same view of data, buyers and sellers can work interactively to collaborate across the Internet.

Cost Management enables you to manage costs throughout your supply chain, including goods in production as well as finished goods.

Features include comprehensive analysis capabilities, flexible overhead allocation, and accurate accounting and reporting.

Demand Planning is a tool to create demand forecasts based on statistical analysis of demand history, causal factors such as events and promotions, and collaborative input from both employees and trading partners.

eBill Payment provides a fully integrated, electronic bill presentation and payment package for both B2B and B2C transactions. eBill Payment tells customers everything they need to know about their accounts. Customers can monitor their account status, view recent transactions and invoices, and make payments over the Internet.

Engineering allows you to access and share product content over the Web while retaining control over design product structures. In addition, embedded workflow greatly improves the change order process, reducing the cycle time to release engineering change orders.

Enterprise Planning offers an advanced planning and scheduling application that uses Web-based access to provide optimization of enterprise-wide procurement, distribution, and production resources. The functionality is designed for global manufacturing and distribution companies.

Enterprise Warehouse provides the tools and technology to manage enterprise-wide information for reporting and analysis.

eProcurement is an Internet solution for the decentralization, automation, and control of the purchasing of goods and services. With eProcurement, you can reduce costs with spending controls and best-price information, improve supplier relationships by reducing returns and customer support costs, and empower employees to make better, faster, more informed decisions.

eProduct Management provides an easy and secure method to share product and engineering information across the supply chain. Suppliers use this tool to participate in the engineering change-order process. The result is shorter lead times for implementing changes and greater collaborative efforts with your suppliers.

eSupplier Connection is an external-facing application that makes strategic information available from back-end ERP systems in real time to your suppliers, improving business collaboration, supplier response capability, and employee productivity. With eSupplier Connection, buyers and sellers work collaboratively by sharing the same view of data across the Internet.

Flow Production targets customers looking to implement the best flow manufacturing practices. Based on the principles of flow manufacturing, this module delivers methods for managing production and replenishing material in a pull environment. With Flow Production, you can manage electronic kanban signals that communicate production, as well as material signals to your inventory, feeder line, and supplier locations.

Inventory provides real-time information over any Web browser so that you can minimize carrying costs, increase inventory accuracy and customer service levels, and reduce labor costs and inventory write-offs. Inventory also includes bar code generation and bar code management capabilities.

Inventory Planning calculates time-phased order quantities and safety stocks using selected inventory strategies. You can do what-if analyses and compare the current inventory policy with simulated scenarios. In addition, Inventory Planning employs realistic forecasts from Demand Planning to plan sound inventory levels across the enterprise.

Order Management provides streamlined order processing and tracking, a flexible customer information system, and management tools for returned goods.

Order Promising enables you do business in multiple currencies and languages. With Order Promising, you can commit ship dates and quote prices to customers based on both uncommitted inventory and available capacities across the supply chain, all while on the telephone. Order Promising ensures on-time delivery by determining the available material and capacity before establishing a promise date.

Product Configurator connects your customers, service reps, and warehouse managers in the selection, creation, and tracking of unique product configurations. This module can also develop automated business processes based on the way you order, validate, price, cost, and build configured products.

Production Management synchronizes the planning and execution of production processes allowing quick response to customer requests and order changes. You can manage production for any manufacturing environment, centralize or decentralize key business functions, create production IDs to track discrete work orders, and use production schedules to manage production by day or shift.

Promotions Management offers a flexible, comprehensive system for managing and optimizing your trade spending funds. By integrating supply chain and financial systems, Promotions Management provides promotions forecasting, planning, tracking, reporting, and execution.

Purchasing streamlines your procurement process by using automated sourcing of requisitions, workflow approvals, exception-based workflow notifications, and electronic commerce, including XML, EDI transactions, e-mail, automatic faxing, and sourcing of items through electronic catalogs.

Quality enables you to configure an unlimited number of measurement and control plans. Use statistical process control to determine measurement acceptance and electronically route violations to the appropriate personnel. In addition, you can maintain a complete set of history, including traceability, corrective action, and free-form comments.

SCM Portal Pack provides an intuitive view of your SCM application data and transactions via a set of prebuilt pagelets. Displayed on your Enterprise Portal homepage, Portal Pack pagelets provide SCM application functionality, reports, and related content.

Services Procurement automates the process of procuring and managing contract services. This Internet solution enables you to procure both requisition- and project-based resources, aggregate service suppliers, and optimize business processes.

Strategic Sourcing streamlines RFx (request for quote, request for proposal, and so forth) processes, enabling you to conduct real-time auctions and strategically award contracts and purchase orders.

Supply Chain Warehouse provides the tools and technology to manage supply chain information needed for analytic reporting and analysis.

Trading Exchange Services allows the enterprise to set up and define its trading partner relationships, manage product catalogs, and hold on-line auctions. Trading Exchange Services seamlessly integrates your applications with those of your trading partners.

Index

A